For Chris this Christ[mas]
with appreciation for your e[xcellen]t
assistance in Arts Promotion, and
the loyalty and friendship given me.

I'm grateful,
Phyllis Pearson

Fashion

FROM ANCIENT EGYPT TO THE PRESENT DAY

Roman sandals. Bas-relief. Civic Museum, Avezzano

Following page: Accessories in a woman's wardrobe. Roman bas-relief. Civic Museum, Avezzano

Fashion

FROM ANCIENT EGYPT TO THE PRESENT DAY

By MILA CONTINI

Edited by JAMES LAVER

Foreword by COUNT EMILIO PUCCI

Introduction by JANEY IRONSIDE
PROFESSOR OF FASHION DESIGN, ROYAL COLLEGE OF ART, LONDON

CRESCENT BOOKS · NEW YORK

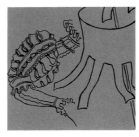

ORLANDO DI COLLALTO

Frieze of cosmetic jars. First century. Spoleto Museum

CONTENTS

DVM PVER ALVEOLO FVRATVR MELLA CV·
FVRATI DIGITVM CVSPITE FIXIT APIS
SIC ETIA NOBIS BREVIS ET PERITVRA VOLVP·
QVA PETIMVS TRISTI MIXTA DOLORE NO

FOREWORD

In the past, only a small and highly privileged group of individuals were interested in what we call fashion.

Today, what once concerned a minority has become a matter of general interest—not only in clothing, but in all expressions of contemporary living, from architecture to interior decoration, from the automobile to the refrigerator. The pervasive influence of television, profusely illustrated and well-produced magazines, window displays in modern shops, and fast, easy air transportation, have made fashion today one of the determining factors in civilised living.

Entire populations of countries have a visual acquaintance with what is produced in the clothing field. The result has been a most desirable democratisation of taste. And, because seeing is comparing, then weighing, vast numbers of individuals are, for the first time, making independent value judgements based on the two essential elements of fashion: form and colour.

Not only does fashion today reach more people than ever; it draws entire peoples together. Allow me to make a statement which may seem exaggerated: Having shown my collection in every country in the world, from Austria to America, from Cuba to Canada, from Greece to Japan, from Uruguay to the Soviet Union, and having observed, close up, the impressions and reactions of their diverse citizens, I can say that fashion is one of the principal factors in arriving at an understanding among the peoples of the world.

This most interesting book, realised with great sensitivity and particular subtlety, is one for which there has long been a need. It is for all who are interested in the wonderful phenomenon of fashion. It is a quick but detailed excursion across centuries of past history into the marvellous world of aesthetics. It is for all who feel in the things of today a sense of progress and achievement. It will appeal to those who look back with nostalgia on past eras, and to the young who, in their continual search for the new, will see the 'newness' discovered by youth many centuries ago, motivated by the same desire for fresh discovery they feel today.

Count Emilio Pucci

A parallel between fashion and the visual arts. *Left:* A fashion plate. *Right:* A painting by Paul Cézanne

Left: 'Venus and Cupid'. Detail. Lucas Cranach. Galleria Borghese, Rome

INTRODUCTION

A history of fashion is a history of life: 'To be out of fashion is to be out of life,' said Colley Cibber in the eighteenth century and this, like many semi-ironical statements, is true. The way people dress is a reflection of their times as well as of their class, financial status and of the local weather.

Starting with ancient Egypt, Greece and Rome—those countries we call the 'cradle' of civilisation—this book provides a fascinating study of life and the evolution of taste and fashion up to the present time.

Today fashion is not just international; it is intercontinental and, subject to local variations in material, colour or climate, it will become increasingly so in our rapidly shrinking world. Some people may deplore this trend and maintain a nostalgic attitude towards the picturesque garments of other ages, but such garments outgrow their usefulness, just as do outdated machines. Beautiful but voluminous, hampering and uncomfortable clothes now belong in museums or at fancy-dress parties—just as

veteran motor cars are cherished for rallies. Costly and inconvenient clothes were once a sign of wealth and class; now differences in dress are disappearing.

In the twentieth century, techniques of mass production, the emancipation of women and the invention of man-made fibres have effected a revolution in style, made plain by these pictures. Although our evening dresses still bear some relationship to the more formal periods in history, our daytime clothes do not. Excessive ornamentation and cumbersome design hardly belong to a civilisation run by machines—and people—in a hurry.

Perusing this book, two quite different points impress me. Firstly, how little standards of physical beauty, both masculine and feminine, have changed through the ages, in spite of minor oddities in the way of coiffure and corsetry. Secondly, how obvious and revealing of our era are the recent changes in dress design.

This is the fascination of studying a history of fashion: it *is* the study of life.

Janey Ironside
Professor of Fashion Design,
Royal College of Art,
London

Egyptian dancer. New Kingdom. The Egyptian Museum

Egypt

The word Egypt evokes the names of three women as if by magic: Hatshepsut, Nefertiti, Cleopatra. These women, separated by thousands of years, nevertheless epitomise the history and traditions of Egypt. This is so partly because woman in ancient Egypt was always honoured and treated with respect. In a papyrus of the time this precept appears: 'Never forget your mother. . . . Remember you burdened her womb for a long time, and when her time had passed she gave birth to you. For three long years she carried you on her shoulders and offered her breast to your mouth. She reared you and was not offended by your dirty ways. When you went to school and received instruction there in writing and counting, she came daily to your teacher with bread and beer brought from home.' The great consideration shown to Egyptian women in ancient times almost certainly stemmed from the quasi-matriarchal structure of Egyptian society. In fact the woman was the real master of the home, and the husband transferred all his property and future revenue to his wife as part of the marriage contract.

Hatshepsut more than any other queen might be considered as the prototype of the Egyptian woman. She was the daughter of Pharaoh Thutmosis I, and shared the throne with her father during his lifetime. When Thutmosis I died, she reigned together with Thutmosis II, her half-brother as well as husband (marriage between blood-relations was quite usual in Pharaonic dynasties); and at his death, setting aside Thutmosis III (her husband's son by a concubine) she reigned over the land for twenty-two years. Tradition demanded that a Pharaoh should be of divine descent, so Hatshepsut accordingly circulated the legend of her divine birth, which held that she was the daughter of Ahmasi (the legitimate wife of Thutmosis I) and the god Amon. She also decided to change her sex, and wore on her chin the false beard of the Pharaohs, and on monuments and bas-reliefs had herself represented without breasts, like a warrior. She chose as her attributes 'Son of the Sun' and 'Lord of the Two Lands'.

She was a great queen, who managed to keep order at home without becoming a tyrant, and peace abroad without terrible sacrifices. She encouraged commerce, and developed new links with other countries; she embellished the town of Karnak with two obelisks dedicated to Amon, and she realised a dream of her father's by building a magnificent temple in Deir el-Bahri. She restored many ancient temples which the Hyksos kings had damaged. Her achievements enabled her to proudly claim 'I rebuilt what I found in ruins, I completed what had been left

unfinished.' Moreover she had built for herself a secret tomb amongst the sandhills on the western bank of the Nile, which became the first of the famous tombs of the 'Valley of Kings'.

Legend says that her life was marked by an episode which was to have immeasurable consequences. One day she went with her maids for her usual ablutions in the Nile waters, and she saw floating on the stream a basket containing a new-born baby. (In those times it was usual to entrust unwanted babies to the great river, placing them in baskets of woven reeds.) The baby looked healthy and had perfect features: she picked him up, and took him to the royal palace, where she brought him up, giving him the name of Moses.

We can still admire two very famous portraits of Nefertiti, King Akhenaten's bride, who lived during the New Kingdom (1580–950 B.C.). One is in the Cairo Museum, and is an unfinished head in crystalline, orange-coloured sandstone touched up in ink; the other one is in Berlin and is a polychrome bust. The queen, who joined her husband in the cult of an only god, the Sun God Aten, and who had six daughters, appears to us with her head polished like one of the ivory balls with which her little daughters

Left: Egyptian head with formal hair style. *Below*: Pharaoh's head. Louvre

Following pages: Bedouins from the tomb of Khnumhotep, wearing brightly patterned woollen tunics. XIIth Dynasty. Oriental Institute, Chicago

Thoth, god of wisdom, dressed in a triangular, stiffened skirt. New Kingdom. Cairo Museum

played. In various bas-reliefs we can see her prettily nestling on Akhenaten's lap, dressed in a transparent pleated linen two-piece dress.

Cleopatra, the 'Queen of Kings' (69–30 B.C.) seduced Caesar, then Anthony, then Octavian, with her intelligence, her wealth, her beauty and her elegance. She had dresses of linen woven with gold, wigs of every colour, splendid jewels.

For three thousand years the Egyptian style of dress did not change very much, as we can see from the portraits of these three queens. Egypt is an unchanging land of even landscapes; her river every year swells and overflows to fertilise its banks; the sun blazing down on her is never veiled by mist. In this immutable setting the Egyptian spirit developed. Art, philosophy, culture, styles of dress and costume are fundamentally dominated by a static conception of life, unchanging both in its external features and in its religion.

This religion, which continued unalterably for thousands of years and was founded on the cult of eternity, prevented any fundamental change in the culture of the Egyptian people for about three thousand years. Quarrels and wars, triumphs and defeats, periods of mourning and periods of joy, everything was governed by a deep religious compulsion that made Egyptians the most devout men in the world, as recorded by Herodotus, the famed chronicler of antiquity. Next to Pharaoh, and sometimes even before him, the Great Priest with all his court held power in the land. Every act in life or death was accompanied by ritual ceremony. The mass of the people were not, however, concerned in these ceremonies which were reserved to the Pharaoh, the nobility, and the warriors. Religion, with its crowd of gods, half human, half animal, led believers towards immortality, the life beyond, the next world. Because of this the temples, the royal palaces, the pyramids were built so as to resist, as indeed they have, the attacks of time and of men.

We can still see all the various aspects of ancient Egyptian life inscribed on the walls of the temples, palaces, and pyramids, which might be likened to the pages of an exceptional encyclopedia. It is precisely from the examination of these 'pages' that we derive our knowledge of both masculine and feminine attire, apparently unchanging or at least changing slowly, throughout the thousands of years.

In the beginning the only garment was a loincloth. It would be made of linen for the Pharaoh, for the Great Priest, or for men of importance; of leather or woven vegetable fibres (never of sheep's wool, as the animal was considered unclean) for the common people. Often the royal loincloth would be enriched with golden threads; one or more very transparent skirts might be worn over it, secured at the waist by a belt. These skirts could be long, down below the knee, or else short, in which case they would be triangular and stiffened, not unlike the shape of the pyramids. The Great Priest would throw a leopard skin over his pleated skirt.

Elegant Egyptian men wore no beard; a smooth chin was a sign of distinction and the everyday use of a copper razor was recommended. Only in a period of mourning, or during a journey abroad was it per-missible not to shave. And yet a beard could be a sign of distinction. All the gods had beards 'like lapis-lazuli'. Thus kings, who were children of the gods, would on ceremonial occasions wear thin lozenge-shaped false beards, prettily curled and always perfumed.

The women were dressed—or undressed—more or less like the men. Their garments were always of the finest linen, very transparent, often pleated (in a type of 'sun-ray' pleating). Queen Nefertiti is repre-sented in what is almost a fashion plate, wearing a long tight dress, and over it a kind of pleated tunic with bat-wing sleeves, the belt very high under the bosom (Empire fashion), and a wide collar composed of many strands of necklaces. This is a particularly modest attire, because the same queen liked to wear

Nefretere, wife of Amosis I, wearing a linen tunic with bat-wing sleeves. Fresco. Thebes

Bas-relief. Temple of Komb Ombo

19

Jewel box. Tomb of El Kubaine. XIth or XIIth Dynasty.
Vienna Museum

Left: The Queen Ankhesenamun putting finishing
touches to King Tutankhamen's toilet. Back of the gold-
plated throne. Cairo Museum

Egyptian necklace of gold and amethysts

a transparent tunic, open from the navel downwards,
over a diminutive loincloth. This veiled the breasts
but revealed the figure, which in any case was never
much concealed, as the fabrics used were always
extremely transparent. The women dancers would
perform their acrobatic dances wearing only a belt
made of pearls and gold which emphasised their
smooth nakedness (Egyptian women did not tolerate
any hair at all on their body, and got rid of it by daily
use of pumice stone).

The women of the common people would take off
their tunics completely unabashed, in order to gain
freedom of movement. Merit, the friend of Sinuhe
'the lonely', the very famous physician, would not
hesitate to remove her tunic when she was helping
her 'master' as a nurse, just because she did not want
to spoil it. And nobody minded.

Quite often women's dresses had a very deep neckline, held by wide shoulder straps. Then came the
fashion of having one shoulder bare, as in the time of
the mythical Amazons, the warrior women.

All the colours of the rainbow were used in Egyptian fabrics, except for black, which was confined
only to wigs. Red was generally not favoured, except
as the colour of the Pharaoh's 'Northern Crown'. At
best red meant 'dreadful violence', at worst 'perverse
wickedness'. Red-haired men, ginger dogs and donkeys were accursed; a red thing was considered a
noxious thing, and the scribes would write in red ink
the words of ill omen on their papyrus. White was a
happy colour, the colour of the 'Southern Crown';
blue reminded one of the skin of Amon, god of the
air; green stood for life and youth; yellow was the
symbol of gold, the flesh of immortal gods. Though

red was excluded, magenta was quite in order for
gowns, belts, or wigs.

The wig played a fundamental part in the Egyptian
wardrobe, both for men and for women. To have a
shining, shaven head was a sign of nobility, but
fashion demanded that it should be covered with a
wig of real hair, sometimes lined with vegetable
fibres. Even coloured or gilded wigs might be worn.
The relatives of a dead person placed his wigs in his
tomb, together with all the other accessories necessary to his daily life and adornment. Whether
natural or false, hair was parted in little plaits and
locks according to a custom clearly African. In order
to be elegant it was essential to look after one's hair.

Nubian ring of gold and semi-precious stones

Above: Wooden chest. Egyptian Museum, Turin

Right: Women at their toilet. From a sarcophagus. Cairo Museum

Below: A couple at table. Tomb of Raurose. Thebes

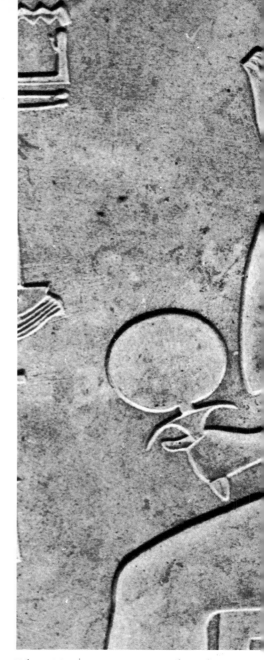

Below: King Zoser, wearing an elegantly trimmed beard. Metropolitan Museum, New York

A woman in love writes 'My heart can think of nothing but your love . . . I run swiftly towards you, neglecting my appearance . . . But I will curl my hair . . . and be ready at any moment.' In the medical papyri we find prescriptions for creams to nourish the scalp, lotions to fight baldness, dyes to eliminate white hair, perfumes and fixatives. There were also gala wigs, to be worn as one would wear a hat, over the real hair.

The men's hair style was usually of a round shape following the lines of the head. This haircut, more or less short, went through many variations: the ears could be hidden or else uncovered, the hair might be combed down on the nape of the neck (as the Beatles

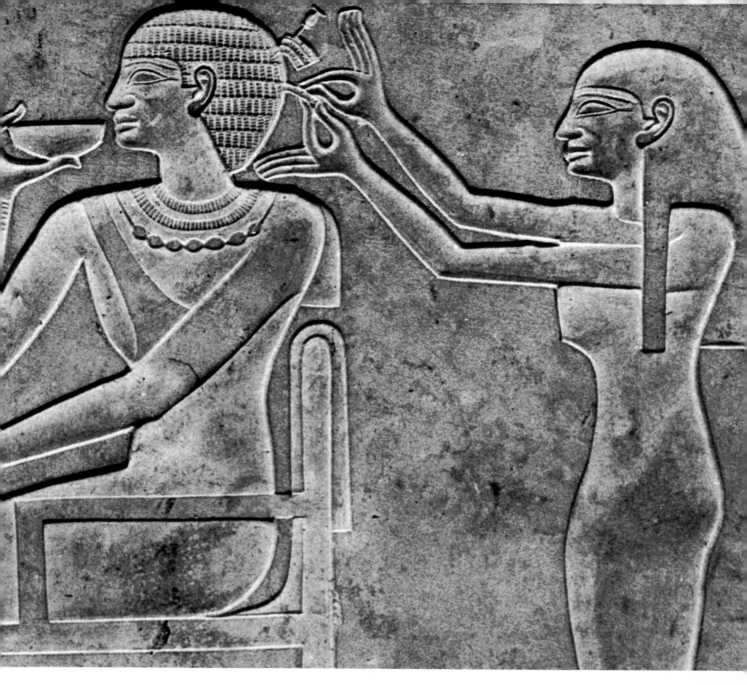

do today) or else away from the face. In frescoes and bas-reliefs sometimes we also see longer hair styles and wigs, shoulder-length or curling down to chest level. Women in general preferred to wear their hair long, like the goddesses, but would often happily follow a new fashion and cut it to shoulder length, or else adopt the round masculine haircut. During the Old Kingdom elegant women tended to imitate the masculine fashions; during the New Kingdom the opposite was true. Moreover ornaments were very popular: jewels, golden braids on the forehead, clasps, bangles, flowers (especially the lotus) and coloured ribbons in the hair.

The lotus flower, symbol of Egypt as the tulip is of

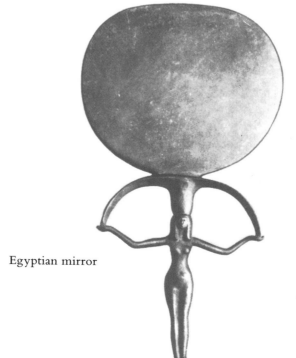

Egyptian mirror

23

Perfume container in alabaster. Cairo Museum

cate sweet scent, and the unscented white lotus flowered on stagnant waters by the edge of the deserts, on canals, and on the banks of the Nile. In temples the capital of columns and pillars represented a cluster of budding lotus blossoms. Beautiful women were compared to the *nenuphar*, the lotus. The rhizome of the flower was considered a delicacy and was the basis of exquisite dishes.

Around 1400 B.C. fashion decreed that heads should have an elongated shape, and princesses actually polished their heads to enhance the elegance of their profile. This fashion was reputed to have been launched by Nefertiti's six daughters, of whom it was said that witch doctors had elongated and narrowed their heads during birth, so as to spare their mother the worst pains of labour. When the girls grew up, the Court ladies wore false pieces on their necks to modify the shape of their own heads in imitation.

The ultimate refinement for the most fashionable women (and men too) was to place at the top of their heads a cone of scented grease, which would slowly melt with the heat of the body and the warm atmosphere, so that head and shoulders would slowly become bathed in rare perfumes, the skin growing oily and glistening, the clothes clinging to the body, revealing all its shape. As a reaction to these extravagances the priests started shaving their heads and keeping them smooth. Children usually wore a curled lock on their right temple. This is the reason why in Egyptian writing the hieroglyphic meaning 'child' is represented by a stylised curl.

An essential characteristic of Egyptian elegance was the care of the body. Queen Nitocris believed an elegant person should bathe every morning; and wash his hands, arms and neck before and after meals (teeth are not mentioned) with water containing natron (natural calcium carbonate) and a detergent

Holland, was present everywhere in Egyptian life. A great lotus growing from the primeval waters was the cradle of the sun on the First Morning, according to one of the numerous traditions concerning the creation of the universe. The blue lotus, with its deli-

Below: Wooden cosmetic pots. Louvre

Right: Torso, supposedly of Nefertiti, wearing finely pleated tunic. Louvre

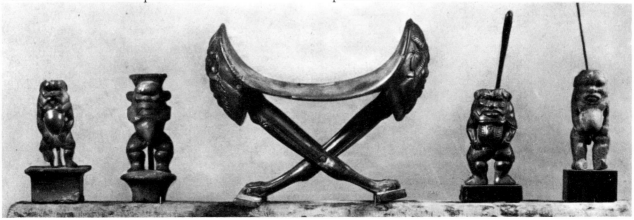

paste composed of clay and ashes. She also recommended daily massage to keep slim, the use of pumice stone on knees and elbows to soften the skin (still recommended by modern beauticians today) and frictions with scented oils to avoid the danger of sunburn and insect bites. There were many perfumes, extracted from different resins; myrrh with its delicate fragrance, *stibid*, a very expensive perfume extracted from acacia and teak seeds, and reasonably priced incense with its mild aroma.

Make-up was very important and every woman would know how to apply it herself, choosing what suited her most. It was fashionable to smear the face with a white foundation, a creamy paste based on white lead paint (rather dangerous to health, as its basis is lead carbonate). Women would colour their lips with an orangy lipstick, delicately outlining them with a little brush; a touch of the same shade would be applied to the cheeks, starting from the cheekbones and working out towards the temples. Eyes were considered the most important part of the face; they were so important that they were reproduced on amulets. The eye of the god was a charm against sterility, believed to give perfect health and clairvoyant powers to the wearer. This amulet was also placed on mummies, above the abdominal incision which the embalmer had cut in the body to extract the viscera.

Eye make-up was a most important part of the daily toilette. The eye would be lengthened and enlarged with a line of coal-black kohl (the same still used by Bedouin women nowadays), shaded on the upper and lower eyelid with a green malachite powder; the eyebrows would be enhanced and lengthened with a dark grey antimony powder, the line arching down on to the cheek in an arabesque. This arabesque was the symbol of clairvoyancy. Both finger nails and toe nails would be lacquered. Perfumes, cosmetics, creams and lotions were contained in little jars and pots, little bottles and boxes, which made a woman's dressing table (or a man's) look like a bazaar, as they often do today. A well-groomed person would also own a battery of little brushes and sticks for outlining the eyes, mirrors, combs made of copper and gold and gadgets to manicure the nails.

Jewels were numerous and of varied shapes and sizes, and gold was the favourite metal. It was valued not only on account of its high price but also because of its symbolic meaning. Gold was thought of as the brilliant and incorruptible flesh of the Sun, and of the gods that were his sons. The goddess Hathor—

'support and body of the heavens, living soul of the trees, goddess with a cow body, wet-nurse of sovereign Egypt, mother of Horus and Isis'—was gold made flesh. Gold, the divine metal, had the power of conferring eternal survival, which is why mummies were given golden masks. The King in the New Kingdom decorated his personal warriors with medals that were 'golden flies', and rewarded his ministers with golden trinkets.

Women of course wore jewels, and heaped their jewel boxes with necklaces of hollowed gold beads, delicately worked crowns, rings, breastplates, finely decorated rectangular plates hanging from a chain, belts made of golden shells, circlets to be worn on the forehead, dangling earrings, cylindrical rings. Many modern jewels are imitations of antique trinkets that belonged to distinguished princesses like the princess of Dahshur, or aspiring court ladies like Senebtisi. Silver was also used; it was called the 'white metal' and considered the substance 'of which are made the bones of the gold-fleshed gods'. But it was more generally used for ornamentation; in the shape of hammered thin plates and encrustations it was applied to decorate statues, furniture and trinkets.

Excavations have also yielded jewels which were precious because of the workmanship and not because of the high value of the materials used. For instance coloured beads were made of pottery and wrapped in strands around mummies; the beads would have various shapes, making up necklaces that looked like collars, blue or green amulets, little statues representing divine mummies, amulets to wear round the neck to keep away evil spirits.

Of glass, 'the stone that melts', Egyptian craftsmen would make trinkets as light as a breath, coloured in blue, green, purple and red. These ancient forerunners of tiny Venetian glass beads could be made into necklaces, bracelets, earrings. Glass was utilised in the making of many other objects, such as iridescent, fragile, precious perfume bottles. Several samples of such work have been found in the Pharaoh tombs, and together with the frescoes and the bas-reliefs they show the love that Egyptians had for life; a love which made them think of death as 'a painful event' although it led to a life beyond this world. On the walls of the Theban catacombs we can still admire the intimate reunions of the living and the dead, together gravely inhaling the scent of the blue lotus flower which emanates from a glass cup: a gesture which combines sensuous pleasure with the magic of rebirth in spring.

Greek ring with figure of Hera. Fourth century. Victoria and Albert Museum, London

Crete and Greece

She is called the *Parisienne*, but nobody knows her real name. She has a little upturned French nose (which is why she was nicknamed the 'Parisian' girl), a slim figure, a full bosom and a narrow waist sheathed in a leather corset. She wears a long flounced skirt, covered by a half skirt so short it barely reaches the hips. Her bodice has sleeves down to the elbows but leaves her breasts uncovered. This is the dress of the girl who lived in Crete around 1700 B.C., and is today admired in the frescoes of Cnossos Palace.

Cretan women were free, strong-willed creatures; they had a taste for frivolity and spent long hours in beautifying themselves, earning a reputation as the best-dressed women in the known world. They were rather fickle, and their fashions were forever changing: full skirts, bell-shaped, trimmed with layers of flounces or trimmed with coloured stripes—but they always retained the skin-tight bodice and bare breasts, occasionally veiling them with an extremely transparent material, woven of gold and silver thread. Sometimes dresses were covered with innumerable little gold plates joined together in shapes like a cuttlefish, a butterfly, or a palm leaf.

Women combed their long hair in spiral curls (the spiral was the characteristic decorative motif of Cretan art) and wore it in a pony tail down the neck. They had small, tall complicated little hats which were fixed on to the head with long gold hat pins. They spent an enormous amount of time in making up, and also in gossiping. They were incredibly vain and sewed their own dresses, to make sure these were exclusive models.

The beautiful women who still live for us in the frescoes of the Minoan palace obviously loved jewels very much. They are shown with long, thin necklaces that encircled the neck two and three times; jingling gold earrings; strands of pearls to braid in their hair; and engraved belts made of precious metals.

Cretan men were as elegant and coquettish as their women. Their loincloths were short and simple, but different from the Egyptian ones, because the lower corner of the fold fell down in front into an oblique point, often weighted by a net of pearls. Men were very proud of their wasp waists, and would pull in their midriffs with wide leather belts to make their chests stand out. They wore very decorative knee-high boots, and like the women they shaved carefully, had a daily bath and oiled their bodies.

Cretan houses were not merely impressive: they were luxuriously comfortable. The breeze could freely enter the windows and ventilate the rooms. A perfect system of central heating and plumbing allowed constant use of hot and cold water, that flowed from silver taps into solid silver basins. The walls were decorated in bright colours and so was the tableware. Flowers, leaves and butterflies were the recurrent decorative motifs.

The Cretans made sacrifices to a creature, half-bull, half-man, hidden in a labyrinth at Cnossos. Each month, amidst laughter, songs and dances, beautiful children and virgins proficient in the dance with the bulls were dedicated to him. These bulls, considered sacred animals, were reared in the 'house of the bulls', a citadel with arena, stalls, lawns, school houses, and quarters for the priests. Every day the young initiates performed acrobatic turns on the backs and between the horns of the bulls, risking their lives. They danced completely naked, shining with aromatic oil, as any garment would have hampered their agile movements.

Incapable of keeping a promise or speaking the truth (the proverbial reprimand was 'he lies like a Cretan'), gay and vivacious, with the reputation for

Graceful head of Artemis wearing a chignon. From a frieze on the Parthenon. Acropolis Museum, Athens

Left: Detail showing head of the bride of King Peirithoös. Temple of Zeus. Museum, Olympia

29

Women dressing. Decoration on a plate. Hermitage Museum, Leningrad

being vain revellers, the Cretan people nevertheless gave life to a splendid civilisation, which disappeared when the island was invaded by the Greeks, who landed there about the year 1100 B.C., armed with the new victorious metal: iron.

The Hellenic World

The life of an Athenian was divided into four stages: *pais, ephebos, aner, geron*—the child, adolescent, man and old man. From the age of six the 'free' Greek would attend school, accompanied by a slave, his *paidagogos*. He would continue his studies even after the age of fourteen or sixteen, often spurred on by a sandalwood birch, with which the teacher would inculcate love of learning. The education of the young Greek would include writing, music and gymnastics, to which in later centuries drawing and painting were added. Gymnastics were considered a fundamental element of education; as well as gymnastics a number of other sports were taught—hunting, throwing the javelin, wrestling, running and jumping—to develop their bodies.

Greek women, perhaps not as beautiful as the statues that depict them, were rather plump and not very tall, although still graceful. Their life unfolded itself in the *gynaeceum*, the women's quarters. Spartan women, however, trained like men at competitive games. Women's education was almost completely limited to home management, and was given within the confines of the home by their mother or nurse, who would teach them how to read, write, reckon, spin, weave, sew and embroider. To acquire a graceful body they would learn how to dance, and for the entertainment of their future husbands they would learn music and singing.

The mass of Greek women lived in complete anonymity. 'The slave has no will of his own; the child has a will, but an incomplete one; woman too has a will, but it is impotent', was the opinion of Aristotle. Women had only one safeguard, the practice of monogamy. Marriage was arranged by the parents of the bride and bridegroom, and the

Minoan women, showing typical dress, hair styles and jewellery. Fresco from the Palace of Minos, Cnossus

contract was based on the economic status of the woman, on whom her father had to settle a dowry in money, jewellery, a trousseau and slaves.

The nuptial ceremonies were always complicated; after reaching agreement on the dowry, the marriage was celebrated in the bride's father's home, in the presence of witnesses, but not necessarily of the bride. After a few days there was another feast, again in the bride's home, a feast which was preceded by the ritual bathing of the couple. During the reception, according to a custom which is still in existence in many villages in the south of Greece, the men congregated on one side of the room, while women remained on the opposite side. There would be feasting, with cakes and wine in plenty. Then the bridegroom would invite the bride, veiled and dressed in white, to step into a chariot that would bring her to his father's house, accompanied by his friends, and by women playing the lyre and singing songs celebrating Hymen. As a symbol of possession, the bridegroom, before entering the house, would pick the bride up in his arms, and put her down in the presence of his parents. After further ritual, such as the initiation into the worship of the family gods, the married couple could withdraw to their bridal-chamber, although they would still be accompanied by young men and women singing the epithalamium. And there, alone at last, the husband could contemplate the face, until then hidden from him, of the woman who was to be his life-companion.

Greek Fashion

Hairdressing was always of great importance. The first hint of the cult of hairdressing in the Greek world can be found in the Iliad, when Homer,

Cretan jewellery

describing the details of the customs of his own day rather than those of the Heroic Age, describes the toilet of the Goddess Juno:

Her chamber then she sought, by Vulcan built . . .
And with ambrosia first her lovely skin
She purified, with fragrant oil anointing . . .
Combed out her flaming locks, and with her hand
Wreathed the thick masses of the glossy hair,
Immortal, bright, that crowned the imperial head,
A robe ambrosial thin, by Pallas wrought,
She donned, with many a curious pattern traced,
With golden brooch beneath her breast confined.
Her gown, from which a hundred tassels hung,
She girt about her; in three bright drops,
Her glittering gems suspended from her ears . . .
Then o'er her head the imperial Goddess threw
A beauteous veil, new-wrought, as sunlight white;
And on her well-turned feet her sandals bound.

Dress from a drawing in a shrine. Cnossus

33

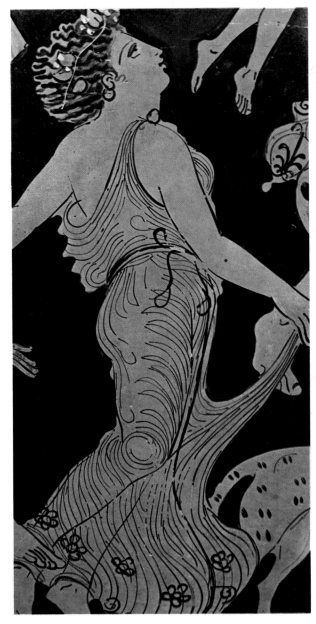

Above: Exekias, showing the simplicity of archaic dress. Vase from Volci. The Etruscan-Gregorian Museum, Vatican City. *Above right*: Dancing Maenad. Painting on a vase. National Museum, Naples. *Right*: A woman at a fountain. Detail from a vase. British Museum, London

Athenian women always wore their hair long, combed into a knot on the back of the head; Spartan women wore their hair in a pony tail. In the Doric period, the bride would have her hair cut, on the day of her marriage, as a sign of humility and renunciation of personal vanity. An unfaithful wife might have her head shaved by her husband. Later on hair-

34

Votive relief used in the cult of Persephone. From Locri. National Museum, Taranto

dressing became more subtle, more of an art in itself: hair was gathered in a small net on the nape of the neck, then swathed in bands; or else it would be fixed in a great chignon supported by a band that passed round the forehead; or it could be gathered on the nape of the neck and held in place by a narrow band. A simple style without any band left the hair in a pad on the forehead and temples, flowing in loose locks at the back. Another variation was a great knot at the top of the head, with the hair combed up and arranged in a cascade of curls. In the small Tanagra figurines hair is gathered into a chignon and then divided with a parting into soft waves.

Elegant women used spirals of gold, or silver or bronze bands as ornaments in their hair. Wigs and false pieces of hair were also known, which Aristophanes and Lucian derisively called 'false heads', 'helmets', or 'bags of hair'. In ancient times hair also had a religious significance. During the marriage ceremony virgins offered a lock of hair to the goddesses. Berenice is supposed to have sacrificed her luxuriant blonde hair as an offering, to ensure her husband's safe return from the wars.

Men also took great care of their hair, dressing it elegantly and adorning it with trinkets. Hair styles, at first very complicated, with curls like a crown all

Details showing Greek hair styles. *Left*: Head of Kouros. National Museum, Athens. *Centre*: Head of a youth. Museum of the Acropolis, Athens. *Right*: Head of a horseman, 'the Rampin head', found on the Athenian Acropolis. Louvre. *Below*: Archaic Greek bas-relief

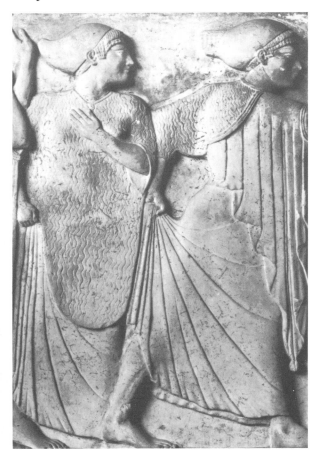

round the forehead, or plaits bound around the head, later became very simple, with the hair caught up in a tie, which was sometimes made of metal. In Athens, young men would cut their hair ceremonially as an offering to Hercules. From then onwards the *epheboi* wore their hair short, jutting over their forehead and over the nape of the neck, like a 'bed of curly hyacinths'. Adults also wore their hair short, cut in different styles: for example the *kepos*, cut like a garden; the *Hectorean* style, with the hair combed backwards into curls; the *Theseid* cut, with hair worn short on the forehead and worn long at the back of the neck; in locks, which was considered rather effeminate; or with a circular cut like that of monks.

To balance the hair style, the beard could be cut into a rounded or a pointed shape, or it could also be a false one. The beard had a symbolic meaning: historians would wear it short; the Epicureans would wear it long, to match their long curly hair; the Stoics would go unshaven. After the victory at Marathon Greek men began to cut their hair; after the reign of Alexander the Great they shaved their beards and moustaches with razors shaped like sickles, so that they could not be seized by their beard in battle.

The Greeks were largely a dark-haired people. Blonde hair was a much admired rarity, and both men and women bleached their hair with potash water, washed it with infusions of yellow flowers, and dried it in the sun, to make it lighter in colour. To give their hair a sheen they used pomades and oils, scented with floral essences: rose oil *amaricium*, from the island of Cos, or an extract of elder and

Details of chiton and sleeves of the goddesses Aphrodite and Artemis. Eastern frieze of the Siphnian Treasury. Marble. Museum, Delphi

marjoram. These oils and pomades were not only used in Greece, but were also exported to various countries throughout the known world.

Greek men often went about bare-headed in the open air but various kinds of headgear were some-times worn: the *pilos*, a skull cap without a brim, which could also be worn under the helmet; the *petasos* (the prerogative of the distinguished) with a brim turned upwards or downwards, and a flap falling on one ear, which was fastened round the neck by a ribbon, hanging down the back; on festive days it was embellished with several brightly-coloured

Details showing different styles of headgear. *Above left*: Head in terracotta, possibly of Persephone. National Museum, Syracuse. *Above centre*: Hermes. Terracotta from Boetia. Louvre. *Above right*: Terracotta statuette from Tanagra. Louvre. *Centre left*: Horseman. Interior of cup (now destroyed). Pinakothek, Munich. *Centre right*: Seated figure. Rhodes

streamers. The Greek hat could also have other shapes, such as a truncated cone, a cone with a small brim, a bonnet, an elongated truncated cone (this last imported from Egypt), a pagoda shape (perhaps introduced by Alexander the Great after his campaign in the Far East), and the Phrygian bonnets.

Greeks, both men and women, were very fond of perfumes, so much so that Socrates bitterly criticised the excessive use that men made of them. Women also were often quite immoderately made up. A lover protested: 'If you go out in summertime two black rivulets descend from your eyes; sweat produces red streaks on your cheeks and neck; and when your hair touches your face it gets all dirty with white paint.' But these reproaches went unheeded! Most women continued to use depilatories, to spread

Athenian plate from Volci. Sixth century B.C. British Museum, London

creams and oils on their skin, and to spray themselves with essences of mint, myrrh, marjoram, thyme. On the advice of Hippocrates, women would sing at the top of their voices to develop their bust; but sometimes they also had recourse to padding. To look slimmer they would swathe themselves with tight bands, and the brassière was not unknown. To appear taller they would fix cork soles to their shoes.

Greek dress, both for men and women, was based on the chiton: originally plain like a Doric capital, then fluted with pleats and tucks in the Ionic period,

and later amply draped in the period which created the ornamented Corinthian capital.

During the Archaic Period the chiton was a simple woollen tunic, which could be fastened on the left shoulder, leaving the right shoulder bare, or it would cover both shoulders, and was kept in place by two clasps. Women wore a wider chiton than that of the men, and they draped it in a different manner, according to their personal taste and skill. They sometimes made false sleeves out of its widths, or created the effect of a blouse with the help of two

Tanagra statuettes showing the chiton

The chiton was often draped to form false sleeves

Sometimes a belt was used to gather the chiton at the waist

A loose fold of the chiton doubled on the shoulders was also used as a hood. Louvre

belts, fastened around the waist and around the hips. Often the surplus material would be doubled on the shoulders. This fold, originally part of the main garment, in a later period became a separate little cape, oval or rectangular in shape, with a circular opening through which the head could pass.

Men's cloaks were either short garments like the *chlamys*, worn doubled over the shoulders, or else very full like the *himation*, which would float freely with the movement of the body. The warriors preferred a short cloak, with geometric patterns on the border, which they wore over a completely naked body. More modest people would wear a brief, pleated loincloth originally in white, later in red, purple or violet, a fashion set by Alcibiades.

Solon's severe sumptuary laws went unheeded, and clothes became ever more elaborate during this period. The chiton was transformed into the peplum, a long piece of woollen material like a gown. On Greek vases they were depicted like a cylindrical petticoat formed by a rectangle of material sewn down one side. The upper part was folded over the rest, so that the gown reached only up to the shoulders, where two clasps passing through four thicknesses of material fastened the front and back of the gown together. In this way the top half of the garment had three openings: two for the arms and one for the head. The folded material formed two layers that covered the breast.

Towards the end of the Archaic Period (between 550 and 480 B.C.) the Ionic influence began to make itself felt, and linen took the place of wool, which was only used for winter garments. (Herodotus, as usual, is our source here.) In order to make the dress cling to the body, the Greeks used little oval weights sewn inside the hem. Often the peplum was completely open on one side. It was quite possible to wear it without a belt, and this gained Spartan women the nickname of 'women who show their hips'. During the Hellenic period, after Alexander the Great's campaign in India, Eastern influences were seen in Greek dress. New fibres, hitherto unknown, were mixed with linen, cotton and silk, and almost transparent fabrics were woven with these. Embroidery made its appearance, but was later abandoned because it was considered 'barbaric'. Women wore sandals of purple leather to show off their naked feet. Men preferred boots, short or long, of black leather, which they would take off before going into their homes.

As time passed the lives of the Greeks became more and more luxurious. Men and women covered themselves in jewels to show off their newly acquired riches, or to deceive their neighbours as to their economic position. Men collected walking sticks with gold and silver heads. Women were laden with trinkets, and wore jewelled ribbons around their ankles, and on their thighs, where later garters were worn. Laws were created to put a stop to such wasteful living: for instance, women were forbidden to take more than three dresses on their journeys, but these laws were rarely observed. In fact peplums became richer and richer, and more and more heavily draped and pleated, in anticipation of some of the fashions of modern times.

Onyx cameo with the heads of the Emperors Claudius
and Germanicus and their wives. First century. Nelson
Gallery, Kansas City

The
Etruscans and Romans

Theopompus, a fourth century Roman writer of comedy, described the Etruscans as effeminate and licentious men. The women were no better; they were very vain of their bodies and did not think it unbecoming to appear naked in public. Other historians and writers, however, like Posidonius of Apamea, Diodorus Siculus, who lived in Caesar's time, and even Virgil, recognised that Etruscans were courageous and gifted people. But there must have been some truth in the description handed down to us by Theopompus, because even those who appreciated the qualities of the Etruscans could not help noting the shameless behaviour of their courtesans and the often obscene obesity of their musicians and intellectuals.

The women in Etruscan society had almost absolute authority, and they practised—albeit discreetly—a kind of matriarchy. Their family name was always preceded by their own name; whereas a Roman woman was known as a Claudia or a Cornelia, Etruscan women retained their own personal name: Ramtha, Tanaquil or Velia.

Greek and Roman women remained in their homes for most of their lives, and were content to influence their men by exercising their tact, to manage their slaves, and to distribute the family's goods—which were, however, purchased in the market by the father or the husband. Etruscan women, on the other hand, would venture out without blushing (as Livy noted) at being exposed to male glances. It was the privilege of ladies, as well as of courtesans, to take part at banquets, reclining on couches in the *triclinium* alongside the men. This privilege was denied to Greek women; during family meals they sat modestly behind the master of the house, ready to get up to serve him. Etruscan women were also free to attend dances, concerts or athletic contests, and from their places in a special stand they would often preside at races and boxing contests.

Another female privilege was to occupy the most important place in the family tomb, a sarcophagus placed to the right of the funeral bed reserved for the husband. The chattels found in the tomb (great amphoras for wine, silver tableware—Etruscans were great eaters and drinkers, and were concerned that they should be well provided for even in the next life) almost always had the name of the proprietress engraved on them: Larthia, or Vetusia. Women's privileged position originated in the Etruscan cult of the worship of Mother Earth.

We find in Etruscan history quite a number of

Left: Woman's head showing Etruscan hair style. Sarcophagus from Cerveteri

ambitious women who made their mark in society. Tanaquilla, an aristocrat, married Lucumon, the son of a rich Greek refugee. As she was very ambitious and wanted to improve her social position after her *mésalliance*, she persuaded her husband to leave Tarquinia and go to Rome, where she thought he would be certain to achieve distinction. At the gates of the city, which at that time was an agglomeration of villages scattered over seven hillsides, an eagle snatched the hat from Lucumon's head, and then replaced it. This omen, which had frightened her husband, gave Tanaquilla, superstitious as were all Etruscan women, 'great and high hopes'. And indeed Lucumon, after changing his name to Lucius Tarquinius Priscus, became the founder of a family of Roman kings.

Urgulania, through her friendship with Livia, wife of Emperor Augustus, attained a position which 'put her above the law'. She was the wife of Plautius, and she succeeded in having her son M. Plautius Sylvanus

Figures wearing typical Etruscan dress in a frieze from Cerveteri. Louvre

Procession of women wearing cloaks. Etruscan Fresco. National Museum, Naples

Dancer. End of sixth century, B.C. Museum of Fine Arts, Boston

elected consul. She intrigued to obtain favours for her numerous relations, and even managed to get one of her granddaughters married to the Emperor Claudius.

Tullia major and Tullia minor, daughters of Servius Tullius, were two sisters with very different temperaments: the one violent, the other submissive. According to legend, their husbands, sons of Tarquinius Priscus, had similarly contrasting temperaments, but each failed to choose the woman who matched his own character. The two good partners in these marriages were murdered at the instigation of Tullia major, so that the two violent ones were able to marry and ensure that Lucius Tarquinius, the future Tarquin the Proud, inherited the royal crown.

The Etruscan Wardrobe

Notwithstanding their masculine character, Etruscan women paid great attention to their attire, as did also the men. In general they followed the Greek fashion, but during the Archaic Period they adopted very different styles: long and sumptuous tight-waisted dresses, worn with a heavy jacket in brilliant colours —bright red or pinky-orange covered with little circles and crosses; full, bell-shaped skirts with horizontal bands under the waist and around the hem that echoed the colours of the bodice; much embroidery and kimono sleeves that made the shoulders look broader and the waist more slender.

They used materials of every kind and colour, pleated, gathered, stiffened; skirts were made wider and fuller with hoops. All the new fashions were quickly adopted by elegant women. When they started wearing the chiton, often of the same vivid pinky-orange and embroidered with small flowers, they covered it with a great scarlet cloak, with blue

Gold trinket from Prenesto. Etruscan-Gregorian Museum, Rome

Below left: Etruscan jewels. Fourth century, B.C. Museum of Tarquinia. *Below right*: Cosmetic pots. Museum of Tarquinia

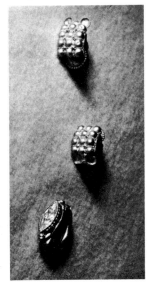

lapels that hung down in front like the long ends of a pelerine. As far as hats were concerned, though they had the pyramid-shaped *tutulus*, in general they preferred to go out hatless. Head coverings were generally worn by warriors, and also the peasants, and were of varying shapes.

Rather than a cloak, men preferred to wear a brightly-coloured scarf, which might be orange, pale green or royal blue, with a wide embroidered border both inside and outside in a contrasting colour—yellow or blue, pale yellow with a brown saw-teeth motif, or white with red dots. The *lacerna* was another type of cloak, almost always made of wool, short and narrow, worn as an outer garment. The *tebenna*, from which originated the Roman toga, was a cloak of small dimensions, worn only by the king and the more powerful citizens. At first it was very short, and was worn over a white embroidered tunic hemmed in red; later it became knee-length, and finally full-length; it was either purple, black (for funeral ceremonies) or white.

On their feet Etruscan men and women wore slippers of red, green or brown cloth, open in front, and high and pointed behind the ankle, which were obviously Eastern in origin. Also fashionable were boots which were open in front and fastened with straps round the ankle; they also wore small boots coming up to mid-calf, and light sandals fastened with crossed straps.

If the Etruscan temperament was reflected in the way they dressed their hair, one would have to conclude that they were a very changeable people, as their hair-styles underwent frequent transformations. Women usually bleached their hair, and then adorned it with bronze or golden spirals and pins capped with bone, ivory or precious metals. They had corkscrew curls which formed a skull cap over the temples and forehead; long plaits either hanging to the shoulders or else wrapped in a *tutulus*, that is a pyramid shape like the hat of the same name. The hair was also worn gathered into a net on the nape of the neck, with curls on the forehead and over the ears; or enclosed in a sheath that would touch the ground behind the back, while the cheeks were surrounded by puffed up locks. Very fashionable was a 'wind-swept' hair style, with a parting in the middle and the hair waved down each side of the face.

Etruscan women loved jewellery as passionately as Greek or Roman women did. Their coffers overflowed with brooches and clasps, rings and bracelets, necklaces and earrings. The workmanship was

Funerary statue of a warrior from Capestrano. Sixth century, B.C. National Museum, Chieti

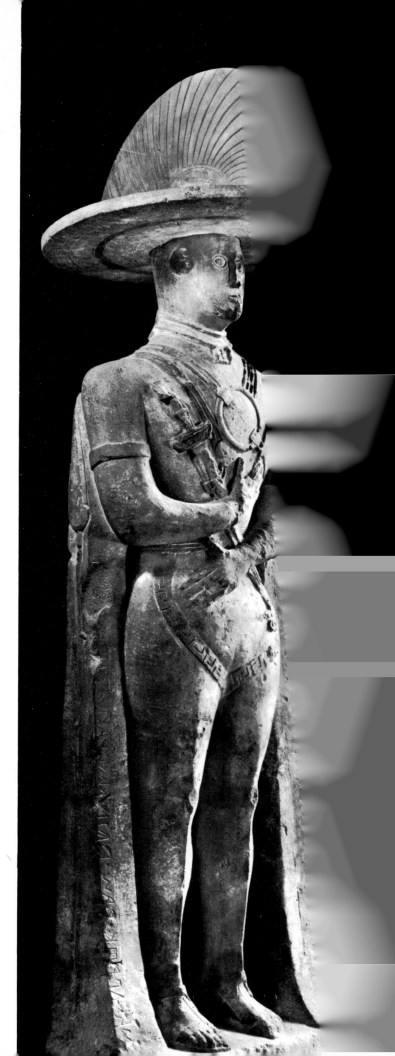

Roman jewels from a mosaic. Piazza Armerina, Sicily

Roman Life and Fashion

Roman women and men loved to adorn themselves heavily with jewellery. Roman taste turned from the Etruscan influence towards oriental jewellery, which was richer and more elaborate. At first jewels were offered to the gods, but later were used for personal adornment. According to Pliny, who like Herodotus was an excellent observer of contemporary fashions, the first oriental stones were imported into Rome at the time of Silius, and immediately caused a sensation. Diamonds were highly valued, but not much used as the art of cutting them was unknown. The gem most commonly in use was the emerald, but also popular were aquamarines and opals. The most popular of all were certainly pearls, used in earrings, for embroidering fabrics, and for decorating footwear, which consisted almost invariably of white leather sandals. The largest pearls were used for necklaces and earrings, of which some were known as *crotali*: these were double pendants with a pearl at each tip, mounted in such a way that they tinkled prettily at every movement. Solid gold bracelets shaped like snakes, fibulae and brooches were also decorated with pearls. The value of the jewel was increased if the history of the previous owners was known or if they were supposed to possess some magic power, such as the power of prolonging life, preserving good health, or prolonging youth.

Emperors and their wives made lavish use of precious stones. Diocletian was supposed to have offered his foot to his subjects to kiss, so that he could show off his sandals decorated with precious stones. Anthony amazed even Cleopatra, who was by no means unsophisticated, when he presented himself to her in a purple tunic covered with emeralds, pearls and opals. Caligula had the mane and the tail of his favourite horse plaited with brilliant stones. Antonia, the widow of Drusus, fastened jewels to the exotic fish in her aquarium, so that their darting movements were emphasised.

superb, and certain of their techniques are still unknown today, such as their way of sprinkling the surface of a jewel with a fine gold powder (thousands of miscroscopic gold grains) and attaching these to the jewel with a solder whose secret we have yet to discover. Jewels were enriched with small engravings of animals, from the lion to the duck, little heads, floral volutes, arabesques. Earrings were always important, some of them masterpieces of the craft. Very long (sometimes as long as three inches), often fashioned like a snake with a human head, they dangled against the cheek and reached to the shoulder.

Onyx cameo with Roman eagle. End of first century, A.D. Kunsthistorisches Museum, Vienna

Rings were the most popular form of jewellery. Several of them were worn on each finger, covering up the lower joint and the knuckles, but the middle finger was left bare for superstitious reasons. Rings were worn even on the toes. Many of them must have been extremely heavy, as they were enormous in size, with very big stones and decorative settings, but there was a distinction between rings worn in the summer, which were lighter, and the heavier winter ones. The simplest of all rings was the engagement

Right: Portrait of a Roman lady. Archaeological Museum, Florence

ring, which the bridegroom placed on the ring finger of his future bride, as it was believed that from this finger a special nerve led directly to the heart. It was a simple iron circle, often covered in gold, and its value was entirely symbolic.

The dress of Roman women in early times was a simple toga, very like the one that men wore. This was cut out of a rectangle of material, six to seven yards long and two and a half yards wide, its corners trimmed to form a round or oval shape; the garment was then folded to about a third of its width, and swathed around the arms and body. As time passed, women left the wearing of the toga to men, and followed the Greek fashion, modifying it to their own taste.

A tunic made out of wool, cotton or silk, was worn next to the naked body; this was very full, short-sleeved and sometimes held in place by a belt. The *zona*, a band worn under the breasts, had the same function as a brassière. The *stola*, a long robe cut wider than the tunic, but with shorter sleeves, was pulled in by one or two belts. The *palla* was a long and narrow rectangular piece used as a scarf, or a double rectangle which fell down over the chest and back, fastened on the shoulders by a seam or by a fibula. This large number of garments was very necessary, especially in winter, as the climate was much less mild than in Greece. Several tunics were often worn together when it was very cold.

There were no hats for matrons, but only veils which could be arranged in different ways but always fall on the shoulders in soft folds. Roman

Above: Detail showing Roman togas, from the Ara Pacis. Vatican Museum, Rome

Left: Detail showing robe worn by Roman actor. Wall-painting transferred to panel (from Herculaneum). National Museum, Naples

women dressed according to the occasion, sumptuously for banquets and religious ceremonies, in embroidered robes with great bands of colour; soberly for journeys, in purple tunics that would not show stains or creases; or scantily, for physical exercise and sport: for this they would wear a simple bikini, which left the movements free, and revealed the graceful body.

In the Classical Period, the Roman woman was proud of being the *domina* in her own home and the *regina* of her husband's clients who crowded into his office, but she always remained confined to her *gynaeceum*, very busy with her spinning, weaving, and organising of the preparation and storage of provisions, distributing them as necessary, and showing a proverbial parsimony. She did not participate in public life, nor did she share officially in the life of her husband. But as time went by, she began to emancipate herself, particularly if she was a rich woman. At the time of her marriage she automatically came of age, and her husband had no claim on her personal possessions, nor did he benefit from her income. Her estate could not be touched even in the event of her husband's bankruptcy, and Augustus and Claudius made laws to prevent wives from becoming guarantors for their husbands.

Very many satirists aimed their barbs at rich women: 'A woman thinks she can do as she pleases, and nothing will make her blush, when she is wearing an emerald necklace, and large pearls are stretching her ear-lobes.' 'Nothing is more insufferable than a rich woman.' 'Why does Censennia's husband remain silent? Because she brought him a million sesterces. He is paid to extol her chastity.' Many marriages were purely formal, unions between rich women and poor men designed only as evasions of the celibacy law.

Men were preoccupied with the accumulation of wealth and the conquest of new lands, and in their turn were very fastidious about their dress. At home they wore only a short-sleeved simple tunic, but when they were conducting their business or attended any festivity, when they celebrated victory or honoured the gods, they would wear a long tunic, made of wool or cotton or silk, often interwoven with gold and silver threads, and decorated with embroidery, over which they would fling their toga. The colour of the toga was symbolic of rank: pure white or *candida* for those who were candidates for public office; *praetexta* with purple bands for priests, magistrates, and the sons of freemen until they came of age (that is when they shaved the down on their faces for the first time); *picta*, purple with gold

embroidery for victorious captains; *vitrea*, made of a transparent fabric, popular with effeminate men; *palmata*, embroidered in gold palm leaves for the victorious *dux*. And then there were the purple bands which passed over the shoulders, crossing the full length of the tunic, the distinctive dress of senators and aristocrats.

Both men and women had a passion for the *thermae*, which were public baths where one would go daily for hygienic purposes, and also to conclude business deals, arrange marriages, and spread gossip. They were open in the morning for women and in the afternoon for men. One writer of this time advised matrons that they should always be accompanied by a female slave to carry all their oils and unguents, which were often kept in a glass ball with

Girl dressed for gymnastics. Roman mosaic. Piazza Armerina, Sicily

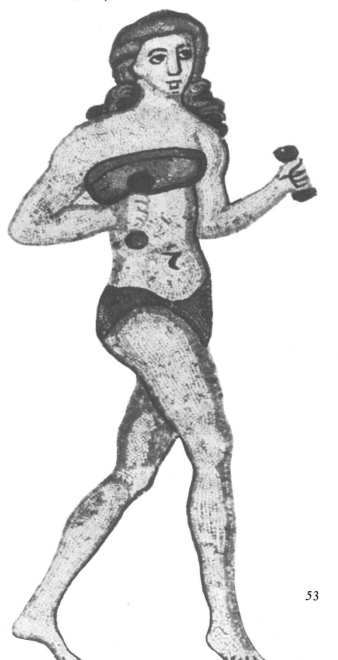

53

Roman matron having her hair dressed. Bas-relief. Museum of Treviri

Statuary showing feminine hair styles, in the time of Imperial Rome

Previous pages: Togas worn by Roman women. Pompeian fresco. National Museum, Naples

a rope handle that could be hung over the arm.

The bath was taken in four stages, preceded by physical exercises chosen according to the age, mood and physical fitness of the individual. Running, lifting dumb-bells and playing with hoops were particularly recommended. After this one sweated in the *sudatorium*, and then moved to the very much hotter *calidarium*. A brief rest in the *tepidarium* followed, so that the body was not subjected to too great a shock from the *frigidarium*, the icy cold baths. During all these stages, the female slave was expected to massage, rub and currycomb the body of her mistress; currycombs were made of ivory or bone for delicate skins, and of iron, copper or silver for tougher hides.

The very refined ladies of the time of the Roman Empire were quite different from their ancestors, the women who lived in the Archaic and Republican periods. Ovid wrote: 'Perhaps under the reign of Tatius the Sabine women were more concerned with tending their husbands' estates than with themselves. In those days the ruddy-faced matron sat uncomfortably on a high chair, spinning endlessly while she looked after her many heavy tasks; it was she who penned the sheep that her daughter had taken out to graze in the fields; she who kept alive with faggots and chopped wood the fire in the hearth. But *your* mothers have given birth to delicate daughters; you have to dress in golden brocade; you have to continually change your elegantly perfumed hair styles, and to show-off the glittering stones on your hands. Your neck is hung with pearls that have come from the orient, so heavy and rich that you can hardly bear the weight of them. But we are hardly in a position to scold you for the care you take to please us, considering that so many men take as much trouble over their own appearance. Husbands follow the fashions of their wives, and the bride can hardly find anything to add to this extravagance.'

At the time of the Empire Roman women had great aspirations to culture: they learnt how to read and write; they studied Greek and voguishly introduced foreign words into conversation; they were taught how to spin wool and to sew. Though the Romans had little talent for music and dancing, girls were taught singing because 'if a woman wants to please, she must know how to hold the viol in her left hand and the bow in her right'. As well they took dancing lessons; simple and pretty rhythmic movements of arms and torso were gracefully performed to the sound of music.

Some Roman women were so cultured and pedantic that Juvenal complained: 'There is nothing more boring than women who, as soon as they sit down

Plotina, wife of Hadrian. National Museum, Naples

Julia daughter of Titus. Capitoline Museum, Rome

at table, start praising Virgil, justifying Dido's death, drawing parallels between poets, comparing Virgil with Homer.' They were familiar with the work of Horace, and devoured the texts of Ovid who was nicknamed 'the women's writer', as well as Propertius and Tibullus, who were forbidden to very young girls because they were considered too daring. Novels sold like hot cakes, particularly the Milesian Fables, a collection of salacious stories originating in Miletus, a town in Asia Minor, which had the honour of supplying the harems of the oriental kings.

Women were interested in philosophy, and a philosophic treatise was dedicated to Octavia. Many influential ladies had their own personal philosophers, and were knowledgeable also about astrology and mathematics. Poppea was accompanied on her travels by so-called 'mathematicians' whose function was to predict her future. Livia, when she was left a widow by Drusus, was comforted by the philosopher Areus, her husband's friend. Agrippina Minor wrote her memoirs, and Augustus Caesar warned her, 'Take care lest you should write and speak in an affected manner.'

Aristocratic ladies competed among themselves not only over the number of their slaves, and the luxury of their dress and home, but also over the size and quality of their libraries. Most books were in the form of scrolls, the codex or bound book being unusual until a considerably later period. The scrolls were kept in large cases of cedar wood, which were usually part of the luggage taken on the various journeys, long or short, that Roman women made, either on holiday or when they followed their husbands on their expeditions.

A woman of a certain social status did not move from her home unless she were attended by a crowd of servants, slaves and friends. Always present was her *procurator*, who administered her estate, and perhaps her *cicisbeo*, and a load of luggage that would ensure her every comfort, including gold and silver tableware, curtains, furniture, precious materials, and all that was needed for her toilet. Poppea used to trail five hundred female donkeys around after her, using their milk for her daily bath.

Women usually travelled in litters, which were much more comfortable than the ordinary conveyances. During halts they would rest in their tents, or perhaps in the houses of friends or of public officials, or in hotels. But hotels, though they advertised 'Good service, baths and comforts like those of the Capital', were often disreputable places and always infested by fleas. It became necessary for a law to be passed that protected travellers and held hotel-keepers responsible for any harm that came to their clients during their stay in the hotel.

Even during their journeys women did not neglect their toilet, which was meticulous and very time-consuming. They used face packs, which often had a pestilential stink because they were made of sheep fat and breadcrumbs soaked in milk (a 'Poppean recipe'), which after a few hours became rancid. Ovid advised barley, vetch, ten eggs, powdered stag's antler, twelve narcissus bulbs, gum and honey, to give the complexion 'a shining whiteness'; and lupins, broad beans, white lead paint, red nitrate, orris root, kingfisher guano, perfumed myrrh, tree sap, honey, dried rose petals, salts of ammonia and barley infusions to eliminate pimples.

After she had attended to the removal of superfluous hair and applied her cosmetics, the fashionable Roman woman concentrated on dressing her hair. Roman women made great use of hair dyes, and coloured their hair black 'like the Bretons', red or blonde 'like the Germans', but never brassy yellow or blue, as these colours were used only by courtesans. The delicate operation of dressing the hair was always performed by a skilled slave, who might be scolded, punished, slapped, and tortured or jabbed with pins if a lock was out of place or the parting was not perfect.

Hair styles underwent numerous transformations. According to Ovid '. . . it would be easier to count the acorns on an oak tree, the Hyblaean bees, or the wild animals that live in the Alps, than the infinite number of hair styles and new fashions that appear every day.' He advised every woman to choose her hair style to suit her face: '. . . a long face requires a parting on the forehead; a light knot at the top of the head, leaving the ears uncovered, is more suitable for round faces.' Even if Ovid was exaggerating, it is quite true that fashion in hair styles did change continuously, so much so that sculptors commissioned to carve portraits were forced to make a special marble wig of the hair, which would be fitted to the head every time the fashion changed. However, it is possible to distinguish three main hair styles: the sober style of Octavia, the simple curls of Agrippina Major and the very complicated style of Messalina. The chief ornaments were tortoise-shell combs and large hairpins, often hollow so they could hold perfumes or poisons. One of the most attractive head ornaments was a band of pearls, worn Byzantine-fashion, which was decorated more and more heavily, until it became a diadem.

Detail of panel with St Ursula. Twelfth century. Museum of Catalan Art, Barcelona

The Middle Ages

The Byzantine Influence

The essence of the Byzantine age is contained in the name of a single woman: Theodora. Daughter of Acacius, a bear-feeder of the amphitheatre at Constantinople, she was extremely beautiful, and while still of tender years became a well-known courtesan. She acquired fame as 'the naked dancer of Subura', but escaped from this quarter of the city when Hecebolus, governor of Pentapolis in North Africa, fell in love with her. She accompanied him to Pentapolis, but having quarrelled they parted, and Theodora travelled through the cities of Asia Minor back to Constantinople. Here she returned to her licentious habits, until Justinian became fascinated by her strong personality.

Very intelligent and ambitious, this 'most beautiful woman of Byzantium' won the love of Justinian, nephew of the Emperor Justin and heir-presumptive to the throne. Roman law forbade marriage between a patrician and a courtesan, but Theodora managed to persuade her lover to have this law repealed. At the age of twenty-one she married Justinian, and at the age of twenty-seven she became Empress. Small but perfectly proportioned, with a delicate complexion, she was gifted with an imperious personality and great natural cunning, and used her influence over her husband with sagacity and skill. Notwithstanding her humble origins and free life, she reigned as a true empress over her loyal subjects.

Within her palace was found every luxury that was produced in Constantinople or that could be procured from foreign lands: silver columns, curtains of purple (the technique of purple dye was a secret jealously guarded by the Imperial manufacturers), Chinese scent burners, silver tables encrusted with mother-of-pearl and ivory, precious mosaics in which gold predominated, marble floors and gardens with marble paving stones, where enormous bronze dragons watched over ibis, peacocks and pheasants, and where fountains jetted cascades of scented water.

Her throne was of solid gold, encrusted with precious stones, with purple cushions that matched her footwear. Her coach, gold-plated, was pulled by four white horses; her dresses, cut very austerely with long, tight sleeves and a modest neckline, were always made of silk, enriched by splendid embroideries, which repeated typically Eastern geometrical patterns of stylised flowers, and were adorned with precious stones. Over the Byzantine tunic, the Empress wore the stole, and over it the

Left: The Emperor Arcadius. Istanbul Museum

palla (mantle), interwoven with fine gold threads. She also wore a gold collar, covered with pearls and gems. On her head she carried a heavy diadem of gold and pearls with cascades of pearls and emeralds reaching down to her breast. She also wore a necklace of large pearls set alternately with rubies and emeralds.

She was dressed like a goddess, but she knew all the refinements of the art of entertaining. She would offer Greek and Italian wines to her guests; with dessert she would serve wine from Lebanon, Falernian wine sweetened with Hymettus honey and Cos wine mixed with sea water. One of the subtle dishes which was served at her table was a roast peacock which had been fed with opium, according to an Indian custom.

If the Empress was fond of luxuries, the Emperor more than shared her enthusiasm. Over purple silk hose he wore a full-length Byzantine tunic, richly embroidered and covered with pearls, then a second tunic with a border of gold; a huge cloak covered this, embroidered in gold and precious stones, with a magnificent *clavus* (band). On his head he wore a splendid diadem, and his hair was cut short over the forehead but left long at the nape of the neck.

Beauty contests are reputed to have originated at this time introduced by another Empress: Theodosia, with the consent of her husband Basil II, sought a suitable wife for her son Leo by gathering together in her palace the twelve most beautiful girls in the Empire. The winner was a girl of sixteen, her perfect features framed by a helmet of hair in which was entwined a double strand of pearls.

As early as the year 441, the Empress Pulcheria had looked for a bride for her brother, Prince Theodosius,

School of Cassino. Twelfth century. Detail of fresco of St Angelo in Formis, Capua

Mourners. Detail of scene on side of sarcophagus. About 1300. From the Church of Mahaud. Burgos Museum of Catalan Art, Barcelona

amongst a group of girls one more beautiful than the other. But her plans did not succeed because in the meantime, while the candidates were collecting in the palace, Theodosius had fallen in love with a remarkable girl of twenty, Athenaïs, and had married her. In 788 the Empress Irene, too, had had recourse to a beauty contest to find a wife for her son Constantine. Messengers were sent throughout the whole of the Empire, and they collected a crowd of beauties. The prize of Constantine's hand went to Maria Dilumnia. Unfortunately the union was not a happy one, as after a few years the Emperor, to the great scandal of Christendom, repudiated his wife and married one of his mother's ladies-in-waiting.

Byzantine women took great care of their beauty, and used pomades and cosmetics of every kind. The Empress Zoë had brought to her from Ethiopia and India all the products she needed to keep young and slim, and her remedies were so successful that she appeared to be a mere thirty when she was already more than fifty, so that her contemporaries believed that she had managed to discover the secret of eternal youth. In any case, the beautiful Zoë, in order to

Right: Hunting scene. From a mosaic in the Villa Imperiale, Piazza Armerina, Sicily. *Below*: Detail from a group of Virgins in the Church of Sant' Apollinare Nuovo, Ravenna. *Below right*: Frederick II. Miniature from *Tractatus de Arte Venandi cum Avibus*. Thirteenth century

protect her skin, hardly ever went out of her palace, believing that fresh air was harmful.

The Early Middle Ages

Byzantine fashion spread throughout the world, and influenced the styles of the early Middle Ages. The pearl diadems became lower and heavier, but were always encrusted with precious stones. Jewellery became increasingly massive, and often included gold and silver crosses. The use of fans also became popular, though they were already known to the Egyptians, who used them to cool the air, and to the Chinese, who used them to drive away flies. Theodolinda, the Lombard queen, had a fan which became famous; made with pleated parchment all round, it had a handle and a sheath of finely carved ivory. She wore it dangling from her belt, as was then the fashion.

Men wore their hair longer, and the face was either clean-shaven or adorned with a short beard. Women never cut their hair, as their long plaits were considered one of the most important attributes of their beauty. Bertrada, the future wife of Pepin, King of France, was not only young and beautiful, but was the proud possessor of two very long plaits, which enchanted all who beheld them.

The son of Pepin and Bertrada was Charlemagne, born in 742; he proved an exceptional emperor, and his reign witnessed a revival of arts and letters and an increased interest in fashion. On ceremonial occasions he would go about in raiment woven of gold, his shoes covered with precious stones, his cloak fastened with a gold clasp, and he would adorn himself also with a golden diadem encrusted with stones. On any other day he hated wearing clothes which differed from the dress of the common people. He would dress very simply, and his furs were not ermine, fox, sable or marten, but sheep and rabbit. His womenfolk (he had five legitimate wives and four concubines) on the other hand were free to follow the fashion that prescribed dresses of subtly patterned silk; or woollen dresses of homespun, dyed red according to the newest techniques, using cinnabar or oak apples. The colours were fixed with the ammonia contained in the droppings of birds and in urine.

The nightgown was unknown in the Middle Ages: people either slept naked or in their shirts and shifts, the shift being the feminine version of the shirt, the same garment, but longer. It was a sign of wealth to possess a number of shifts. It is recorded that Gibertina, a Venetian lady, owned as many as five, embroidered round the neck and the sleeves with gold.

The Empress Irene. St Sophia, Istanbul

John II Comnenus. St Sophia, Istanbul

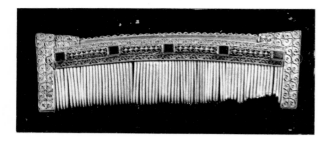

Comb and jewelled coronet belonging to Queen Theodolinda. Museum of the Basilica of San Giovanni, Monza

Typical medieval dress. From an illuminated manuscript in the Marciana Library, Venice

The Northern nations with their passion for heraldry introduced the fashion of two-coloured garments: the right half was different from the left half, and charged with heraldic emblems. The wealthy possessed the *crosna*, a fur overcoat. At wedding ceremonies the bridegroom, after the celebration of the vow, would offer a *crosna* to the bride, who promptly returned it to him as they crossed the marital threshold, because the garment was used both by men and women.

One of the main preoccupations for women of the early Middle Ages was the kitchen, particularly as meals were abundant. As luxury increased the tables

of wealthy people were covered with a cloth, hanging in folds, so that guests could wipe their hands and mouth on its folds. There would be three main courses—hors d'oeuvre and soup, meat and game, sweets and fruit. Not more than ten to fifteen hors-d'oeuvre were served, so that the guests' appetite was not spoiled: salads, often of hollyhock and hops, salt and pickled pork, and vegetables from the garden. Soup was highly esteemed, but chicken soup was eschewed by puritanical people, as it was thought to have aphrodisiac powers. Much of the poultry eaten was so tough that it could only be digested if boiled with sharp-tasting sauces. Considered delicious were plovers and doves, especially if cooked without taking out the entrails. Goose was very popular, the geese being fattened with bread soaked in lukewarm milk for three days before they were killed. Peacocks, the prince's meat, and swans were considered delicacies. Birds were served each one on a round piece

Right: Salome. Mosaic in St Mark's, Venice

Queen Theodolinda's fan. Pleated parchment with ivory holder. Museum of the Basilica of San Giovanni, Monza

of bread, arranged in a pyramid, so that each guest could take as many as he liked. Amongst vegetables, beans, broad beans, and peas were eaten, but not lentils which were considered indigestible and the cause of nightmares. The condiments most in use were garlic, onions, parsley, mint, fennel, aniseed and coriander.

Queens, princesses and noble ladies had many privileges, especially in the realm of fashion. They knew all the artifices necessary to make themselves attractive, and had a thousand ways with their veils. Queen Uta, one of the twelve founders of Naumburg Cathedral, according to her mood or the occasion would arrange her veil in a dramatic fashion (Byzantine), in a mysterious one (oriental) or a naive one, like the peasants' style.

Queens, princesses and noble ladies were, however, sometimes no more than pawns in the political struggles of the age: they were used to strengthen alliances, enlarge fiefs, or satisfy violent passions, such as those of Robert II, king of France, the son of Hugh Capet. At the age of eighteen Robert had been obliged for political reasons to marry Rosala, who was thirty-four years older than he. He repudiated her immediately after the marriage, and until the

age of twenty-two he lived as a virtuous and chaste bachelor. At that age he fell in love with Bertha, the wife of Eudes I, Count of Blois, and mother of five children. To win her, the king thought it necessary to declare war on his rival; Eudes, however, died of influenza, the war ended, and the king was able to marry the woman of his choice.

He had not reckoned, however, with the Pope, Gregory V, who excommunicated him because he had married his third cousin. In those times, marriage between even remote blood relations was considered incestuous. Bertha went through five years of humiliation and moral anguish, and finally her health began to suffer to such an extent that her husband was driven to give her up. He was then told that he must look for another wife with no blood ties to himself.

Robert then married Constance of Castille. She was so busy and self-absorbed that she never noticed the attachment which still existed between her husband and Bertha. She spent her time in the company of troubadours, whom she had brought with her from the South: 'Men with short hair and short trousers, hairless chins, and pointed shoes.' The troubadours, who originally came from Provence, went from court to court and from castle to castle,

Margaret of Provence. Louvre

Scenes from medieval life in an illumination in the Manesse manuscript. Thirteenth century. Heidelberg University Library

together with musicians who accompanied their verses on the viol or the lute. The troubadours were messengers of love, but they also performed the task of relaying news and gossip.

The patroness of troudabours was Eleanor of Aquitaine. 'God save Dame Eleanor the Queen, who is judge of honour, of spirit and beauty, of generosity and loyalty,' sang Philippe of Thaun. Eleanor was a woman of very individual tastes. She was the first to adopt the medieval fashion of a dress with a train and very wide sleeves, often so long that they touched the ground (the use of many yards of material was supposed to demonstrate the wealth and nobility of the wearer). Her dresses were made of the complicated silk weave known as samite; her embroideries were picked out in pearls set in gold; her *bandinella* was of linen, and her cloaks were of wool dyed with indigo; the seams of her clothes were concealed by strands of pearls; and she wore the most refined of jewels, veils, and other accessories.

At the age of fourteen, having been left an orphan by her father, William of Aquitaine, Eleanor married Prince Louis who became Louis VII of France. She followed him to the Holy Land during the Second Crusade, where she began to seriously consider divorcing her husband. She returned to France and

Glove in the Coronation regalia of the Holy Roman Emperors. Twelfth century. Imperial Treasury, Vienna

Falconer with plumed hat and saddle cloth. Capodilista Codex, Padua

their marriage was annulled in 1151 by mutual consent. She was married again, this time to Henry of Anjou, bringing as a dowry the immense territories inherited from her father. From this event stems the strife between England and France, which shaped medieval history. Henry, the grandson of William the Conqueror, succeeded to the English throne in 1154, and Eleanor's dowry became part of the domain of the crown of England.

In London the queen was sad, far away from the French landscape and sunshine. She spent her days spinning wool, playing the viol, and weeping. But her tears were quenched on the day that she met Bernard de Ventadour, the famous troubadour. She went back with him to France, and with him she set up the 'Court of Love' where, together with twenty other ladies, splendidly dressed in *cendal* (a type of taffeta), with long plaits down to their waists, she gravely discussed the 'Code of Love', composed of thirty-one articles, some of which were curious and bold: 'Love never lives in a house of avarice; marriage is not a legitimate bar against love; the lover who survives his beloved must mourn for two years; the true lover is always shy; and there is nothing to prevent a woman being loved by two men, or a man being loved by two women.'

Left: Queen Uta. Naumburg Cathedral

Below: Detail from a corbel. Duomo, Modena

There were discussions on particular problems such as whether true love can exist between husband and wife. The answer they arrived at was that love cannot exist between two persons bound by marriage; true lovers give everything to one another graciously, without being obliged to do so by the law; love disappears where husband and wife have the *duty* of submitting to each other's will, and never refusing each other anything.

The 'Court of Love' organised tournaments, in which heavily armoured knights wearing the colours of their lady on their helmets took part, mounted on horses splendidly caparisoned. At the Court of Love they discussed the feats of King Arthur, read romances like the *Roman de la Rose*, commented on the exploits of the valiant Orlando, or talked of the scandals of the day, like the affair of Genevieve of Brabant, who was accused of committing adultery with her steward, a man many years younger than her.

Because of her royal duties, Eleanor was obliged, however, to go to and fro between London and Poitiers, a city always dear to her heart, not only because Bernard de Ventadour lived there, but also because it was the centre of her territories, which she governed with wise firmness. Her relationship with her husband deteriorated at this time to the point of hatred. When her children rebelled against their father in 1173, she took their part. She was made a prisoner by the English, and confined in the castle at Salisbury, where she lived as a prisoner for sixteen years; Richard, her favourite son, set her free at the death of Henry II. After a long career of political importance, Eleanor, who signed herself 'Queen of England by the wrath of God', died at the age of eighty-two and was buried at Fontevrault.

Her story takes place at the time of the great re-awakening of mankind which occurred after the year 1000. Men and women freed themselves from the nightmare of disastrous prophecies which had preceded the end of the millennium, and experienced new hope for the future.

Arts and crafts flourished again, and there were fewer savage incursions into the territory of neighbouring lords, fewer senseless duels, life became a little milder and hunting was preferred to war. Castles were built with windows; sanitary services were installed; carpets covered the floors of hard earth, which poor people had insulated with layers of dead leaves in winter; walls were enriched by hanging tapestries.

St Julia. The Scaligeri Tomb. Middle of the twelfth century. Verona

From the altar of the Church of San Vicenzo. Twelfth century. Museum of Catalan Art. Barcelona.

Physical comfort became more important, especially in relation to sleep: woollen mattresses replaced the heap of leaves on the floor. During the summer a single mattress, longer than the body, so that a third of it was folded over to form a head-rest, gave sufficient comfort; during the winter the four poster bed, single or double, was preferred, on which people slept swathed tightly in sheets and blankets. The pillow might be many-coloured, and the mattress was always raised so that the sleeper rested comfortably half sitting up. A lamp was sometimes suspended from the ceiling and kept alight all through the night to drive away evil spirits.

This was the age of superstition. If a bride on her wedding day crossed the path of a dishevelled woman, a hare, a dog or a blind man, a lame man or a snake, she was sure that her marriage would always be unhappy. It was also a common belief that if a person made a knot in a string, a ribbon, or even a hair behind the backs of the newly wedded couple, while reciting the *miserere* backwards, the marriage would come to a disastrous end. In order to reverse the evil spell, the bridegroom had to wear, throughout the wedding ceremony, two shirts inside out.

The Age of Chivalry

The age was redeemed by the institution of chivalry which, whatever its shortcomings in practice, did set up an ideal to be followed. A long preparation was needed to become a knight: a noble youth would, at the age of ten or eleven, come to live at the court of a prince or a feudal lord. For about four years he would fulfil the duties of a page to his lord, and acquire the necessary education: he would train at sports—riding, swimming, archery, fencing and hunting—as well as learn the art of writing poetry and playing chess. If he distinguished himself in these arts, he would be promoted to the rank of squire, and could follow his feudal lord in battle. At the age of twenty-one he would be dubbed knight with a ceremony as solemn as it was splendid; when Frederick Barbarossa had his two sons ordained as knights, he gave such a magnificent feast that it was remembered for years to come.

Knights were clothed in a woollen tunic that came just below the knee, over which they wore a coat of mail, a shorter tunic made of a network of metal rings. A heavy sword hung on the left side from a wide leather belt, with a strap on the right shoulder. On the head was worn an iron helmet, in the shape of a pointed cupola, or round with a little brim. Their chief weapons were a long double-edged sword, bow and arrows, lances of various types and a heavy iron club. A knight carried also a shield on which was depicted the coat of arms of the fief to which he owed allegiance or the emblems of his beloved.

The spirit of chivalry had a profound moral effect on the age. Besides the strict code of honour which governed a knight's behaviour, one of his ideals was to honour and cherish the female sex. In an age when women counted for so little that it was believed they did not possess a soul, and were deprived of any rights over their children (in Frisia, a child who lost his father at the age of nine was granted emancipation

Above: Andrea Bonaiuti. Detail from *Glorie dei Domeni-cani*. Santa Maria Novella, Florence

Above: School of Benedetto Antelami. Detail of figure representing September in the 'Allegory of the Months'. Baptistery, Parma. *Below*: Herbalist. Medieval miniature from *Tacuinum Sanitatis*

and thus became the guardian of his own mother); in an age when women were regarded as chattels (in Norway husbands could sell their wives to pay their debts or could give them away to their friends) knights rendered homage both to noblewomen and common women, elevating them to the rank of 'lady and dame'.

This attitude is reflected in the writings of Abelard, the unhappy lover of Eloise. The Breton philosopher in his letters and essays had always praised women in this way: 'God's kindness, when he prepared his grandiose plan of creation, reserved without any

doubt a special place for woman. From the very fact that he created her after Adam, we must see man as a means, woman as an end in herself. Our knights, today, enfold woman with sweet admiration. Have women perhaps changed? I see them proud, passionate, exacting, and every day I see men spending all their energies to gain their woman's heart. This is a new state of affairs which shows how advanced and pious our civilisation must be. Women, you have said "No" to brutality, and to your credit the century to come will be a century of sweetness.'

The new position of women in society encouraged them to abandon the uniform and rather monotonous—even if graceful—draping of their dresses, and to desire greater elegance. This greatly stimulated trade in cloth, since they wore an increasing number of undergarments and outer garments, all of them very full.

The most sought-after cloth came from Flanders, and this was usually scarlet and green with patterns in squares, circles and dots. Silk was manufactured in Genoa, Florence and Lucca. Raw materials were imported into Paris and then finished by spinners organised into guilds. Oriental motifs were abandoned and replaced by western designs, both religious and secular in character.

In Italy women began to wear a second tunic, tight at the waist and fuller at the hem, over a long undertunic. Sleeves which were narrow where they were set into the shoulder, became wide towards the wrist, so that a glimpse was caught of the under-tunic of a different colour. The neckline was square and deep; the skirt, sleeves and neck had borders of coloured materials, often embroidered; bodices were worn on the outside. A Sicilian poet describing the girl he loved wrote: 'With her *wiscia* [leather bodice embroidered with pearls and other gems], her veil and her jewels she seems, to whoever gazes at her, like a sun clothed in splendour, crowned by thick darkness and surrounded by stars.'

Instead of pockets, which were still unknown, both men and women carried bags which could be hung on a shoulder strap or else suspended from the belt; they were either square or rectangular. Men wore a short tunic over a longer one, brightly coloured, made either of wool, linen or silk heavily embroidered or striped in many different colours; this shorter garment was slit up the sides to make movements easier. A leather belt was worn round the waist, adorned with metal studs: the fashion for buttons began in the thirteenth century. The nether garments consisted of long knitted stockings which matched the tunic and were quite often red. For older people fashion prescribed a tunic down to the ankles but tight around the hips, and a full robe open in front with wide short sleeves; this had no belt, but a narrow collar, fur-trimmed in winter.

Above: Container decorated with peacocks and gazelles. First half fourteenth century. Palazzo Venezia Museum, Rome. *Left*: Detail of landscape showing an Italian town. Ambrogio Lorenzetti. Art Gallery, Siena. *Right*: St Nicholas saves three women condemned to death (detail). Correr Museum, Venice

Medieval shoes.

French women wore the *chainse*, a full-length undergarment which they took off at night before going to bed. The dress was shorter, full, with wide sleeves, embroidered and held in at the waist by a belt made of cloth or metal. Often the bodice was cut at the waist to allow for a fuller skirt. This dress was abandoned when the *surcot* came into vogue; this was a garment that was very wide and very long, its fullness gathered in at the waist. On the shoulders a rectangular or semi-circular cloak was worn, fastened by cords. French women invented the fashion for two-coloured dresses, a fashion which spread to Italy and England.

Their hair was worn loose on their shoulders or divided by a parting; it was covered by a *guimpe*, a veil that was swathed around the neck. Towards the end of the thirteenth century women started to cut their hair, and some even shaved it off completely. They also used stockings in winter, and had low, pointed shoes. Men wore the *chainse* like the women, but soldiers had breast-plates of various types, or else a short tunic entirely covered with metal mesh or plaited with metal strips, a helmet with a moveable visor, metal greaves, knee-caps, metal shoes with spurs and metal gloves.

Northern women were influenced by French and Italian fashions, though they often wore over their dresses another sleeveless tunic, open on the hips below the waist so that the contrasting colour of the garment underneath could be seen. This fashion was later taken up by the men, who adopted it, with some modifications, for their cloaks. The head-dress terminated in a stylised crown, and the face was framed by a small net which passed under the chin. From the North spread the fashion for furs, which were also obtained from Asia, after the first Crusades. Bear, sable and marten were very expensive, and so they often used lamb, fox, hare, cat and even dog. There were long furs down to the ground, fur linings for cloaks (Graziano Gradenigo in his wardrobe inventory included: 'a big fur of hare covered in vermilion cloth'), fur borders for collars and sleeves. White skins were sometimes dyed, usually a brilliant scarlet; ermine was adorned with the little black tufts at the end of the little animal's tail.

Gloves were already known to the Romans and even earlier. Xenophon noted that the Persians used gloves with separate fingers, but medieval gloves were probably of German origin. They were a symbol of authority as well as of feudal investiture. To give a glove was a sign of trust; to throw a glove or to deal a blow with a glove was an act of provocation, a challenge which was followed by a duel. Gloves in the thirteenth century were made of iron for soldiers, or of leather, specially reinforced, for falconry. The fashion for gloves was quickly taken up by women, who had them made up in silk, leather, hemp, skin, fastened at the wrist by buttons or with turn-ups often lined with fur. Later they were adorned with embroidery and precious stones. The skins were often treated with perfumes, and sometimes with poisonous substances for less romantic purposes. Strict rules regulated when gloves were to be worn: it was forbidden to appear in the presence of the feudal lord, or to enter a church, to salute, to dance or to render homage in any other way while wearing gloves.

The care of feminine beauty was felt to be a subject of particular importance. Trotula, a woman doctor of the School of Salerno, who lived in the year 1100, gave advice which was followed for many years to

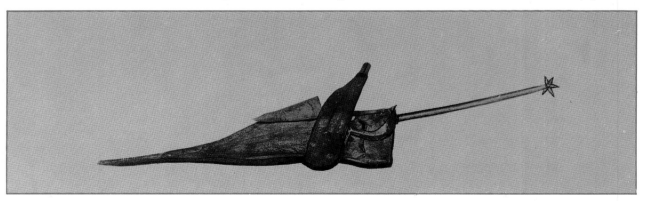

The cobbler's shop. Medieval miniature. Fourteenth century

come. To keep slim, a problem which preoccupied women even in those days, Dame Trot (as she was called in England) prescribed bathing in sea water, and using as a deodorant infusions of herbs, such as bayleaves, calamint, absinthe and hyssop. For the more generously built women, she recommended the application of frictions with cow dung dissolved in good wine, followed by a prolonged stay in the 'stove', a small chamber which was heated with a fire of elder-wood to such a temperature that profuse sweating was obtained; after this, a good bath and relaxation in bed improved the circulation. 'Sand graves [sand baths] near the sea bed', it was suggested, would achieve the same effect.

There were further prescriptions to prevent wrinkles; to whiten the skin through the application of leeches, which were supposed to reduce unsightly

The month of April. Detail of the 'Allegory of the Constellations'. The sign of Taurus. Hall of the Palazzo Comunale, Padua

redness; to keep gums healthy by rinsing the mouth with lukewarm wine; to make lips firm by coating them with honey; to remove superfluous hair with quicklime; to make hair blonde by rinsing it in henna, gorse flowers, saffron, eggs or calf's kidneys; to soften hair by rubbing the scalp with the body of a lizard boiled in olive oil; to perfume the hair with dried roses, nutmeg, caraway and cardamoms all dissolved in rose water, or with watermelon juice, iris juice, lily pods, vine tendrils, or a mixture of eggs, breadcrumbs and vinegar.

Medical prescriptions were equally fanciful, but scrupulously applied. To combat fever a little bag containing a green frog would be hung round the patient's neck. Against epilepsy it was enough to hang round the sufferer's neck a medal on which were engraved the names of the three Wise Men, Caspar, Melchior and Balthazar. Migraine would disappear if a piece of rope used by a hangman was tied around the head. To lessen labour pains a woman was encouraged to wear her husband's socks; he was advised to climb the nearest bell tower, encircle the biggest bell with his wife's belt, and make it ring three times.

There were numerous remedies against vermin: the bed was brought into the open air, and beaten with a hazel twig on Good Friday; or one could keep alight all the year round the embers of a fire lighted on St John's Day; or sweep the room from the outside inwards towards the fireplace on Ash Wednesday Eve; or beat the beds three times with a hazel sprig, in the spring, at the first croaking of the frogs.

Towards the end of the eleventh century the feudal system was modified by the trend towards self-government, which resulted in the establishment of Craft-guilds and Communes. Noblemen and burghers reached a compromise, a sworn pact which was the basis of the city's government. The burghers organised themselves; and the tradesmen and the artisans formed Guilds. The Roman Guilds were the earliest known Guilds, but because they became rebellious and mutinous clans, they were in great part abolished by Julius Caesar; later they were reorganised by Augustus, who, however, put them under the control of the State, so that they did not transcend their function of protecting production and labour. The Guilds had a period of decadence during the barbaric invasions and the feudal system, but were revived in the Communes, first as simple associations, later as compulsory organisations of producers

Right: Detail of a procession, showing headgear. Lombard school, fourteenth century. Trivulzio collection, Milan

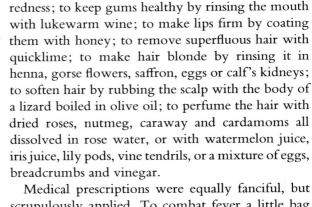

Detail of fresco from the hall of the Castle of Manta, Saluzzo

who wanted to protect the interests of their group. The early Guilds were almost all connected with the textile industry; amongst those who first organised themselves thus we find the weavers and the dyers.

At this time, ladies wore soft flowing garments, with very high waists to enhance the beauty of the breasts. Sleeves were narrow, almost tight fitting; skirts were slit on one side to allow a glimpse of the petticoat; the neckline was square and was often bordered with a dark binding. A popular dress was the *dalmatica*, a tunic of uneven length, with slits at the hips, bound with a gold border. The sleeves of this dress were short and caught above the elbow with gold bands, from which ribbons of the material would hang. This tunic was worn over a full-length robe with long narrow sleeves.

In Italy the wealth and social position of women was often indicated by the colour of their clothes. The brighter colours were reserved for fine ladies:

scarlet, green, morello (dark purple) and tawny (orangy yellow). Blue cloth was reserved for workers, white cloth for monks, dark green for clerks, and brown for knights; cloths with multi-coloured stripes were for messengers and pages.

During this period hats took many different shapes and forms: turbans, berets, cones, top hats with wide upturned brim, bonnets or hoods. The hood was often a fold of the cloak passed over the head, a fashion that was popular with women and that the poet Guido Guinizelli praised with these words:

Who has seen Lucia with her hood
Covering her head—oh how it suits her!
There is no man in the Land of Abruzzo
Who wouldn't fall head over heels in love with her.

As time passed clothes became richer and more extravagant than ever before. Dresses had longer

Another detail from the same fresco

trains, jewels became heavier and adorned the body from head to toe; accessories became more precious. Finally sumptuary laws were passed to put an end to this enormous waste. Pope Gregory X, in the second Council of Lyons, amongst other prohibitions forbade women to wear 'ornaments without moderation'. Two years later 'the Pope commanded that pearls be forbidden to women . . . also gold and silver braids'. It was ruled that trains must be shorter and that veils should be worn in place of any other headgear. Very ingeniously women evaded this law by wearing veils of fine linen and silk, interwoven with gold, in which they looked ten times more attractive.

In France, Philippe le Bel forbade dukes, counts, barons and their wives to own more than four garments; and unmarried women could only own one dress, unless they were heiresses who had inherited castles. Moreover he forbade burghers' wives to wear ermine, *petit-gris*, squirrel, gold and precious stones.

Engraving of fifteenth-century castle

But even the King had his small defeat. In his edicts he had forgotten to mention shoes, so that these became a symbol of elegance, especially through the efforts of a certain *sieur* Poulain. He invented a new type of shoe, more or less pointed according to the rank of the wearer. The *poulaine*, as it was called, was as long as two feet for princes and noblemen, one foot for rich people of lower degree and only half a foot for common people.

We cannot leave the Middle Ages without some reference to the role of women in this epoch of transition. In the Middle Ages women from the nobility had a very different position from women of lower degree. Clotilde, the wife of Clovis, played a decisive role in the conversion of France to Catholicism, which of course was an event of radical importance in European history. When there was a weak monarchy and a strong nobility, in the confusion that followed women often fought to preserve their own estates. Widows, on behalf of their children, defended their fiefs when threatened by vassals and enemies with the strength and conviction of men. Eleanor of Aquitaine and Matilda, wife of William the Conqueror, are women of this period who had great political importance. Both governed their own territories in their husband's absence. Ermengard of Narbonne, who kept her numerous husbands to the level of prince consorts, was a patron of the Church and of troubadours; she fought valiantly for many years to defend her inheritance, and was often consulted in difficult feudal disputes. For sixty-five years Flanders was governed by two women, the two sisters Joanna and Margaret; and Margaret's labours restored her country which had been devastated by war. Blanche of Castille, Louis VIII's wife, when she was made a widow, fought against the rebel noblemen in her land; she concluded the peace of Paris, and protected the Jews, and when her son St Louis came of age, she continued to exert her influence on government; her daughter-in-law, Margaret of Provence, though she detested her, followed her example. Women took part in the first two Cru-

sades: Isabella de Conches, Joan of Toulouse and many others. Women who competed with troubadours included Countess Beatrix of Dié and her daughters. Marie de Ventadour was as extraordinary a poet as Joan of Arc was an extraordinary soldier. In Paris one hundred and eight professions were exercised by women: they were weavers and traders, managers of great enterprises in international trade, miniaturists, doctors and embroiderers.

The abbess Hildegard of Bingen considered that the decadence of Church and society in the twelfth century was due to masculine weakness. For this reason, she started a feminine religious movement in the North, which was in the end defeated by the masculine philosophy which knows only one ethic for men and of men; the other half of mankind is considered only in so far as it is useful to men. Thomas Aquinas wrote 'Woman was created to help man only in procreation, because in any other work another man will provide better assistance than a woman.' This was written while women had the full burden of work in the fields and in the towns. In the late Middle Ages, when men took the place of women in several feminine occupations, German towns fell into a period of decadence.

In the courtly civilisation of the twelfth century women had learnt to sing and recite, to write poems and to philosophise; their lives were conducted at a high cultural level. But towards the end of the Middle Ages men believed women were empty vessels with nothing to say, who must be kept silent in church, in the family and in society. Forgotten were the times of the great abbesses and queens, of the great ladies of courtly life, of poetesses and mystics—women had to accept life, men or poverty as they came. From time to time, however, a feminine voice would be raised, high and clear, like that of St Catherine of Siena.

The only resource of most women was fashion, which at the beginning of the Renaissance was to become even more splendid, cumbersome and sophisticated.

Ivory comb from Germany. The carving depicts the fountain of youth. Victoria and Albert Museum, London

The Fifteenth Century

The Early Renaissance

From the crucible of the Middle Ages, through transformations, wars and struggles, was born the Renaissance. The Communes disappeared and the lordships and oligarchies took their place, a new political system supported by the majority of the urban bourgeoisie and by the lower classes themselves, who were tired of continuous internal wars and their tumultuous, disordered life. The Renaissance brought not only a political transformation but also a widespread growth of interest in culture, both Latin and Greek. The revival of learning provided a meeting point for the different social strata.

The interest in classical learning, in those studies that Cicero had described as 'human', gave birth to humanism, which was the perception of the dignity of man as a rational being, a recognition of the essential goodness of man. The spirit of humanism had enormous influence on scholarship, literature, the fine arts, science and philosophy, and on every aspect of everyday life. And the changes in fashion punctiliously underlined this cultural evolution, translating the new taste for beauty into luxurious clothing and splendid furniture. Women, with their intuition and sensitivity, at every turn caught the mood of this new consciousness; however, with few exceptions, they were relegated to a role inferior to that of the man.

Some great feminist intellects, however, shone brilliantly, for example that of Alexandra Mancini Strozzi, a woman of the middle classes, who poured her philosophy of life into her letters, and Isabella d'Este Gonzaga, Marchioness of Mantua, a most accomplished and learned woman.

Her parents, Ercole d'Este and Eleanor of Aragona, carefully educated Isabella in both literature and the arts, and she was one of the most cultured women of her time. From her father she inherited three passions: building palaces, travelling and organising theatrical spectacles. From her mother she learnt the arts of embroidery and of music; she played the harp, violin, clavichord and the lute. She had a great love of literature, and from the days of childhood she learnt to appreciate Italian translations of French novels, Spanish romances, the letters of Pliny, the commentaries of Caesar, Boethius' *Consolation of Philosophy*, and many other Greek and Latin authors such as Euripides, Plutarch, Seneca, Plautus and Terence.

Her erudition was far greater than that of her husband—a man of arms rather than of letters, and

Left: Herodias. Detail of Herod's Feast. Masolino. Baptistery, Castiglione Olona

physically ugly, with a bulldog face—but she loved him faithfully. In her letters Isabella unconsciously showed her proud and sweet character and her passionate interest in all that surrounded her. She conducted a complicated correspondence with the greatest geniuses of her time and with the most powerful princes; ambassadors, Papal Nuncios and the Knights of Rhodes wrote to her about what they saw and heard; Pigafetta described to her his fabulous travels in uncharted seas. The Marchioness also corresponded with craftsmen and merchants who provided her with the best in the international market for the adornment of herself and her ladies-in-waiting, her rooms and her palaces. From France she had sent to her amethysts and fabrics, *toile de Reims* and gold chains, and wooden dolls dressed in the latest fashion, the *mannequins* of the time.

She was interested in everything: affairs of state, the latest fashions in jewels or dresses, the purchase of a turquoise or a Persian cat, a musical instrument or a statue, the news that the last Canto of Ariosto's poem was finished, or that her sister Beatrice owned a belt like that of St Francis, but studded with precious

Illustration from the manuscript *L'Acerba* by Cecco d'Ascoli. Venetian school. Trivulziana Library, Milan

Following pages: 'The Birth of the Virgin'. Detail. Fra Carnevale. Metropolitan Museum, New York

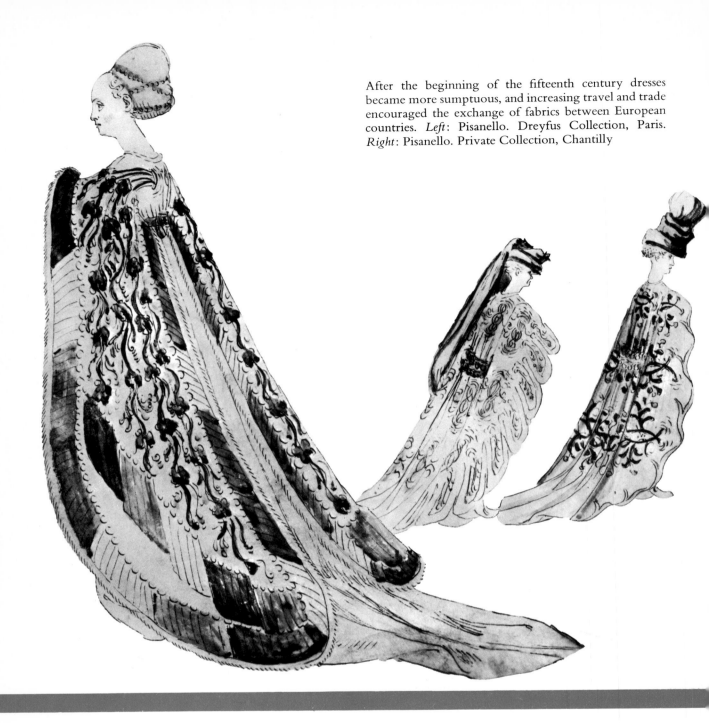

After the beginning of the fifteenth century dresses became more sumptuous, and increasing travel and trade encouraged the exchange of fabrics between European countries. *Left*: Pisanello. Dreyfus Collection, Paris. *Right*: Pisanello. Private Collection, Chantilly

stones. In her letters she went into the minutest details (as later Madame de Sévigné was to do), giving her orders with the same precision and clearsightedness, be it a matter of State defence, or the subject of a painting. 'She most strikingly and perfectly personified the aspirations of the Renaissance.'

A French fashion, launched at the beginning of the fifteenth century by Marie de Clèves, was the *hennin*, a cone balanced on the head, from the tip of which hung a light veil, often woven in gold. A variant of this head-dress was shaped somewhat like a saddle, with a draped veil, which fell on the carefully shaven forehead. The fashion for the *hennin* spread to Italy,

notwithstanding the opposition of the priests who taught the street urchins to run after ladies dressed in this fashion, crying in mockery 'Hennin, hennin'. In France this headgear grew to such enormous sizes that architects were obliged to enlarge the doors of the Castle of Blois to allow the ladies of the Court to pass through comfortably, without having to lower their heads. Isabella of Bavaria wore one of gold brocade a yard long, studded with precious stones, from which hung a veil that covered her shoulders and back. In order to restrain the devotees to this fashion it became necessary to pass a law regulating its size according to the rank of the wearer.

90

The fifteenth century was known for the folly of its headgear: the multiplicity and oddity of its coifs and *hennins* were famous; sometimes made of many-coloured gauzes, or of saffron-scented muslin; or of stiffened Holland cloth stretched over a rigid frame, with finely-pleated trimmings and a veil fixed by a golden brooch; or of turbans studded with gems; or mitre shapes in golden brocade. Amidst such luxury the little hat of Joan of Arc, with a round low crown and a slightly turned-up brim, was modest and simple.

After the first few decades of the fifteenth century dresses became more sumptuous and underwent certain radical changes. The Greeks and Romans had garbed themselves in fabrics without seams, draped in various ways, sometimes to create the illusion of a sleeve. In the Middle Ages, the Barbarians replaced the draping, which was uncomfortable to ride and fight in, with dresses, which were pulled over the head and sewn with coarse stitches each time they were worn. Though in France buttons had been known from the time of the Merovingians, in other countries they were not in common use until the end of the fourteenth century; this was due partly to the feeling that buttons were the symbol of a 'loose' life, as they allowed one to 'loosen' one's garments with greater ease than before.

Frontispiece of illustrated manuscript. A Master of Lombardy. Fifteenth century. Trivulziana Library, Milan

Right: Six illustrations from the *Codice Capodilista*. Civic Museum, Padua

Women's dresses in the early fifteenth century became more sumptuous with the use of new fabrics: damask (so called after the town of Damascus that had inspired its typical patterns) plain coloured but with threads of different texture woven into it; taffeta of Persian origin; Genoese velvet; and fabrics made from the by-products of silk. Improved communications with even very distant lands and more frequent journeys helped the spread of different materials to all parts of Europe.

At this time the dress, usually made in very heavy material, was designed with a high, tight-fitting bodice, supported by ivory or wooden busks that were enamelled, carved or engraved. In France and also in Italy women deepened and widened the neckline, sometimes exposing their bare breasts, as did Eleanor, the favourite of Charles VIII. She was present, thus 'disarrayed', at a banquet organised in her honour during the Italian campaign of the King of France. Eleanor and her rivals in elegance, to enhance the beauty of the bosom, used poppy water, an infusion made of ivy, rose oil and camphor.

The tight-fitting bodice was attached to a skirt which was gathered or flowed in soft pleats. Skirts were often caught up with silver and golden hooks

Figures on a Florentine chest showing the influence of ancient culture on dress. Victoria and Albert Museum, London

Pallas and Arachne. Engraving from Ovid's *Metamorphoses*. Fifteenth century

which were masterpieces of the jeweller's art. Long sleeves attached to the bodice by strings terminating in a gold or silver tip (or *aiguillette*) and passed through open buttonholes in the dress were another refinement, which came of the German influence. In France sleeves were very wide, or shaped like funnels, with fur cuffs. In Italy they had either horizontal or vertical slits, skilfully placed slashings through which the shirt puffed out, or else they were very tight on the forearm, reaching to the wrist.

Isabella of Castille was not only the patroness of Christopher Columbus and co-governor of Spain with her husband Ferdinand; not only was she a great political figure, engaged in waging war against Portugal, and driving the Moors from her own country, but she also introduced the fashion for sleeves slit from top to bottom, or divided into strips and fastened at regular intervals with gold or silver buttons. The chemise was allowed to puff out through the slits.

On a woman's dressing table at this period gold and silver bottles for cosmetics and pomades made a great show, together with ear-cleaners, tooth-cleaners, nail-cleaners and tongue-scrapers—little sticks in wood or precious metals. It was recommended that hands and eyes should be washed in cold water every morning; hot water was used only for a complete bath, which was usually taken once a year in the autumn. (At a later date immersion in hot water became more popular among the aristocracy.) The bath was considered a means of relaxation, especially after a journey, and many ladies used to prolong it to the extent that they had breakfast served to them in their tub. Hair was washed every week, and Lucrezia Borgia had her journey from Rome to Ferrara—where her fiancé Duke Alfonso was waiting for her—postponed for several days, in order to

allow time for herself and her maids-in-waiting to perform the complicated task of washing their hair.

The trains on dresses that had caused so many sermons—a century before, a bishop had thundered from his pulpit: 'If women had needed a tail, God would have provided them with one'—grew longer and longer, and were often made heavier with embroidery or precious stones, so that they had to be carried by pages. Thirteen-year-old Margaret, niece of Francis, on the day of her wedding with the Duke of Cleves, had to be carried bodily to the church because her dress, woven with gold and studded with precious stones, was so heavy.

Many materials were embellished not only with formal designs of Eastern origin but also with patterns of leaves and flowers. Nettle leaves were embroidered in white velvet on a black silk background for the cloaks of French princes; silver nettle leaves were appliquéd to the violet cloaks of the Sieurs d'Armagnac; pale green nettle leaves decorated the dark green *huque*, a short sleeveless tunic, to contrast with the red skirt, the white sleeves and stockings of Joan of Arc. The 'smallest soldier of France' (she was only five feet four inches) owned a wardrobe of which chroniclers have given us many details: a black doublet with a little collar, tight-fitting breeches (which were considered shocking because they were worn by a woman, albeit a woman soldier), a short lead-grey tunic and a woollen beret. When Joan met the Dauphin of France in Chinon, she wore a dress of vermilion silk and a *huque* of dark green, the gift of Charles, Duc d'Orléans, for her good service against the English. Another of her dresses was red woollen cloth of Flemish origin, lined with white silk, encrusted with eighty-three nettle leaves of green cloth, with full sleeves gathered at the wrists and trimmed with marten; these elegant but very practical sleeves she used as pockets in the fashion of the time.

Joan of Arc was a soldier, a woman with a mystical and masculine soul, but Margaret of Scotland, the first wife of Louis XI, who was born about 1425, was a weak woman, soon to be broken by her tumultuous life and by the unjust jealousy of her husband. Her husband, the only king of France who was never dominated by women, but had two wives and ten favourites, had married Margaret when she was ten and he only fourteen. His impetuous and imperious character pushed him into numerous adventures, both amorous and warlike, so that Louis neglected his wife. She found comfort in her long periods of

Right: 'Allegory of the Months'. Detail. Francesco Cossa. Schifanoia Palace, Ferrara

94

95

Women's hair styles. Pisanello. Albertina Library, Vienna

'Portrait of a Lady.' Domenico Veneziano

loneliness by composing love poems and having innocent discussions with her ladies on the *tendre amour,* part of the tradition of chivalry.

In these superstitious times the recipe for gaining the heart of one's beloved was to capture a toad on a Friday night 'while Venus was shining', dry it, reduce it to powder, put the powder in a little bag made of soft linen, and put the little bag for three days at the foot of an altar where Mass was celebrated. This powder was sprinkled on a bouquet of flowers which was offered to the girl; she would smell the flowers and inhale the powder, and would immediately burn with love. Love and fidelity were kept at a constant pitch by burning a lock of hair of the beloved, by spreading honey on her bed and sprinkling this with the ashes. If a man fell in love with a woman who persisted in fidelity to her husband, all he had to do was to put a magnet under her bed.

Louis XI did not in the least appreciate the pastimes of his queen. Not a very cultured man, suspicious, indifferent to the 'Paradise of Love', he was incited by his chamberlain Jamet du Tillay, and became embittered because he had no heir. His cruelty reduced his wife to a state of neurasthenia; though she ate basketfuls of unripe apples and drank pints of vinegar —remedies which according to common belief encouraged pregnancy—Margaret never wore the necklace of green-coloured diamonds which were supposed to help in labour. She passed away at the

age of eighteen, expressing her bitterness with the words, 'Fie upon life; speak to me no more of it.' The funeral oration of Louis was cynically concise: 'Our spouse has died of excess of poetry.'

He soon consoled himself by falling in love with Marguerite de Sassenages, who pursued him very cleverly. The story goes that she lingered in a corridor where the King had to pass, and lifted her skirt, pretending to have lost her garter, and in this way made

Jeanne de Laval, second wife of René d'Anjou. Medallion. Luciano Laurana. Bibliothèque Nationale

Left: After the disappearance of the *hennin* the hair was bound in ribbons in the classical manner. 'Portrait of Margherita Gonzaga'. Detail. Pisanello. Louvre

A Jewish wedding. Illustration from a manuscript. Jacob ben Essen. Vatican Library, Rome

him notice her. The garter had been an adjunct to feminine elegance since the fourteenth century. According to legend, it was the garter lost by the Countess of Salisbury during a ball, and picked up by Edward III, King of England, which gave birth to the Order of the Garter, to which twenty-five knights were elected, the King himself presiding. When Edward III picked up the countess' little accessory, the courtiers couldn't help laughing at the confusion of the lady. Very gallantly the King, lifting up the little circlet of brocade, pronounced the historic sentence 'Honi soit qui mal y pense.'

During the Renaissance the garter—nowadays seldom worn—was not always popular. The Duchess of Orleans, however, had a whole collection of garters, of which some were of gold and enamel work, with designs that signified her sorrow in her widowhood. Mourning did not show itself only in such eccentricities, often of dubious taste, but for centuries had had well-defined rules.

Wearing black was the most usual expression of grief. Women wore a dark cloak with a hood, and wound bands of pure white cloth around their faces. In an elegy, composed in Arabic on the occasion of the death of the son of Roger the Frank, Prince of Sicily, the mourning was described thus: 'They had been gaily dressed like doves, but they came back in their mourning like ravens.' In 1187 the news that after the victory of Saladin, Jerusalem had fallen into the hands of the Muslims, was brought to Italy by messengers clad in dark clothes. Often women in mourning would cut off their hair, as did the wife of William, Duke of Puglia, when she was widowed.

During the Renaissance mourning practices underwent considerable changes, due in part to Anne of Brittany. This daughter of Margaret de Foix had had at her feet Louis of Orleans, who made her promise that she would be his bride as soon as he could bring about the annulment of his marriage to Joan, the unattractive daughter of Louis XI. This project did not meet with the approval of Anne de Beaujeu, who became Regent at the death of the King until the Dauphin could ascend the throne. She wanted the Dauphin to marry Anne of Brittany, and her intrigues started a war. The allies in opposition to Anne de Beaujeu numbered seven: the Duke of Buckingham, the son of the Duke of Rohan, Jean de Chalons, the Prince of Orange, the Infanta of Spain, Maximilian of Austria—father of Margaret—and Alain d'Albret. They all were claimants for the hand of

little Anne of Brittany, charmed by her childish beauty, and even more by her dowry.

The allies lost the war and soon afterwards the death of her father left Anne of Brittany helpless amongst the many who claimed her hand. Anne sought the protection of Maximilian of Austria, and asked him to marry her. The wedding was celebrated by proxy in Rennes with a peculiar and somewhat unorthodox ceremony. The bride had to lie down in a splendid four-poster bed, and the Austrian Ambassador, Zolfang de Polhain, keeping in his hand the Royal Act that named him proxy, uncovered his right leg, which for a moment he introduced naked into Anne's bed.

Anne de Beaujeu, 'the least foolish of all the women of France' as her father had described her, a woman-hater although a libertine, was still actively manipulating the pawns in the marriage game, and she succeeded in having the marriage of Anne of Brittany annulled and a new one celebrated between her and King Charles VIII. The union, even if due to political necessity, was quite happy, though the husband was repeatedly unfaithful. When he died, perhaps having eaten a poisoned orange, the queen shut herself in her rooms, touching no food, in floods of tears, screaming and tearing her dress.

On the day Anne finally decided to leave her rooms, the Court was taken aback with surprise. Instead of wearing white for her mourning, according to the tradition that demanded the wearing of this colour by widowed queens (called 'white queens', because white was the symbol of fidelity to the dead husband), Anne appeared swathed from head to foot in a black robe, a colour that expressed her mood, because it 'did not fade with time'. Although royal mourning never changed colour, the queen's mood did, because she finally married Louis XII, who had just repudiated Joan of France.

German armour. Fifteenth century

Left: Portrait of Lionello d'Este, Marquis of Ferrara. Pisanello. Carrara Academy, Bergamo

Anne was very beautiful, if slightly lame (she hid this imperfection by wearing one shoe with a very high sole), and she knew all the feminine artifices to make herself more attractive. Indifferent, like all the elegant ladies of her time, to masculine jeers and to sermons from the pulpit, she used to shave her eyebrows, and to paint a darker arch in their place; she made up her eyes and cheeks, and she underlined with a blue pencil the veins on her forehead, to enhance the transparency and delicacy of her skin.

Her face-pack consisted of raw veal cutlets, soaked in milk, and then applied to her face with bandages. To eliminate the blonde down on her face, she rubbed it with a powder made from fifty eggshells pounded in a mortar with rose water; to polish her finger nails she rubbed them with special sticks, and she kept her hands soft by massaging them every evening with a paste made from malmsey, musk-rat, benzoin, ambergris and musk; and she wore gloves at night.

Jewels at this time were the passion of men and women alike. They adorned their fingers with many rings, and sometimes they even wore them on the

Illustration from 'The Legend of the True Cross.' Michele di Matteo. Accademia, Venice

thumb of the left hand. Rings were also worn over gloves, and often gloves were perforated so that the rings inside could shine through. Men and women both wore heavy gold necklaces studded with precious stones; gold chains, to keep in place the splendid cloaks that women threw round their shoulders when they went out; gold belts to ornament women's dresses or from which men could hang their swords, their hunting horns or their daggers. Earrings, which had disappeared during the Middle Ages, became fashionable again, and were worn even by men. There were diadems of every kind, large ornamental clasps to fasten cloaks and enamelled brooches studded with gems. Very often almost magical powers were attributed to precious stones: opals would protect all men who were called James, onyx and jade were lucky, and pearls protected chastity.

Hair styles became important again after the disappearance of the *hennin*, which had hidden all the hair. In Tuscany women adorned themselves with garlands of fresh flowers, or with bands wound round the head in the classical manner, in imitation of the Greek women who had tied their hair with narrow ribbons. Included in girls' trousseaux were whole coffers filled with bands, veils and tiny veils for the hair, which Petrarch had praised in describing Laura's

'The son of Umberto de Socrati.' Detail. Baldassare Estense. Alte Pinakothek, Munich

Florentine velvet, with a chestnut branch design. Musée des Arts décoratifs, Paris

hair style. There were gold nets studded with pearls and ribbons set with precious stones. Hair was worn long, gathered at the nape, and combed to frame the face, with straight tresses to contrast with the waving hair at the temples, held back with bandeaux.

Though there was great variety in hair styles, women no longer deserved the satirical words of St Bernard, who jeered at them because they had 'more heads than the Devil'. Courtesans dressed their hair with curls all round the face, while the rest of the hair was gathered in a knot at the top of the head.

Very fashionable was blonde hair, whether true or false. Men were almost always clean shaven; the first time an adolescent shaved his beard was a family event of some importance, as it had been in ancient Greek times. Those who preferred not to be clean shaven could choose among a variety of beards: pointed beards, beards shaped like brushes, goatees, imperials, bowl-shaped, or even forked beards. To keep the beard in shape and the hair in place, men used resins or else the white of an egg.

Men's hats were often similar to the women's, but of more modest proportions: turbans and cones made of felt, manufactured in Lombardy, caps falling back on to the shoulders, and hoods. The latter were of Tuscan origin. Florentines never took them off out of politeness because 'the hood is never taken off in greeting or paying respect to anybody unless it be a bishop or a cardinal; in front of magistrates, knights, doctors or canons it can be raised slightly with two fingers, while the wearer bends down his head as a token of humility.' A little hat was reserved for the common people, while rich people would wear one on top of their hood. In the fourteenth century, the hat had been considered an object of luxury: in Rome at the time of Rienzi it had become a sign of great authority to wear a hat '. . . and those who did not wear a hat were considered of no importance at all'.

'The Legend of the True Cross.' Detail. Piero della Francesca. Church of San Francesco, Arezzo

Florentine engraving. Fifteenth century

Engraving. Dürer. Albertina Library, Vienna

'The Marriage of Boccaccio Adimari and Lisa Ricasoli.' Detail. Cassone Adimari. Accademia, Florence

In Italy a very common covering for the head was the *mazzocchio*, from which a brim went down to the left shoulder and a point hung down the back, often to the ground so that it could 'be wound round the neck and round the head . . . a protection against the winds and the many subtle draughts of air'. *Mazzocchio* was also the technical term for the pad on which the metal crown of a nobleman was placed. For women, the *mazzocchio* was 'a padded circle of cloth, which swathes the head all around, and is lined with cloth on the inside; it covers the whole head'. It was different from the *balzo* or *rebalzo*, a kind of large round toque, usually made of velvet, which was worn to conceal the hair and enhance the beauty of line of a woman's neck.

In the fifteenth century men's hats became more and more important, and so did their shoes. These were made of leather, and reached the ankles in two triangular pieces; the tip was narrow and pointed, according to a fashion which originated in the East. Towards the end of the century shoes had a square tip, like a duck's beak, a fashion launched by Charles

Drawings by Dürer showing the more severe style adopted by women of northern Europe. Albertina Library, Vienna

Right: Studies of the dress of women from Nuremberg. Dürer. 1527

'Portrait of a Lady'. Roger van der Weyden. Circa 1450. National Gallery, Washington

VIII of France, to hide the imperfection of one of his feet which had six toes. Boots were also worn. Women preferred to wear low shoes, closed at the ankle, or else fastened with a strap; French women chose to wear shoes shaped like slippers, which were very highly embroidered.

A very important item in male attire was the cuirass, so perfectly designed that it had to be moulded on the body of the future wearer. It was made of tempered steel, to give it maximum durability, and consisted of various parts fastened together: a collar-plate, breast-plate and back-plate. At the sides it had two hip-plates, to which were joined the thigh-pieces, the knee-plates and the greaves; on the shoulders were shoulder-plates, to which were joined the armlets which ended in gauntlets for the protection of the hand. The helmet, also made of steel, was moulded on the head of the warrior, who in battle, however, would use a helmet with a visor. Afterwards followed the fashion for the basinet, with a back-piece to protect the neck. Towards the end of the fifteenth century the helmet with movable or

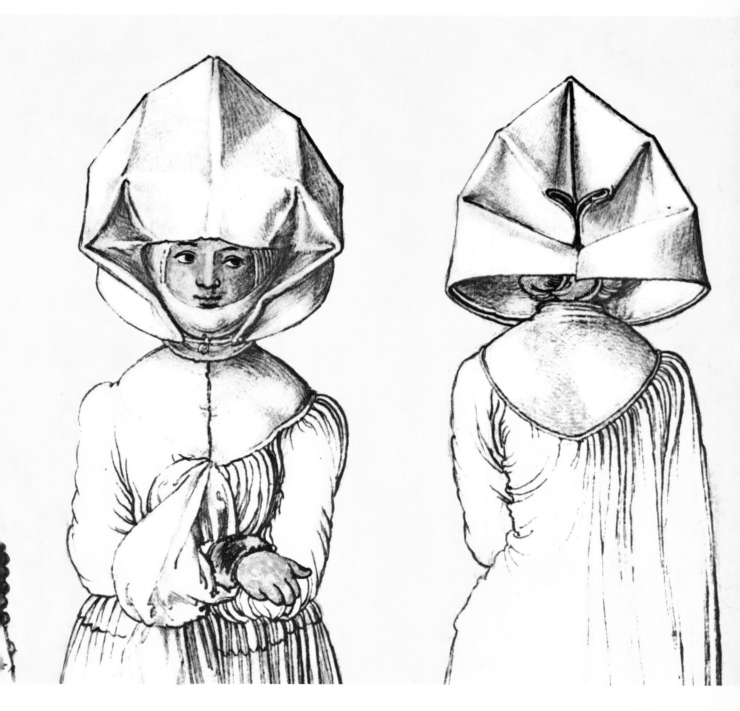

'The Moneylender and his Wife.' Detail. Quentin Matsys. Louvre

fixed visor was embellished by the crest, with plumes, or veils of different colours which had symbolic meaning. The fashionable young men who did not go to war transformed the cuirass into a fanciful garment, even although it was made of metal. They wore hats with enormous brims around a low crown; shoulder-plates over a steel coat of mail; guards for the elbows; very high leggings with rounded, blunted spurs over shoes made of articulated steel. The weapons in use were shields, lances, swords, daggers and cross-bows. The invention of gunpowder led to the use of different kinds of firearms, and in the end made protective armour useless.

Men continued, as they had done in the fourteenth century, to prefer brightly coloured garments, and even wore clothes with patches in different colours, stripes, squares and triangles. The heads of great families, however, expressed their preferences for certain colours, just as Amadeus VI and Amadeus VII

of Savoy had done, so that they were called respectively the 'Green Count' and the 'Red Count', because of their liking for these colours.

In the fifteenth century men's garments became shorter, while their stockings, which were always coloured or striped, were longer and reached their hips; young men abolished the short skirt, and adopted the French fashion of the doublet, which was often open down to the waist, with wide lapels in a different material fastened by a thin cord laced through parallel buttonholes. Sleeves often had vertical slits, through which a pure white shirt would show, as it did at the neck.

While women tightened their waists to make them more slender, men padded their coats with hay, to make their shoulders and chest seem broader, and tightened their waists with a belt. The doublet had borders of braid and fur. Fur became increasingly fashionable, and was also used to line capes and cloaks.

In Paris in the fifteenth century there were more than four hundred furriers. While young men followed the changing fashion and adopted short skirts, older people preferred long garments with full sleeves.

Cloaks were very rich, although shorter than the ones worn by women; they were always semicircular and in one piece, or they had two slits bordered with fur; some had two wide lapels, from behind which the sleeves emerged. The sleeves were often double, with pleats, sewn to the shoulders as if they were wings, made heavier with embroidered borders and studded with gems. These sleeves were sometimes false (that is the arms did not pass through them, but were clad in narrower sleeves) and fell loosely on the hips, trailing down.

During the Renaissance, accessories became more elegant and important. It was at this time that handkerchiefs were rediscovered. They had formerly been used by the Romans, who usually had two when they went out: one on the left wrist and the other one tucked in at the waist or round the neck. In the fifteenth century the handkerchief was for a time allowed only to the nobility, and special laws were made to enforce this; later they became more generally used. Handbags became necessary to hold the handkerchief and cosmetics used to touch up one's make-up (which, according to the author of the *Roman de la Rose*, should always be done in private). Handbags became more and more splendid, with embroideries in relief and trimmings of braid and precious stones. Another feminine accessory which changed was the fan, which took the shape of a pennant, a square or a triangle of material attached to a decorative handle, carved or engraved. Hand mirrors, too, were often shaped like this, though there was always a preference for the flat, rounded French shape, with the back decorated with paintings of battle scenes, or the Arabic style of wrought bronze.

The little caskets in which family documents were preserved, protected by complicated locks, and provided with a handle to facilitate carrying, also became more ornate. There were special boxes, usually cylindrical in shape, to hold cosmetics and playing cards. The cards for playing *tarot* were very expensive, sometimes costing as much as fifteen hundred gold pieces, because they were made of illuminated parchment. Dice were made of ivory, and dice games had to be played in company, as the law forbade throwing dice alone.

Table settings also began to follow a new fashion. Knives had ebony handles during Lent, to indicate by their colour a time of penance; during Easter, handles were made of a different material, often of ivory; handles used on Whitsunday had to be in two colours, half black and half white 'to express the half-happy, half-sad nature of this event'. Table settings began to include forks and spoons. Queen Clemence, the wife of Henry the Obstinate, owned forty-two spoons. Forks, which had two prongs only, were recommended for eating fruit. Hands could be used when eating so long as great care was taken, when helping oneself from the main serving dish, to plunge into the sauce only the first joints of three fingers.

Furniture became more elaborate: chests had carved fronts and movable tops. Sideboards were made of expensive wood and decorated with carving. Portable escritoires, writing-desks shaped like triangular cases, were suspended from men's belts and contained their writing materials.

Sewing equipment was kept in a small wooden casket, divided into compartments to hold the scissors, thimble, needles and thread of every colour. The fireplace was the woman's special corner in the home; decorated with marble, wood or stone, it was furnished with stools and cushions, brackets and iron points on which to place candles. Women would retire to this corner to read their favourite books: *Novellino* by Masuccio Salernitano, *Le livre d'heures de Troyes* (very dear to Margaret of York), *The Defence of the Conception of the Virgin* and *The Treasure of the City of the Ladies*. This last was written by Christine de Pisan, the first woman who 'dared to write like a man', not only to earn her living (she had been left a widow with several children at the age of twenty-five) but also in order to affirm the rights and position of women: 'Woman is equal to man . . . his inferior in physical prowess, she possesses as much moral strength and intellectual ability.' But Christine did not devote herself solely to trying to improve women's status; she also gave advice on the best way to become a good housewife and to keep a husband's

love. She even wrote some recipes, among them one for the preparation of food for convalescents; she suggested that the meat of a day-old chicken should be boiled, strained in a sieve and mixed with almonds.

Not only Italian, French and Spanish women but also the women of the North were dominated by the laws of fashion, modifying them, however, to the climate and customs of colder countries. In Holland clothes were more austere, especially the headgear, a large coif consisting of two stiffened horns which covered a net confining the hair and held in place by the stiff embroidered fabric and by jewels, often pear-shaped pendants. Men wore berets of every kind, often falling to a point at the back. In Flanders, the most conservative of European provinces, women swathed their heads in fillets which were often arranged to stand out like wings, and looked like nun's coifs. Stiffened with wire frames or starched, these fillets took many shapes: very high or wide, or wound around the face forming a kind of chinstrap, or standing up in two points, reminiscent of the saddle-shaped *hennin*. Hair, always hidden, was confined in a coif, a portion of which jutted out over the forehead, keeping the head-dress in shape.

In the Northern countries clothes were severe, often embellished with gathering and draping, with full sleeves, but they were never exaggerated. The wide neckline, deep in the front and back, was always filled in right up to the neck with thinner stiffened material. The train was shorter than in France or in Italy, and was often attached at the neckline with loose, closely-set pleats. In contrast to this austere mode of dress is Savonarola's comment on contemporary dress in Italy. He was a Dominican monk who, shocked by the corruption in his country, believed himself to have been chosen by God to regenerate the Church and Italy. He was the inspirer of many bonfires of 'vanities'. On to an improvised pyre he would throw precious veils and cosmetics, licentious books and ornaments. At first his words were taken as prophecies, for some were justified by the terrible events of the age, such as the invasion of Italy by Charles VIII; then he was condemned by the Pope. He succeeded in escaping from his pursuers, but when he was abandoned by the common people, the rulers of Florence had him arrested and tried and finally committed to death at the stake.

Despite the sermons, the sumptuary laws and the bonfires of 'vanities', feminine (and masculine) fashions continued to become more and more luxurious and ostentatious, enriched in the sixteenth century by Spanish and French influences, and by the expensive Italian fabrics.

Pendant. Venetian design. Sixteenth century. Victoria and Albert Museum, London

The Sixteenth Century

The High Renaissance

The sixteenth century is usually accepted as the beginning of modern history. The dreams of the Middle Ages were abandoned, and the weak feudal kingships replaced by States jealous of their independence. The Renaissance and the love for ancient learning which had been born in the fifteenth century deepened and came to its full flower.

Europe's new world role was determined by the great discoveries and the foundation of the first maritime empires. The discovery of North America brought new customs into Europe, even in the field of nutrition: maize and potatoes (which first were thought to be a variety of truffles) were introduced and tobacco became fashionable, especially as it was used by Catherine de' Medici, Queen of France, who first received it as a gift from the Ambassador at the Portuguese Court, Jean Nicot.

In this century the foundations of modern medicine—especially in the field of surgery—were laid with the work of an ex-barber, Ambroise Paré, chief physician of the *Hôtel Dieu,* the largest hospital in Paris. This man, surgeon to four French kings, from Henry II to Henry III, wrote a treatise, *La méthode de traicter les playes faetes par les arquebuses et aultres bastons à feu,* which was about the aseptic care of wounds, and was revolutionary for its time, as it had been believed that the only way of sterilising wounds was to 'rinse' them in boiling oil. Modest in his greatness, Paré at each 'miraculous' cure would say to the people who complimented him: 'I bandage the wound, but God cures it.' He was so much admired that, though a Huguenot, he was saved from the famous Night of St Bartholomew by Charles IX, who hid him in his own bedroom to guard him from the massacre that took place.

From America, discovered almost by accident by Christopher Columbus, and revisited by Amerigo Vespucci (who gave her his name) not only new foods and new poisons, like tobacco and cola, were imported, but also novelties which fashion soon made her own: gold and silver in plenty, and the plumage of exotic birds with which fops adorned their hats, and which elegant women used for a new kind of fan. It was at this time that parrots first appeared in Europe, replacing the talking magpies which had been all the rage in the last century. And it was in this century that animals of every kind—cats, dogs, squirrels, birds—took possession of the palaces, and studies were devoted to their care and breeding.

Left: 'The Man with the Glove'. Detail. Titian. Louvre

Leonardo da Vinci, the friend of the Marchioness of Mantua and one of the greatest artists of his time, painter, sculptor and thinker, gave a new impetus to science with his inventions and studies of anatomy, hydraulics and architecture. He was the first since the mythical Icarus to consider human flight as a possibility. His studies in this field are astonishing even today for their precision of analysis and their prophetic anticipation of inventions of the future.

Throughout the whole of Europe there was an explosion of genius. In France Pierre Ronsard, one of the greatest French poets, devoted himself to studies of the ancient world, and founded the *Pléiade*—a poetic circle which produced hymns, eclogues and elegies whose main theme was love. In Spain Cervantes, in his novel *Don Quixote,* ridiculed the old romances of chivalry, and created a masterpiece of a new kind. In Italy there was a flowering of great minds in the tradition of Dante and Petrarch: Ariosto, Aretino, Bandello, Machiavelli and many others. Among these are the names of many women, such as Gaspara Stampa. She was a noble lady from Padua, who used her poetic gift to express her passionate but unhappy love for the Conte Collaltino di Collalto. Vittoria Colonna, Marchesa di Pescara, is another personality of this period, whom her contemporaries admired for the melancholy lyrics she wrote in memory of her husband Ferdinando d'Avalos, who died prematurely.

Portrait of a man wearing a ruff, short breeches and hose

Following pages: Sumptuously dressed woman of Giustiniani family with her nurse. Detail of mural by Veronese. Villa Giacomelli, Maser

Donzella da Marito.

Nobile moderna

As always, fashion reflected the mood of the age, especially where masculine attire was concerned: the small skirts and tunics vanished, and were replaced by padded doublets topped with ruffs. The doublet was lavishly trimmed with gold or silver buttons, precious stones and diamonds. Breeches, very different from the loose trousers which came from the East, became very close-fitting tights, with a cod-piece which later ages considered indecent. The cod-piece was lavishly decorated and was sometimes used also as a purse.

All accessories assumed greater importance than ever before. Gloves became more and more exquisite: those belonging to Charles V were supple and close fitting, made of cloth of gold encrusted with hundreds of pearls; those of Queen Elizabeth were embroidered with animal figures; Duke Jacques de Nemours, grand master of elegance, wore two pairs, one on top of the other; he even owned gloves to wear at night, lined with scented herbs and pomades to soften his hands. Charles VIII was con-

sidered uncouth because he only used gloves for falconry and boar-hunting.

Perfumes also became extremely popular. Whereas in the thirteenth century lavender was the favourite, and in the fifteenth century violet and musk were most popular, in the sixteenth century all perfumes were fashionable: many objects were scented, from horse saddles to shoes and stockings. The Italians and the Spanish were masters of this art, and each Court had its own perfumer. In Portugal, it was reckoned that to every four teachers in the country, there were eight glove perfumers and twelve specialists in the art of cosmetics. Love of hygiene, however, was apparently very rare: Guido Postumo, writing about Isabella d'Este, said '. . . here [in France] women are rather dirty, with scabies on their hands and other kinds of dirtiness, but they have beautiful faces.'

Women's dresses in Italy during this period had tightly fitting bodices stiffened by bones, to which very richly gathered skirts were attached, sometimes

Venetian engraving. Cesare Vecellio

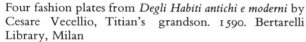

Four fashion plates from *Degli Habiti antichi e moderni* by Cesare Vecellio, Titian's grandson. 1590. Bertarelli Library, Milan

Giouine maritata

caught up on one side and in front to give a glimpse of a petticoat. Décolletages were generous but not immodest, and sleeves were close fitting, puffed at the armhole and sumptuously embroidered.

In Venice women dressed in a distinctive style but with increasing ostentation. Cesare Vecellio, Titian's grandson, who issued hundreds of plates illustrating the costumes of the world, gave a place of eminence to Venetian fashions, which stipulated different clothes according to the social rank of the wearer. The young girl who was eligible for marriage wore a long, full skirt, and over it a kind of apron open down one side; the deep décolletage of the bodice was modestly filled in, and the sleeves had slits to reveal the shift. The up-to-date noble-woman, on the other hand, was clad in a robe of precious material, which allowed her little clogs to be seen. Her head was swathed in a coif covered with fresh flowers, and she wore fresh flowers at her breast. This fashion, introduced by Henry III of France, made floral decoration so popular that it even became

117

customary to strew the floor with petals and leaves. Florentine women adorned their beds, as well as their hair, with garlands of flowers.

After marriage Venetian women would adopt a fashion which was Spanish in origin: the bodice was padded with wool or hair, and was shaped like the 'breast of a duck', lengthened at the abdomen; the skirt of brocade or printed velvet revealed the under-skirt, and sleeves were made in double, the outer ones very wide and almost reaching to the ground, the inner ones much tighter and fastened at the wrist with lace. Not all Venetian women were satisfied with the conventional fashions of the day, however splendid. There were a number of exaggerations, for example the hair style with vertical curls on the forehead, almost like horns. Necklines plunged precipitously and breasts were lifted up by a support, shaped like 'a little balcony'. Clogs (called *chopines* in French) often had very high soles, six inches or more, which jeopardised the balance and made it necessary for the very elegant to walk supported by a husband or maid. Venetian women, whether virtuous or not, started the custom of wearing over their dresses a black veil, which came down from the head over the shoulders, covering the whole body. This veil later became a black silk cape, and later a shawl, the typical *zendado*.

Venetian men also dressed in great splendour. They wore close-fitting knitted tights which replaced the tights made of material, but were only worn by the very rich as they were very expensive; these were secured round the knee by a garter, and attached to the doublet with hooks or double pins. Over the tights the *zipone* was worn, a tunic which buttoned up and came to just above the knee. The *zornea* was a little cape with wide sleeves, tightened round the waist by a belt. But the favourite cape was the 'Turkish' one, which came down to the feet and had very full sleeves. The 'toga' was another garment which was typically Venetian, but had nothing in common with the Roman toga except that here, too, it was used as a symbol of authority; it was a long flowing garment with open sleeves, and a band of material, the 'stole', of the same colour as the main garment; as in Roman times the colour was symbolic also: purple for Senators, violet for scholars, red for the Heads of the Council of Ten, black for the nobility, doctors and magistrates.

In the sixteenth century shifts became one of the most important items in a feminine wardrobe: Lucrezia Borgia owned two hundred, and although Bianca Maria Sforza owned less—only eighty-three—they were all extremely fine: eight had decorations in gold and silk, another fifty were plain and twenty-five embroidered in black silk. Black was a favourite colour for personal linen: Margaret of Navarre used black sheets to enhance the pure white-ness of her skin and the grace of her body. The habit of putting on a shift before going to bed was considered indecent, because people were accustomed to sleeping completely naked.

Knickers were also considered indecent, and were worn only by courtesans, for whom they were made of cloth of gold and silver. Later respectable women began to wear them after Catherine de' Medici had launched the fashion. This 'little duchess', daughter of one of the richest bankers in Florence, highly edu-cated, with an extensive knowledge of Greek and Latin, was the niece of Pope Clement VII, who arranged her marriage to the son of Francis I, King of France; the King wanted this marriage in order to limit the increasing power of the Emperor Charles V, and so had formed alliances with the sultan Suleiman and Henry VIII of England. He needed another ally, Catholic and more powerful, and he obtained this by marrying his second son, the future Henry II, to Catherine de' Medici.

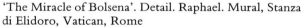

'The Miracle of Bolsena'. Detail. Raphael. Mural, Stanza di Elidoro, Vatican, Rome

Costume plates
Above: Engraving by Teodoro Viero
Below: From *Degli Habiti antichi e moderni* by Cesare Vecellio
Below right: From *Le Costume historique* by M. A. Racinet

Right: Venetian dress and high-heeled shoes in the six-teenth century. Musée de Cluny, Paris

'Small in stature, thin, with coarse features and bulging eyes', Catherine failed to keep the love of her adolescent husband, who was already secretly enamoured of Diane de Poitiers, a woman older than him by twenty-one years, extremely clever and cunning, with a taste for court intrigue. Catherine lived a quiet life, with little authority until she was appointed regent during the minority of her second son, Charles IX. The astrologers who at her birth prophesied that she would be the cause of great misfortunes proved accurate. She was a neglectful mother; a faithful, but not an obedient wife; and a cruel woman: the chief responsibility for the Night of St Bartholomew, when thousands of Huguenots were massacred, rests with her. The King was publicly unfaithful to her, and even at the coronation ceremony not only paid homage to his mistress by wearing a tunic of *azuré* silk, strewn with golden lilies and embroidered monograms of the royal initials linked with those of Diane de Poitiers, but even demanded that his mistress should be given the place of honour.

Catherine was left a widow at the age of forty-one, when Henry II died in a duel with the Comte Gabriel de Montgomery, while wearing the black and white colours of the beautiful Diane. The queen of France had ten children, but her progeny brought her much unhappiness: six died at a tender age: Francis II, who had a very weak constitution, died at the age of sixteen; Charles IX died of tuberculosis at the age of twenty-four; Henry III, unable to overcome his despair at the death of Marie de Clèves, the woman he loved, fell into a mild madness, taking up feminine occupations and passing his time with the *mignons*—effeminate, powdered young aristocrats, bedecked

with jewels, clad in sumptuous garments—who surrounded him. Margaret had as weak a character as her brothers, but she survived all of them.

Though he had a difficult temperament, Catherine was constant in her love for Henry II. She was fully aware that she could not compete with Diane de Poitiers, who had the harmonious grace of great beauty. With feminine cunning, Catherine tried to turn to good account the best part of her body—her legs. In those days women rode on horse-back, comfortably seated, with both feet resting on a foot-rest. Catherine invented the way of riding known as side-saddle; in this new position the skirt did not always stay in place, and it was therefore necessary to wear the *caleçon*. This garment provoked a great scandal among many who vainly objected to women wearing a masculine garment.

The most important event in the sixteenth century was the revolutionary religious movement, the Reformation. The origin of this movement is to be found in Luther's revolt against the practice of selling indulgences. He quickly found followers in Germany, but the movement might not have spread to England if Henry VIII had not wished to divorce Catherine of Aragon in order to marry Anne Boleyn, the second of his six wives. The Pope forbade this union, and for this reason the King of England decided to defy the Church of Rome and set himself up as Head of the Church. He never, however, abandoned the Catholic faith, and continued to burn heretics until the end of his reign in the tradition of Rome.

In the sixteenth century the Papacy was not only a spiritual but a political power. Catholicism at this time was exposed to the influences of a new pagan spirit: the values of humanism easily penetrated the Papacy, since they had the same Latin origin. At this time the Church was weakened by the same decadence that affected the princes; the deep corruption of the Church, which took from humanism its materialistic values, was no whit behind the secular princes in violence and deceit.

Pope Leo X is said to have lived like a spectacular Roman prince, although he was less corrupt than Pope Alexander VI, and less able than Pope Julius II, who had tried to restore the power of the Papacy and free Italy from foreign influences: the son of Lorenzo

Above left: 'Portrait of Laura Battiferri'. Agnolo Bronzino. Palazzo Vecchio, Florence

Left: Dress worn by peasant women. From *Diversarum Nationum Habitus*. Pietro Bertelli. 1592. Bertarelli Collection, Milan

Right: Portrait of Bartolomeo Panciatichi. Jacopo Pontormo. Uffizi Gallery, Florence

Drawings of German women showing the more conservative styles of northern European dress. Melchior Lork. John Evelyn Collection

Two women from Lübeck, 1567.
Melchior Lork

the Magnificent, Leo was more a patron of the arts than a Pope, more a reveller than a Shepherd of Souls. He loved good cooking and jokes—such as when he had a seedy little poet called Barabello crowned with laurel leaves in the Capitol.

Partly as the result of the shortcomings of the Church, the Reformation, both as a political and a religious force, spread through almost all the countries of Northern Europe, even reaching France and Switzerland, but did not have any following in Italy, because for Italian people it represented the negation of their intellectual and political progress. Nevertheless it dealt a deadly blow to the Church, ending in the sack of Rome by the Imperial army. The German soldiers not only brought the plague with them into Italy, but also a new fashion—the slashed coat.

This fashion was invented not by the Germans, but by the Swiss troops after their victory over the Burgundians at the Battle of Grandson. Seizing

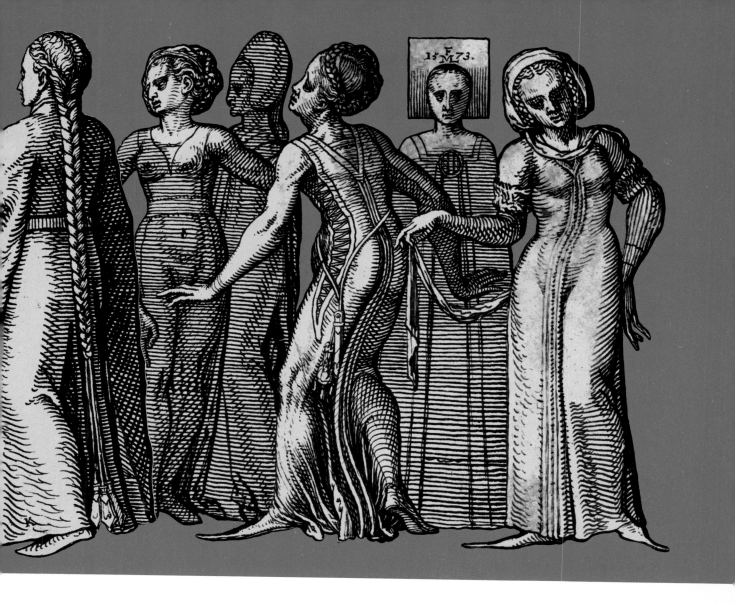

the coats of their defeated enemies, the Swiss tried to put them on, but were prevented by their tightness; thus they came to slash them, and slits became fashionable. Later they became so elaborate and complicated that tailors used hot irons rather than scissors to fray the cloth. The lining, usually of brightly coloured silk, was puffed out through the slits of the coat.

The German troops also launched the fashion for 'lattice' breeches: these were breeches made of wide strips of material separated from each other and reaching from the hip to the knee. This costume is worn even nowadays by the Papal Swiss Guard in Vatican City, and it is said that it was Michelangelo himself who designed this garment.

The fashion for beards at this time had been launched involuntarily by Francis I. On the 6th January 1521, the King of France was in Romorantin, the house of his favourite, Madame d'Angoulême, when he learnt that the Comte de Saint-Pol had been crowned King, after he had found a broad bean in his slice of cake. In those days, on the Feast of Epiphany, it was usual to play at *tirer les rois*: a large cake was prepared in which a broad bean was hidden; the guest who was lucky enough to get this in his portion was supposed to be elected King.

The story is told that Francis I decided to punish

his rival. Together with the band of courtiers who were his followers, he arrived beneath the windows of his château, and started to throw snowballs. These were answered by a shower of apples, pears and eggs. Unfortunately one of the guests of the Comte de Saint-Pol threw a hot ember which fell on the King's head, burning him so severely that he was dangerously ill for several days. The doctors had to cut his curls, which were thick and long, to tend his wounds. When he recovered, Francis found he was bald and disfigured by scars, which he hid by growing a beard. Thus changed the masculine fashion which in the fifteenth century had stipulated a shaven face and long hair; in the sixteenth century a beard became the sign of nobility. This was often divided into two points, or it could be full, and was sometimes complemented by a moustache. To have a 'strong, clean and attractive' appearance men cut their beards under the chin, and combed their hair down on the forehead. There were also eccentrics who wore their beards long on one side and short on the other, so as to have two profiles to present to the world.

By the middle of the century masculine dress all over Europe reflected a marked Spanish influence, which was especially shown in the ruff. At first the ruff was simply a gathered collar which adorned the shirt. According to the advice of the *Royal Mirror*, a Norwegian handbook of fashion, shirts had to be the correct length, shorter than the coat, but showing at the wrist and throat. Then the *fraise* or ruff grew to such enormous proportions that the handle of spoons had to be lengthened, otherwise the size of the ruff made it difficult to eat.

Men's sleeves became very full near the wrist, where they were adorned by one or more frills. Breeches towards the end of the century became longer and were fastened below the knee with a brightly coloured ribbon, which was replaced later by a gold or metal button. Breeches were padded with horsehair or hay and, reflecting the influence of the French, sometimes had lateral slits. The legs were covered with knitted stockings which became very popular after an Englishman, William Lee, invented a knitting machine which greatly reduced the price of this fashion accessory.

In France, masculine fashion underwent changes and transformations which reflected the taste of the kings who succeeded each other. At the time of Francis I men continued to wear a very close-fitting

Above left: French comb. Sixteenth century. *Left*: Another engraving from *Degli Habiti antichi e moderni*

126

doublet extending to the hips, from which emerged short and very tight-fitting breeches, divided by multicoloured stripes. These breeches came to the knee, and their hem was covered by stockings of a different colour, tied over and under the knee with two embroidered ribbons. Francis I and his court loved expensive clothes, and were accused of displaying on their backs the income from their mills, their forests and their lands. On the occasion of his meeting with Henry VIII, the King of France made his appearance dressed in white, with a gold belt, a crimson doublet, a quantity of jewels and gold leather shoes. His tent of painted cloth, sewn with gold thread, filled with precious things, looked like a fairytale castle, surrounded by knights and horses caparisoned in precious fabrics and elaborate harness.

'The Betrothal'. Lucas van Leyden. Antwerp Museum

During the reign of Charles IX men's shirt collars became fuller and more heavily gathered. With Henry III it became fashionable to wear padded trousers and small semicircular capes which often had short sleeves trimmed with fur, and to use face powder and wear dangling earrings. Men's hats became flatter and shaped like berets, made of velvet or brocade, either with or without a brim, and adorned with gems or plumes. Shoes were fastened round the ankle with bows or little ribbons; sometimes they had two vertical slits, through which one could see the stockings.

The true fashion plate was quite unknown at this period, but there was an increasing interest in costume, and books began to be issued with engravings not only of foreign and ancient costumes but of contemporary dress. These were not without their influence and tended to make fashion more uniform throughout Europe. This development would, of course, have been impossible without the invention

Fashions worn during the reigns of Francis I, Charles IX and Henry IV. Costume Documentation Centre, Paris. *Below*: 'The Tailor'. Detail. Giambattista Moroni. National Gallery, London

of printing by Johannes Gutenberg in the middle of the fifteenth century.

Before Gutenberg almost all education had been the province of the Church. Books were extremely expensive, the task of copying very arduous and the results sometimes inaccurate. Few writers reached a sizable audience before their death. The libraries of the courts, monasteries and colleges were numerous but small. Charles V of France was held in high esteem because he owned 910 volumes; the Priory of Christ Church in Canterbury had the richest library in Europe, comprising 2,000 manuscripts, all illuminated. Among private owners one of the best known was Richard of Bury St Edmunds, who made his own library public (although the books were chained to the lecterns and reading benches) and who expressed his love of books in a treatise called the *Philobiblion*, in which the books themselves spoke in the first person, complaining about the bad treatment inflicted on them by 'those animals on two legs called women'

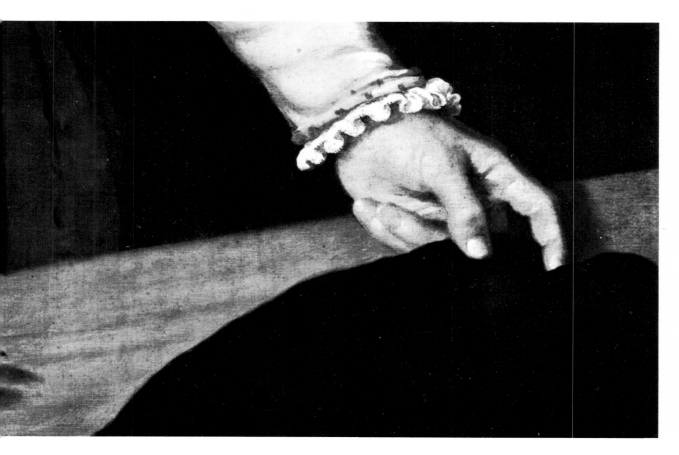

'A Man in Blue'. Titian. National Gallery, London

who continually exchanged them for linens and silks.

Although Gutenberg's invention was opposed by the copyists who were afraid that they would be left without work, and by noblemen who feared that their treasures would depreciate in value, knowledge of printing spread all over the world; it was perfected in Venice by Aldo Manuzio, in Leiden by the Elzevirs, in Paris by the Etiennes. The costume plates most popular in the sixteenth century were those issued by the Frenchman Boissard and by the Italian Vico, and these carried on the function of the French dolls in spreading knowledge about fashion.

Feminine dress in the sixteenth century was greatly influenced by the Spanish farthingale. This garment encircled the lower part of the woman's body with a series of hoops in the shape of a cone; these were sewn in the skirt, which was thus held rigid. In France the farthingale was a *bourrelet,* a roll of felt at the waist which widened the skirt. Marguerite de Valois loved this fashion because it made walking easier, and allowed her to display dresses with a very wide skirt, lavishly decorated with precious stones and embroidery. Margot, as she was usually called, was not only an arbiter of the finer points of fashion, and notorious for her amours, but also a very gifted woman, fond of literature and every refinement in life. She was

Fabric used in an English coat. Sixteenth century. Victoria and Albert Museum, London

Above right: Violet silk brocade embroidered with gold and silver. Sixteenth century. Civic Museum, Turin. *Below right*: English bonnets. Sixteenth century. Victoria and Albert Museum, London

HABITI D' INGHILTERRA.

HABITI D' ONGARIA.   HABITI DI GERMANIA.   HABITI DELLA SPAGNA

A comparison of sixteenth-century fashions in (*on the left*) England, and (*above*) Hungary, Germany and Spain. From *Diversarum Nationum Habitus*. Pietro Bertelli. 1592

surrounded by a talented group of nobles, poets and artists, with whom she spoke an esoteric language intelligible only to the initiate.

Extravagant fashions like the farthingale prompted the passing of new laws which attempted to control the follies of the age. Henry III of France, though he himself had an excessive fondness for fine clothes, forbade the use of gold and silk (imported from foreign countries at very high prices), and compelled women to dress more modestly. Black or tawny velvet, silver and gold buttons, jewels for dresses and silk embroideries were permitted only to noble-women; middle-class women were allowed to use silk only for the borders of their dresses, the lining and mock sleeves. In that period both men and women often had double sleeves: a narrow sleeve, which was attached to the dress, and a fuller, shaped sleeve which was joined to the bodice or doublet, so

that it could be changed easily according to the occasion or the mood.

A chronicler of the time noted that Italian women, more thrifty than their French or Spanish peers, were able with two dresses and ten pairs of sleeves to contrive a number of combinations, and so effect a considerable economy. This was not unlike our modern use of two skirts and a number of separate blouses to enlarge the possibilities of a limited wardrobe.

The edicts of Henry III forbade the wearing of cloth and braid of gold and silver; coloured velvet and trains were allowed only to princesses and to the Queen's ladies-in-waiting; this applied also to silks, the velvet *chaperon* (a headgear that came down over the forehead) and masks. Princesses, especially during journeys, covered their faces with masks to protect them from dust, wind and the glances of strangers. If women of the bourgeoisie wore the farthingale, it had to be kept to certain prescribed measurements; and women of this class were not allowed to spend more than sixty sous on a single dress.

Though the fashion for the farthingale and its variations swept across Spain, France, Italy and England, the women in Northern Europe were not

Following pages: 'Ball at the Court of Henry III of France'. Anonymous. Louvre

Henry II of France. Clouet. British Museum, London

at all influenced by this exotic fashion, and continued to keep their national costume, which was more suitable for their climate and way of life. In Germany women wore long heavy dresses made with many yards of material, so that the female body appeared very sturdy. The bodice was close fitting but not held rigid by busks, according to French fashion. The neckline was modest: round or square, or V-shaped

Philip II of Spain. Detail   William of Orange. Detail

and filled in with a linen triangle; or else reaching right up to the chin. The size of the ruff was not unduly exaggerated. Sleeves, which at first had been very wide, became narrower and narrower until they were close fitting; they were often divided into layers by strips of material sewn horizontally. Towards the end of the century sleeves became funnel-shaped. Skirts were often pleated and covered by a pleated apron, and sometimes showed the underskirt.

To protect themselves from the cold women wore pelerines and long cloaks, usually pleated. These cloaks, which had a characteristically shaped collar, round and narrow, were also draped over the head and in this way covered the whole body. The single frivolity in this garment was that the cape was cut away under the arms to show the dress.

The headgear of German women took various shapes: a nun-like coif (like the one worn by Catherine von Born, the woman who married Luther), a square shape supported by a wire frame, and there were hats shaped like a mitre or a halo.

German women, like many women in the north of Italy, wore their hair long, gathered in a thick plait which hung down the back, or else in two plaits wound around the head. 'Hair is the most beautiful feminine adornment. I like women who let their hair fall on their shoulders; this is a very pleasant sight', wrote Luther, who nevertheless felt that women needed strict discipline; he believed that God had destined women exclusively for 'motherhood, kitchen and church. Take women away from rearing their families, and they are good for nothing.'

In England, as elsewhere in Europe, women were fond of finery. The farthingale was fashionable and also the French *bourrelet,* which became so large that it looked like an enormous plate; and skirts looked like drums. Necklines, previously wide and square under the reign of Mary Tudor, were veiled by a chemise which came high round the neck, and completed by a ruff like a mill wheel, made of several layers, or else pleated over a metal frame like a fan.

The sleeves were puffed like little balloons near the armhole, and then narrowed and became close fitting with the usual ruffle of lace at the wrists. They were also puffed from shoulder to wrist and embellished with embroidery and braids. Sometimes women wore two wings, attached at the shoulders, and made in very thin material, supported by metal wire. In France, where they had originated, these wings were called *conques,* and from them a wide veil, rectangular or oval, fell to the ground. Shoes were closed and shaped like slippers, and were made either of cloth or of leather, and brightly coloured. Cloaks, which were little used, were generally oval, with sleeves which came to the elbow.

The magnificence of feminine attire, which increased as time went by, was partly due to the great variety of colours and the rich materials that were available. Cloth from Milan, Genoese velvet, gold and silver fabrics from Florence, Naples and also from Paris, where Italian artisans had been imported, were popular throughout Europe.

Queen Elizabeth I succeeded her half-sister Mary Tudor in 1558, at the age of twenty-five. Tall, red-haired, thin and bony, unquestionably the most elegant of English women, she owned two thousand dresses, almost all gifts from her subjects who knew of her love of clothes and her thrift. At the age of fifty-three the queen, who loved dancing and hunting, who used to spit and to swear like a soldier, and to beat her fists on the table in frequent bursts of temper, was still very open to flattery and had a special fondness for elaborate dresses: during her reign ruffs, which were stiffened with blue or saffron starch, became enormous.

Elizabeth was a mistress of diplomacy. When the Spanish ambassador visited her to complain about the behaviour of Francis Drake, who had seized a cargo of gold, taken from the treasure ship *Cacafuego*, she feigned great surprise, though it was well known that she herself had financed the enterprise. She decided to go aboard his ship the *Golden Hind* in

Below left: Louis XIII. Anonymous
Below right: Vincenzo Gonzaga. Anonymous. Uffizi Gallery, Florence
Right: Philip II. Titian. National Museum, Naples

'Portrait of a Lady'. Caron. Alte Pinakothek, Munich

Detail, showing fashion for heavy necklaces mounted with precious stones

person, ostensibly to reprimand him. When, however, he knelt before her, she bestowed a knighthood on him. The same ambiguous statesmanship was displayed in her treatment of her cousin, Mary Queen of Scots; Elizabeth saved her life and kept her in jail for seventeen years; eventually she was tried and finally beheaded, but immediately after the execution Elizabeth denied that she had ordered her death.

Elizabeth never married, though her name was romantically linked with two men, Leicester and Essex. It has been suggested also that she was in love with Sir Walter Raleigh, the great explorer, who named the region of America he discovered 'Virginia' after the Virgin Queen.

Masculine costume at this period in England became very refined and elegant: doublets were decorated with precious buttons; rich trunk hose was worn; sleeves were heavily embroidered; coatsleeves were cut so that they fell down the wearer's back, and were often bordered with fur. Men's hair, which was worn short, their beards and moustaches were often perfumed.

In other countries fashions were similar, strongly influenced by the Spanish, but modified also according to the demands of climate and national temperament. In Hungary men still wore the long robe buttoned in front, and pulled in at the waist with a wide leather belt studded with silver and gold, which was of Byzantine origin. Hungarian men wore cloth

Right: Portrait of Catherine Parr, sixth wife of Henry VIII. Hans Holbein the Younger. Novarro Collection. *Above*: Detail, showing hands laden with rings, an important fashion accessory

138

berets with upturned brims, adorned with plumes. Women had multicoloured embroidery on their skirts and aprons and they hid their hair in caps.

In this century a passion for lace spread through Europe; it was called *merletto* in Italy, *spitze* (points) in Germany, and *dentelle* in France, because it was finished off with a pattern of small points or teeth. Already known in Egyptian times (where it was more like embroidery on very fine linen, a type of *broderie anglaise*), lace as we know it is Italian in origin: Christopher Froschauer, in his book on fashion printed in Zurich in 1536, stated that the art of lace made with bobbins had been introduced to Switzerland by Venetian merchants. There are, in fact, two methods of making lace—with a bobbin and also with a needle; the two methods were often used together, for example in *point lacé*, which was composed of strips of lace made with bobbins and joined to each other by needle stitches as fine as gossamer. In England, where the Virgin Queen wore extremely high, stiffened lace collars, this fashion was called 'French', while in France it was known as 'an English exaggeration'. Men also had lace on their attire.

Jewellery, the conspicuous symbol of wealth, was worn by the nobility, particularly in Spain, where the wealthy appeared bedecked like idols, with a profusion of gold, pearls and precious stones imported from faraway lands. Laden with gold chains, their dresses encrusted with gems, their fingers covered with rings, Spanish grandees carried on their persons the immense fortunes that came from the New World

Elizabeth of Austria, Queen of France, wife of Charles IX. Frans Pourbus. Bibliothèque Nationale, Paris

to Europe. In those times to wear one's fortune on one's back was perhaps the best way both to keep it safe and to show off one's possessions. Similarly up to recent times peasant women in the Balkans wore their dowry sewn in a handkerchief which they displayed to advantage on their bosom. Women in the sixteenth century wore very long gold necklaces, with pearls or precious pendants or medallions. These were often the work of great artists like Benvenuto Cellini, who created masterpieces of intricate workmanship. Cameos and coral, emeralds and rubies, diamonds and enamelled jewels amounted to great fortunes, which might change the whole course of a war, as had happened a century before. Charles VIII, King of France, during his Italian campaign, did not have enough money to pay his troops and meet the expenses of the journey. Fortunately, the Marchesa Bianca del Monferrato, who was deeply in love with him, gave up all her jewels to help him and he was able to meet his obligations.

Hair styles in this period tended to make the head look smaller; the eyebrows were shaved off, the high forehead was emphasised with the hair drawn back and often plaited. At the time of Henry IV hair was usually sprinkled with scented powder (middle-class women would use flour). A stiff cap from which hung a veil was worn, or else a round cap on hair that was parted in the middle and gathered in plaits or curled around the temples. The narrow-brimmed *toque*, on which, in accordance with the French mode, was placed a twist of silk decorated with plumes, was very fashionable; also a felt hat over which a coloured shawl was draped. Small hats with large brims drooping down on one side like a dog's ear, were fashionable for men. There were straw hats, turned up in front and behind; and hats made of the white bark of a lime tree, adorned with fringes, braids and peacock or ostrich feathers. For hunting, hats were made of leather and shaped like hoods, often with woollen tassels at the temples.

With increasing knowledge of the customs of so many different peoples, and the spread of culture, a more polished code of manners evolved. Washing one's hands before sitting down at meals became obligatory, and if one glass was shared among many guests, the lips were thoroughly wiped before drinking. If a drink was served in a ewer with several spouts, it was considered polite to put one's lips to the spout that had not been used by the preceding guest. The Countess of Valentinois, in order

Right: Portrait of the Princess of Eboli wearing the universally popular Spanish ruff. Sanchez Coello. Infantado Collection

to show her own importance, drank from the same spout that had been used by the King of France and the Cardinal of Ferrara; this caused scandal and envy among the courtiers present. It was a sign of politeness to pick up bread which had fallen from the table and kiss it before putting it in one's mouth. A person was expected to cross himself if he sneezed.

These were the rules of etiquette for daily life, but Baldassar de Castiglione, in his *Cortegiano*, described in detail what the behaviour of gentlemen should be. According to him the first requisite was position, because unless one were born into the upper classes, it would be difficult to acquire manners and spontaneous grace of body and mind. Therefore the aristocracy seemed to him the repository of good manners, exemplary behaviour and good taste. The education of a gentleman should consist of the study of the arts of war: enthusiasm for the pursuits of peace should not be pushed to the point of weakening men in their character as warriors. Too many wars, he felt, make men brutal, but women could turn men towards gentleness. No court, however brilliant, can flourish without women; no courtier can be brave and courteous, nor undertake chivalrous adventures, if he is not moved by the influence of a woman. Castiglione taught also that in order to fulfil her function, woman must be feminine to the full, and avoid imitating men in behaviour, manners, speech or dress. She must develop graceful movements of her body, and speak gently. She should study music, dancing, literature and the art of entertaining: in this way she can attain that inner beauty which is the object and the stimulus of true love.

With the end of the sixteenth century, the period of the Renaissance may be said to close, a period which had the novelty and creativity, in its new styles of dress and architecture, art and literature, of a new civilisation. This period heralded the beginning of a new attitude towards life, a new sensibility which delighted in pomp, movement, and dramatic emphasis, and was characterised by a love of mystery and artifice: the Baroque movement.

A tailor at work. Engraving. Seventeenth century

The Seventeenth Century

POSVI DEVM ADIVTOREM MEVM

SEMPER EADEM

'Costume is the mirror of history.' So Louis XIV defended the excessive pomp of the French court of that time, a statement which anticipated modern definitions of the function of costume to clothe the body, and also expressed the artistic, social and even economic aspects of an epoch. Costume is the record of a way of life, the expression of a society and of a civilisation; it reveals the character of a people. In its mirror, the great epochs of history are reflected. The study of costume has frequently suggested an explanation of events, when no exact knowledge of their causes and origins was known.

Henry IV

At the beginning of the seventeenth century dress continued to be sober, just as Henry IV, one of the greatest if not the greatest king of France, had desired. A Gascon of vigorous stock with an attractive personality which made him successful with women, he had inherited from Henry III a country weakened by corruption, by religious conflict, by political disorder. His intelligence and fine judgment enabled him to restore the finances of the State, rebuild the villages and roads destroyed by wars and reorganise agriculture (the only book he ever read was the *Théâtre d'Agriculture*). He issued the Edict of Nantes, which authorised the Protestant religion, gave freedom of speech to Protestants and thus ended religious strife in France.

Simple in his manners, brave and untiring, he never paid much attention to dress, but left these pleasures to the ladies of the Court and their effeminate young men. Excessively simple in his dress, he was often blamed by his courtiers because he wore garments that were patched at the elbows. After his divorce from the 'la Reine Margot' he married Maria de' Medici, the daughter of the Grand Duke of Tuscany, a much more polished person than himself. Maria de' Medici, in whose veins flowed the blood of Catherine Sforza, the belligerent woman warrior of the Renaissance who had defended the stronghold of Forli from the Papal troops, had, however, more self-confidence than intelligence, and desired that her Italian favourites should take over the government, and that she should be allowed to live an extravagant life at the court of King Henry.

In the first years of his reign there was no prevailing fashion: continuing the tradition of the sixteenth century, people were free to dress as they wished, though the Spanish influence still predominated. There were a thousand variations of the ruff, the Spanish fashion that had conquered Europe in the previous century. Ruffs were made of extremely fine linen cloth, often adorned with lace, and always wide and stiff. From the *fraise*, a mere pleated linen band which encircled the neck from collar to chin, came the exaggeration of the true ruff, attached to the neckline, and fanning out over the shoulders. The round shape was obtained by using several layers of linen one over the other, pleated like a fan. In order to keep this rigid, a large number of superimposed layers were used, and also a metallic frame inserted between each pleat, which supported, stretched and stiffened the ruff. Ruffs were starched, and the technique of starching became almost an art: at first only rice starch of a pale blue colour was used at the French court, where Henry III, it is said, supervised in person the starching of his ruffs. Then an English woman called Miss Turner invented a starch of a pale yellow colour, and these two colours became immediately popular. They came to have political significance as the blue starch was considered a Papist dye, while the pale yellow was adopted by the Huguenots. In England yellow starch was abandoned when its inventor was accused, perhaps unjustly, of poisoning Sir

Engraving. Callot. 1617. Bertarelli Collection, Milan

Left: Queen Elizabeth of England set the fashion for stiff collars high at the back and open at the front. Crispin de Passe. 1603. Engraving

Following pages: Portrait of the artist and his first wife, Isabella Brandt. Rubens. Circa 1609. Bavarian State Collection, Munich

Thomas Overbury, and was beheaded at the Tower of London. Miss Turner went to the block wearing a dress with a yellow ruff, after which no elegant woman kept a pale yellow ruff in her wardrobe.

The Spanish way of dressing, although sumptuous, was very uncomfortable, not only because of the ruff which imprisoned the neck, but also because of the fullness of the skirts, supported by the farthingale in such a way that walking was difficult; and because of the very tight bodice, which came below the natural waist in the front, with a basque, the seams of which were covered with braids, strands of pearls, and ribbons. This was an extremely expensive

Portrait of Eleonora Gonzaga. Frans Pourbus. Ducal Palace, Venice

fashion, and condemned the wearer to almost complete immobility; although it could be worn by women with leisure, it was very uncomfortable for women in the humbler walks of life. Because of this, when Europe was overwhelmed by that fever of wars which for many long years tormented Germany, France, Holland and England, the Spanish fashions began to die out, especially for men. Men were the first to abandon the ruff, though women stubbornly went on wearing it for some time. A few followed the example set by Elizabeth of England and wore the little 'Stuart' collar, gathered and stiffened, high at the back of the neck but open in front with a rather deep neckline, which was often veiled.

Louis XIII

In the time of Louis XIII, the ruff changed into the falling collar, which fell limply on the shoulders, although many older people continued to be faithful to the ruff which had caused so many scandals in the days of their youth. Spanish dresses in the seventeenth century were almost always black, with only a touch of white at the neck, and brightened by gold and silver braids. As cumbersome as these dresses were the hair styles, often composed of stiff little plaits, as we can see in the paintings of Velasquez.

It was indeed in the reign of Louis XIII that French fashions began to be differentiated from the Spanish. After Richelieu's edict had forbidden the importation of braid and lace from Italy and Belgium, costumes became more sober and more elegant. Women

Maria de' Medici. Rubens. Prado, Madrid. *Left*: Lady wearing an ornate ruff. Van Dyck. Gallery of the Academy of S. Luca, Rome.

wore an embroidered shirt, two petticoats, one under-garment in two pieces (a bodice and skirt) and a dress also in two pieces, open in front to reveal the underskirt. The apron, in lace or silk, was often a sophisticated accessory. Sleeves became very important, enriched by bizarre ornaments, with cuffs of wide lace turned up on the forearm. The collar, no longer of the high 'Stuart' type, lay on the shoulders with the lightness of lace. The farthingale slowly disappeared, and the underskirt, stiffened by a frame of coarse hemp, had a conical shape, the width at the hips being obtained by bunching up the skirt.

While Spanish fashion had preferred dark colours, the French favoured pale shades in all the colours of the rainbow, and these were often given bizarre and fanciful names. Fashionable shades were 'leaf colour' or 'gazelle colour', sea-green, bud-green, brown-green, gay-green, lawn green; and even more fanciful names like 'laughing monkey', 'kiss-me-my-love', 'wasted time' or 'mortal sin'.

Another fashion was born: the fashion for false beauty spots, which had even more fantastic names than the colours, and were bought in Paris at '*La Perle des mouches*' in the Rue St Denis. They were called 'passion' if applied at the outer corner of the eye; 'finery' if they were placed in the middle of the

Portrait of a lady showing the more severe style of ruff worn in northern Europe. Jan van Ravensteyn

cheek; 'boldness' if they adorned a nostril; 'kiss' if they were placed at the corner of the mouth; 'coquetry' if placed directly on the lower lip. This fashion expressed a desire for elegance, but also served to hide an unsightly mole or pimple. Patches were made of velvet or silk, and were kept in special little boxes, carried in the handbag.

The wish to appear original at all costs gave origin to another fashion which lasted only a very short time: the fashion for tinting the lips green or black.

The son of Maria de' Medici, Louis XIII usually wore a doublet ending in a point at the front, with sleeves slit vertically; each slit was adorned with a ribbon ending in a metallic point. He wore no ruff

The ruff was followed by a French fashion for falling collars, which lay limply on the shoulders. 'Portrait of Unknown Man'. Detail. Terborch. National Gallery, London

but a round or square falling collar, hemmed with lace. The doublet was later replaced by a coat fastened with buttons or loops, seamless, with a pointed collar made of lace, and very full slashed sleeves. Men wore breeches more close fitting than before, with lace frills at the bottom, and the seams adorned by bands of braid. These became longer, and were fitted into boots shaped like funnels which hid the stockings. From the boots emerged the linen linings trimmed with lace.

By 1650 people no longer followed the Spanish fashion, but French fashion exerted its influence all over Europe, with the exception of Holland, a very conservative country. Dutch women preferred their

Portrait of Burgomaster Bas and his family, showing fashions worn by three different generations. Santvoort. Amsterdam Museum

staid old costume, puffed up on the hips not because of the farthingale, which they had never adopted, but because the skirt itself was fully gathered. The only bizarre feature was an odd little hat worn on the forehead, made of silk and plumes and shaped somewhat like a tulip, the flower which became the national symbol of the country. Native to Turkey, tulips were first imported into Holland by Ogier Gislain de Busbecq, ambassador of Ferdinand of Austria to the Court of Suleiman the Magnificent. A passion for tulips swept the country, and prices were often extremely high. They were quoted in the Exchange, were accepted as part of the dowry of marriageable girls, and caused sudden wealth and sensational bankruptcies. It became necessary to formulate a law which put an end to speculation in tulips, but the flower nevertheless continued to feature in embroideries, paintings and furniture decoration in Holland.

Louis XIV

French fashion, under the guidance of Louis XIV, the *Roi Soleil,* abandoned simplicity and became more and more extravagant and sumptuous. Gentlemen began to decorate their clothes with ribbons and embroidery; they adopted full short trousers,

which came down to the knee, and were laden with lace hanging over the calves. (These were often the target of Molière's irony.) Boots were replaced by silk stockings and court shoes, but when Louis XIV married Maria Theresa the Infanta of Spain, it seemed for a time that the fashion for boots was coming back. In fact the *Roi Soleil* appeared in court wearing a splendid pair of seamless boots of Levantine leather, lined with silk and adorned with gold lilies. This fashion lasted only as long as the honeymoon, because Louis XIV returned to wearing silk stockings and high-heeled shoes, a style which he never abandoned again. This was probably because stockings showed his legs, which were perfect, and high-heeled shoes allowed him to add inches to his stature, for he was small, being under five feet six inches.

These little shoes were made of silk or velvet, embroidered or encrusted with gems; the edge of the sole and the heels were dyed bright red. Women's shoes were not unlike the men's, but their shoes had white rather than scarlet heels.

Elegant women added a third skirt to the two they wore under their dresses; this was open in front, pleated and puffed on the hips with knotted ribbons, pins or buckles. Very often this third skirt lengthened into a train, which had to be carried by a page. These three skirts had somewhat fanciful names: the inner one was called *la fidèle* and was the *jupe de besoin,*

The wife of the Lord Mayor of London. Wenceslaus Hollar. 1644. *Right*: The fashions for the ruff and the deep collar overlapped for some years. *Le Costume historique.* M. A. Racinet

Medallion portraits on a wardrobe. Anonymous. Seventeenth century. National Museum, Nuremberg

adorned with ribbons and embroideries sewn in the favourite colour of the woman's beloved; the second one, the *friponne,* was the *jupe de parade et d'éclat,* in cloth of gold and silver, heavily embroidered; the third one was known as *la modeste* or *la secrète* according to the *Dictionnaire des Précieuses.* These 'Précieuses', who were satirised in the work of Molière, frequented the salon of Madame de Chevreuse, where all the gossip of court and town was exchanged with eager malice.

Men were often more frivolous in their dress than women. Their garments were often decorated with more than three hundred bows, and they also wore brocades, embroidery in gold and silver, silks that were extravagantly expensive—they cost 'the eyes out of your head,' wrote Madame de Sévigné in one of her letters, describing a *très beau justacorps* of her son-in-law, which had cost a thousand livres. Even on their cloaks, shaped like capes, and made of brocade rather than wool, men loved trimmings of braid and rich embroidery, often spending enormous sums on this extravagance.

In 1656 an edict was passed by Mazarin which forbade the use of gold and silver not only on clothes, but also on coaches, in an attempt to curb the debts and enormous waste of the times. Mazarin brought on himself the hatred of the elegant world for having tried to curb luxury, and he had to repeal his laws

Engraving from *Le Costume historique.* M. A. Racinet. *Left*: English lady wearing a dress with deep lace collar and skirt gathered at the hips. Wenceslaus Hollar. 1640. National Museum, Nuremberg

Following page: Fabric with design in magenta velvet on cream-coloured silk. Seventeenth century. Civic Museum, Turin

154

Young Englishman. Nicholas Hilliard. Victoria and Albert Museum, London

The Empress Margarita of Austria. del Mazo. Prado, Madrid

because of the violent protests of the artisans, who made the braids and embroideries, the buckles and buttons, wove the cloth of gold and silver, and who feared that Mazarin's edicts would be the ruin of their trade and put an end to their prosperity.

During the very long reign of Louis XIV the fashions changed several times, and each wave spread across the whole of Europe, and sometimes even across the ocean, by means of fashion dolls, half or a third the size of the human body, and dressed with every minute detail correct. They came from the Rue St Honoré, and were the only means by which news of the latest fashions could pass through the barrier created by the war between France and England. From 1672, however, fashion news had also been spread through a newspaper, *Le Mercure Galant*,

Dress was severely formal at the Spanish Court. 'The Infanta Margarita'. Velasquez. Prado, Madrid

A cobbler. Abraham Bosse

so that elegant people from Vienna to Venice, from Berlin to Madrid, from London to Brussels, could be informed of the fact that doublets were now long and finely pleated, or whatever fashion's latest whim might have become.

In the course of two years (between 1672 and 1674) the fashion for ornaments on sleeves changed seven or eight times: they were buttoned to the wrist; turned up with coloured ruffles; open the whole length of the arm; loaded with lace and ribbons; decorated with little buttons very close to each other, or ornamented with a double circlet of lace on the forearm and the wrist.

Hats during those years did not change very much: they were wide-brimmed, with a gold cord round the crown. During the summer of 1672 gold-embroidered gloves were fashionable; in the winter of 1674 they were made of dog-skin and covered with fur from the same animal.

Le Mercure Galant stipulated that necklines should no longer be boat-shaped as they were when Maria Theresa was a young bride, but now were more accentuated at the back; it also spread the fashion for skirts *à la Psyché*, which were soft and full and flowing; and cloaks in Indian linen or white or red silk. Women's stockings, made of silk, were either white or flesh coloured at that time, and their little shoes had a square tip and were made of black velvet or of the same fabric as the dress. Amber necklaces and diamond ornaments became the rage, as well as painted linen fans studded with gems and having attached to them silk sachets containing perfumed

Left: The Gallery of the *Palais Royal*, Paris. Abraham Bosse. Engraving

159

Men had swords, breeches were tight fitting at the knee, and sleeves became important. Portrait of the Archduke Albert of Austria. Rubens. Art Museum, São Paulo, Brazil

essences. Furs continued to be fashionable, and many animals were sacrificed to this desire for elegance— sable, otter, marten, fox of every kind, wolf, lamb, cat, hare and rabbit.

Sometimes men's doublets were lined with fur. Muffs were worn by men, hanging from their belts: these were also of fur, tiger, panther, otter or beaver. Muffs had originated in Venice in the fifteenth century but only during the reign of Louis XIV did they become fashionable throughout the world. They were made of silk or brocade, lined with fur, fastened with buttons of crystal or gold, and covered with beads. At first only courtesans wore them but subsequently respectable women took them up. Men's muffs, worn only partly to protect their hands from the cold, were usually rather small, often in black or grey satin and lined with fur. Women wore various shapes according to the fashion of the moment, and sometimes only used them as part of their coquetry. The muff was very useful indeed to conceal the face in delicate moments. Sometimes they were large enough to conceal a lapdog.

From 1674 to 1678 French fashion came to a temporary standstill, owing to royal edicts forbidding luxury and waste, in an attempt to restore the finances of a nation wasted by continuous wars. Later the edicts were forgotten and the creators of fashion launched the typical late seventeenth-century costume. Now the elegant man wore a long coat which clung to his body from the neck to the knees, but was open at the chest to allow a glimpse of a sumptuously

Below: Gloves were an important fashion accessory. English gloves of the seventeenth century. Victoria and Albert Museum, London

Right: A wide sash worn over the shoulder carried the sword, and ribbons gathered the breeches at the knee. 'Portrait of Charles I'. Detail. Van Dyck. Louvre

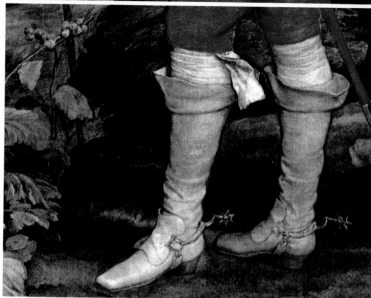

161

embroidered shirt. Round his neck he wore a cravat: a linen collar rectangular in shape, which divided into two and fell down almost to the waist. This masculine accessory had a military origin: it was part of the costume of the mercenaries from Croatia, who had been employed by various European sovereigns since the sixteenth century. These Croatian troops a century later formed part of the army of Louis XIV, and from them stemmed the new masculine fashion.

Elegant men in the seventeenth century wore swords even when not at war, hanging from a heavy scarf which crossed over the coat from one shoulder. The close-fitting breeches, fastened at the knee by a garter, barely showed below the coat. At hip level a rather wide ribbon belt was worn. Earlier, in the 1660s, they had adopted a mode which was German rather than French in origin: Rhinegraves or petticoat-breeches as they were called in England. They were immensely wide in the leg and were pleated or gathered on to a waistband and fell like a divided skirt to the knee; below were flounces of lace.

For women the corsage was open and laced across the front with ribbons. From the bodice full short sleeves belled out, finishing in a ruffle of lace. *La robe de parade*, made of heavy material, was covered by another *robe*, open and secured at the hips by diamond rosettes, bows or circular draperies.

Hair Styles

The most typical hair style of the 1690s was the one launched involuntarily by Mademoiselle de Fontanges. Louis XIV had fallen in love with her when she was only eighteen, and he insisted on having her always near him when riding through the woods on hunting expeditions. On one such hunt, she made her appearance in an amazon costume covered with embroideries and with a fanciful coiffure consisting of ribbons and plumes; when a sudden wind disordered her hair, the young lady simply tied it up with a ribbon. The effect was so attractive that the King begged her not to alter it during the day. Mademoiselle did not need asking twice, and from then on the ladies of the court arranged the curls that had been hanging on their neck and ears with ribbons, plumes and little caps with high crowns stiffened by wires.

Another hair style which was all the rage was one which Madame de Sévigné described to her daughter thus: 'The hair is parted at the sides and arranged in round, soft curls, which must not fall lower than an inch below the ears. The effect is young and pretty, with bunches of hair held at either side of the face.' Women did not hesitate to allow male hair-dressers to dress their hair, in spite of the fact that in 1605 the clergy had threatened to excommunicate women

Engravings of (*from left to right*) a housewife, a gardener, a woman in mourning, a minister and a woman with a large bonnet. *Centre*: Woman carrying a fan. 1670. Strasbourg Almanack. Bertarelli Collection, Milan

162

Illustration on a fan, showing a mock battle in Florence. Callot. 1619. Bertarelli Collection, Milan

Venetian courtesan. Forabosco. Uffizi Gallery, Florence

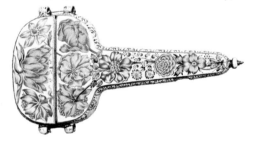

Dutch enamelled scissors case. Seventeenth century. Victoria and Albert Museum, London

Charles I of England and Henrietta of France. Van Dyck. Pitti Palace, Florence

who allowed themselves to have their hair done by men. There was much use of false hair, and the wigs and postiches that Queen Margot had used to hide her baldness came back into fashion.

Wigs have throughout history been used for such a purpose, but Louis XIV in his early years had an excellent head of hair. When this began to fail he adopted a peruke, and so great was his prestige that every fashionable man in Europe began to wear one even if he had no need of it. This strange fashion lasted for more than a century.

The wigs worn by Louis XIV were always very high to make him look taller. Wigs became so popular that Colbert, the Minister of Finance, imposed a new tax on the wig-makers' trade. In this way the very heavy burden of importing cut hair from abroad was set against the export of finished wigs. These were at first the colour of the natural hair of the wearer, and according to their shape they had different names. The *Roi Soleil* was himself clean-shaven and this fashion too he imposed on Europe.

It was in the reign of Louis XIV that the formation of a dressmakers' guild was authorised. Before this, dresses were made at home or else by tailors; towards the end of the seventeenth century Monsieur Regnault and Monsieur Gautier, the most famous fashion creators of their time, were replaced by Madame Charpentier and Madame Villeneuve. They encouraged their clients to lengthen their skirts, to shorten them, to pad them, to load them with gold embroideries, to trim them with braid or embroider them with floral motifs. They suggested new colours: grey, red, blue, yellow, scarlet, brown, purple; and used precious materials like damask, shiny fabrics like satin, soft fabrics like velvet, stiff and gleaming ones like taffeta. They replaced the *palatina*, the silk or fur scarf, launched by Elizabeth Charlotte of Bavaria, which was wound round the neck, with an embroidered *fichu*, or a lace tie. This lace tie was long and narrow, wound round the neck, crossed on the breast and ended in a buttonhole in the bodice. It was called a Steinkirk, as a reminder of the victory won by the Maréchal de Luxembourg over the Prince of Orange. The tie was often made of the French lace called Alençon, after the small town where Richelieu, with the help of an expert, Mademoiselle Gilbert, had founded the first great lace industry. The importing of lace from abroad was restricted to help the tradesmen who had been almost ruined by his earlier

Right: Olimpia Aldobrandini wearing modified Spanish style dress with ribboned sleeves. Anonymous. Doria Pamphili Gallery, Rome

edicts. The passion for lace was such that not only was it used for the robes and shirts specially made for the bath, but it was even used to embellish the bath tub. Fashionable also were sleeves made of two or three layers of Alençon lace, which were called *les engageants*. Lace was used to adorn Spanish leather gloves or the taffeta scarfs used to protect the wig when it rained.

Male tailors exercised their ingenuity in lengthening, widening or shortening men's coats. They made imaginative use of pockets, increasing them from two to four, and cutting them vertically, horizontally, and obliquely. Sometimes pockets were simple, sometimes they were covered with embroidery or braid like the pockets of the trumpet players in a military band and therefore called *à la trompette*. Breeches, which before had not shown below the

Portrait of Amelia of Sölms and child. Detail. A. Kersloot. 1628

Right: Lace collars were worn by men as well as women. 'Portrait of a Gentleman'. Maratta. National Gallery, Rome. *Centre*: 'Portrait of Agatha Gelvinck'. Dirk Dirckszoon. Amsterdam. *Extreme right*: Portrait of Colbert. Bibliothèque Nationale

coat and had been made of the same material, were now made of different fabrics, lighter in colour and embroidered; sometimes this was velvet, and they were also made in white, green or crimson damask, and decorated with embroidery, lace or braid trimming. Lace was also used for shirts, for the 'scissor slash' model which had a slit in front enriched with a fine lace border. Later, breeches were once more made of the same material as the coat, but became much shorter again.

Louis XIV, with his love of finery, often intervened personally to guide fashion in one direction or another. As a symbol of mourning for the death of his father-in-law Philip IV, he ordered that coats should no longer have slashed sleeves, and should be lengthened to the knee. He actually passed a law forbidding the wearing of slashed sleeves except by himself and his courtiers. He continued to wear gold and silver coats, and also founded the 'patent coats' which he distributed to seventy of his favourites: when they wore these blue coats with gold embroidery they could follow the King without needing any further permission. The chosen bodyguard of the King was the corps of mounted musketeers, which at first dressed in a kind of tabard, red with a gold cross on the chest. Then the *grand roi* ordered a new uniform, a blue tabard with a silver cross.

In the seventeenth century there were no great differences between masculine and feminine fashion so far as the materials were concerned, nor in the taste for jewels, accessories and excessive decoration. Only hats were comparatively simple. Men usually carried their hat under their arm, so that it did not interfere with their wig. Hats were of various shapes; there were felt hats, with wide upturned brims, adorned with plumes; hats shaped like cones with rigid brims and white plumes; hats with low crowns and upturned brims and plumes; lop-sided hats to balance the long single curl falling on to the right shoulder of the wearer; three-cornered hats and even two-cornered hats with silver and gold braided edges. The three-cornered hat was worn much larger by Venetian women, but French women, and indeed all elegant women of that epoch, were sparing in their buying of hats, usually preferring not to wear any, except for a small kerchief of white lace (or black

Right: Venetian lace collar. Seventeenth century

for widows) with a point coming down on the forehead, held stiff by wire. Only in the Northern countries did women stay faithful to the hat: sometimes shaped like a cone, made in silk and with a ribbon for married women; or all in white, like a nun's cap, for widows; or wide-brimmed and with a small crown, usually in a dark colour for all other women.

In the seventeenth century we see the beginning of an awareness of fashion for children, copied from adults but slightly simpler. Of course embroidery and lace were used for little bonnets and collars, but no ruffs or farthingales were worn, though skirts were full and long. As long ago as the thirteenth century the question of dressing children had been discussed. In documents of that time we find descriptions of girls' capes and boys' shirts; sumptuary laws passed at that period to curb excessive luxury, still allowed boys up to the age of twelve and unmarried girls to wear embroidery. In the *Vita Nuova* Dante described Beatrice, who was not yet ten years old, in these words: 'She appeared before me dressed in a most noble colour, a humble and honest dark red, dressed and adorned in such a fashion as was befitting her very young age.' Toys of that time were very simple: little bells on the cradles, wooden horses' heads on sticks and dolls made of pottery, paper or plaster of paris were popular with children.

The seventeenth century was in a very real sense the beginning of the Age of Enlightenment, which reached its culmination in the eighteenth century. It saw the beginning of the critical spirit and the rise of inductive philosophies. Galileo proclaimed that the earth went round the sun, and Harvey discovered the circulation of the blood. There were advances in

Left (above): 'Children of Charles I'. Detail. Van Dyck. Sabauda Gallery, Turin. *Left (below)*: 'The Montmort Children'. Detail. Philippe de Champaigne. Beaux Arts Museum, Rheims. *Right*: 'Boy in White'. Detail. Van Dyck. Durazzo Gallery, Genoa

'Prince Frederick of Urbino'. F. Barocci. Palatine Gallery, Florence

every science, and towards the end of the century a diminution of religious fanaticism. Politically and culturally this period was dominated by France, and by the prestige of Louis XIV.

Spain, which had reached the apex of its power in the last century, began to decline. Between 1660 and 1680 European history revolved around France and Louis XIV. Catholic Europe, shaken by the Thirty Years War, weakened by the decadence of Spain and the new Turkish assaults on Austria, abandoned

Left: 'Nurse and Child'. Detail. Frans Hals. Kaiser-friedrich Museum, Berlin. *Right:* 'The Montmort Children'. Detail. Philippe de Champaigne. Beaux Arts Museum, Rheims

all hope of establishing a new Holy Roman Empire. In these circumstances Louis XIV was able to defy rival powers. An absolute monarch who uttered the famous words, *l'état, c'est moi*, he bent to his will the aristocracy, church, parliament and middle classes. A triumph of the rule by Divine Right, he did not recognise any limit to his power, but used it to make his country even greater, not only politically, but also in the fields of art and intellect.

Under the *Roi Soleil* France reached the height of her prestige and intellectual and cultural brilliance. He built Versailles, the triumph of baroque taste, and organised there splendid festivities in honour of Louise La Vallière, his first mistress whom he abandoned for Madame de Montespan, a beautiful and insolent woman. At Versailles the poet Benserade declaimed his verses, Molière produced his comedies,

'Children of Charles I'. Detail. Van Dyck. Sabauda Gallery, Turin

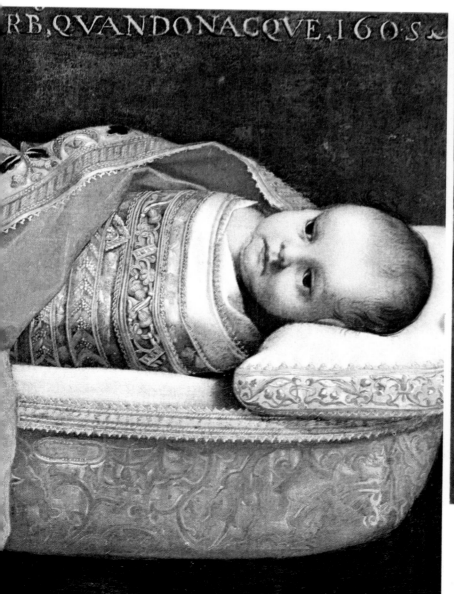 

A musical gathering at the Court of Louis XIV. Engraving

Portrait of Charles Créqui. Daniel Dumonstier. Louvre

The Consul. Another engraving from the Strasbourg Almanack. Circa 1670. Bertarelli Collection, Milan

the Baroque period. The attire of the gentlemen and ladies who lived in this celebrated palace was a triumph of the creativity of French classicism. Courtiers with curled wigs, dressed in ribbons and lace, made tall by their scarlet heels, gallantly attended ladies dressed richly in silks and brocades, their beautiful naked shoulders rising from a foam of lace, their hair styled in the latest fashion, their long train carried by a little black boy. The whole world looked towards France, envied her triumphs and sought to imitate them. But the greatness of France had been built at the price of immense sacrifices by the people.

The advance of rationalism was speeded by the philosophic writings of Descartes, and the same spirit can be detected in the plays of Corneille; in the comedies of Molière with his sharp powers of observation; in Racine, and even in La Fontaine who in his *Fables* invested animals with human thoughts and feelings. This tendency towards rationalism emerged in literature not only in France but in England also.

England

In the reign of Elizabeth, England attained a degree of prestige which she had never enjoyed before. The defeat of the Spanish Armada in 1588 revealed her power. In literature she produced her supreme genius, William Shakespeare, and in science, Francis Bacon. From the struggle of the Civil War in England arose Cromwell who, although hated, certainly made his country respected abroad. The seventeenth century saw the foundation of her empire overseas, and the emergence of England as a European power.

Portrait of Newton. Anonymous. Engraving. Circa 1690

often taking part in them himself, and Lulli produced his operas. The whole Court, five thousand people, the flower of French aristocracy, lived at the Palace; five thousand more people, in the service of the king, were housed in adjoining buildings. The fairy-like fêtes and festivals of Versailles constantly celebrated the glory of the king.

The architectural style of Versailles, given its first impulse by Michelangelo in Italy, replaced the pure lines of the Renaissance with the rounded forms of

Portrait of the Marquis of Drevet. Hyacinthe Rigaud. Versailles Museum

Italy

In Italy, at that time almost entirely under Spanish domination, the seventeenth century was even more the age of reason and criticism, the only field where Italian genius was free. Marcello Malpighi was the founder of microscopic anatomy; Francesco Redi did original work in the field of spontaneous generation; and the impulse which had started with the philosopher Giordano Bruno in the sixteenth century, was carried on by Tommaso Campanella, who first identified nature with thought itself.

Women and Manners

Women found their place in the world of philosophical speculation, and translated into charitable works the urge to free themselves from the spiritual slavery which many felt oppressed them. In a small

Six fashion plates by Bonnart showing the trend towards simpler dress with a more flowing line

village called Dombes, on the initiative of the man who later became St Vincent de Paul, the 'Daughters of Charity' were born. They were pious women, who under the guidance of Louise de Marillac had 'as their convent the homes of the sick', as their 'veil a holy and strict modesty', as 'cloister, obedience'. The 'ladies in grey', so called because they wore dresses of this colour, worked at their charitable

Another engraving from *Le Costume historique*

174

mission in the country, in the towns and on the battlefields helping the sick.

Aristocratic ladies too followed the example of the 'Daughters of Charity'. Ladies of the highest nobility devoted themselves to helping the sick in the *Hôtel-Dieu* and the *Hôpital de la Charité* (the latter was under the protection of Maria de' Medici, Queen of France) and the beggars and the poor people in the *Maison de la pitié*. Those ladies who lacked the courage to nurse the sick as Maria Gonzaga Princess of Mantua did, gave away money to charity. Thus Marguerite de Rouillé founded, under the patronage of the Cardinal de la Rochefoucauld, the Hospital for Incurables in Paris, an establishment which made a great contribution to the support of the chronic sick.

Less pious and more intellectually inclined, the sisters and the niece of the abbess of Port Royal des Champs, Mère Angélique Arnauld, dedicated their lives to the study of theology. Juana Inès de la Cruz, a young Mexican girl who had learnt how to read at the age of three, and to write verses when not yet ten, and who had been called 'the tenth muse' by her contemporaries, chose to hide her intellectual ability in a convent. Gilberte and Jacqueline Pascal, sisters of Blaise Pascal, mathematician, physicist, philosopher and one of the greatest French writers, were no less gifted than their famous brother, even if they are not as well known. Gilberte, who had studied philosophy and history, after bringing up her five children, withdrew from the world and took refuge in Jansenism, the religious movement which opposed the

A shop in Paris. J. Bérain. 1678

moral decadence of the times. Jacqueline, a poetess at the age of eight, a playwright at eleven, took a degree at the age of twenty-five, but ended by following the example of her sister.

In Italy, Cristina Paleotti was one of the most brilliant women of her time. She was surrounded by passionate admirers: the High Constable Lorenzo Onofrio Colonna (the husband of Maria Mancini, who had been tenderly loved by Louis XIV, but had her life sacrificed to political necessity); Count Antonio Trotti; the Count of Pignoranda; the Marchese Guido Pepoli and the Marchese Filippo Barbazza. She received the Cross of the Order of the Empress. She took pleasure in writing poetry, as did also Faustina Maratti Zoppi, another intellectual.

Yet another remarkable woman in the seventeenth century was Christine of Sweden. She was highly cultured—she had read Plato, Tacitus and the early Fathers of the Church, and the philosophy of Descartes, and had gathered in her palace in Stockholm the greatest intellects of her time. Daughter of the great Gustavus Adolphus, she succeeded to the throne when very young, but at the age of twenty-eight she abdicated in favour of her cousin Carl Gustav, because she did not wish to marry and would therefore produce no heirs. Dissatisfied with the Protestantism in which she had been brought up, she became a Catholic convert in the royal chapel in Innsbruck. Subsequently she went to live in Rome where she led a splendid if somewhat unconventional life. She surrounded herself with philosophers and writers and founded the Arcadia, a famous literary society.

When she went to France she was much concerned with the rules of Court etiquette. She made the following notes in her diary: 'Cap not to be worn when visiting somebody important; a duchess when presented at Court has the right to kiss the Queen's dress higher up from the hem than other ladies; gloves must be taken off when offering something to the King or Queen; pavement—men should walk in such a way that women are not splashed by water from the street or the gutters; masks must not be worn in the presence of important people unless one is sitting in their coach; princes have the right to sit down at the royal table at banquets, to offer the king their napkin, to hold the little tray while the King is taking Communion, to take precedence of all the nobility; silence is compulsory when gambling in the royal apartments, even if the King is absent.'

Though there was this interest in etiquette, society lacked refinement. At table guests amused themselves by throwing bread or fruit at each other; cleanliness was ignored and the early morning ablutions consisted of wiping one's face with a handkerchief; the needs of nature were often satisfied in public; cleaning the teeth was done by sucking aromatic lozenges (Louis XIV was always sucking aniseed lozenges to 'freshen his breath'); perfumes were used to neutralise bad smells but never water. Reason, the ruling force in every other field, had not yet expressed itself in the matter of hygiene.

'The Visit'. Detail. Pietro Longhi. Aldo Crespi Collection, Milan

The
Eighteenth Century

The beginning of the eighteenth century was disrupted by the War of the Spanish Succession, by wars in Poland, and by the decadence of the reign of Louis XIV, the absolute monarch who, after having brought France to the height of her power, was responsible also for undermining the institution of monarchy itself. At the time of Louis XIII the Fronde had already begun, a movement to substitute government by law for the monarchy. A second conspiracy, the Fronde of the Princes, had been formed, but it came to nothing in 1653, crushed by Mazarin.

During the War of the Austrian Succession, Prussia had managed to seize Silesia and, fully aware of her own power, was aiming at supremacy over Vienna. Maria Theresa of Hapsburg, Empress of Austria and Queen of Hungary, by means of an alliance with Russia and the Bourbons, struggled to defend her possessions. She also succeeded in extending her power through the marriages of her children, among them Marie Antoinette, who became Queen of France. Frederick the Great, however, helped both by good fortune and his own strategic skill, managed to enlarge his state, which he strengthened by means of important reforms and raised to the status of a great European power.

In this century Russia, under the guidance of Peter the Great, began to make her power felt. Already strong in the Baltic, she now assumed a role of first importance in European politics. England, made rich by the conquest of her American territories, started the conquest of India. She further extended her empire by taking Canada from France, thus becoming a world power. The United States of America declared their independence in 1776, freeing themselves from the rule of George III, King of England.

Wars and political struggles in the first half of the eighteenth century transformed Europe, establishing a new order, and giving birth to new states on the other side of the ocean. But another transformation was being prepared. As early as 1692, a society known as the Arcadia had started in Rome. Its aim was to fight the bombast and bad taste of the century and return to a life of spontaneity, finding inspiration in the simplicity of the shepherds who were supposed to have lived in Arcadia in the Golden Age.

Contemporary with the Arcadia ideal was 'the Enlightenment', a cultural movement of German origin, which spread through the whole of Europe. While the Renaissance had freed the European spirit from submission to church authority in the sphere of politics, economics, science and art, the Enlightenment tried to banish medieval obscurantism and live by the light of reason. Christianity and the Papacy were favourite targets. One of the most important supporters of the Enlightenment was Voltaire, the brilliant writer who led the battle, with his historical essays and tragedies, satirical tales and lampoons, against traditional beliefs.

Educated by the Jesuits, Voltaire was encouraged by his father to follow a career as a lawyer, but he had other ideas. He was twice thrown into prison because of his revolutionary theories. A friend of Frederick of Prussia and of Catherine of Russia, he was also one of the founders of the great French *Encyclopédie*, which had as its aim the spread of education among the people, freeing the spirit from the prejudices of the times. Although it was officially condemned on the appearance of its first volume in 1751, between then and 1772 sixteen further volumes were published. This was an imposing summary of the knowledge of the time, in which Experience and Reason took the place formerly occupied by Revelation.

Masks were a fashion accessory often worn at carnivals and balls. 'Woman with a Mask'. Felice Boscarati. Dino Barozzi Collection, Venice

Left: The extravagance of eighteenth-century fashion is epitomised in this portrait of Marie Antoinette, which was painted shortly before the outbreak of the French Revolution. Elisabeth Vigée-Lebrun. Versailles Museum

Following pages: Men wore wigs and long jackets with embroidered cuffs. 'Louis XIV receiving Frederick Augustus of Saxony'. Louis Silvestre. Versailles Museum

Portrait of Louis XIV. Rigaud. Versailles Museum

'Louis XV'. L. M. van Loo. Versailles Museum

New Fashions

After the death of Louis XIV, dress became simpler, ridding itself of the excessive ornamentation that, instead of adding elegance to the body, merely weighed it down. Fashion was influenced by the painter Antoine Watteau, well known because of the wall-tapestries he had designed for Versailles. Women's dress developed also from a combination of an Italian influence derived from the theatrical tradition and the French influence. The dress consisted of a bodice which came to a point in front, and was stiffened by whalebones, with 'Watteau' pleats which came down from the shoulders. Sleeves had vertical pleats, and were often short, with a ruffle that came to the wrists. The skirt was deeply pleated from the waist, and gave an impression of great fullness. From the back of the neck a little gathered cape was attached at the shoulders, and reached to the ground.

Another innovation was the placing of metallic hoops under the skirt to make it wider. This device

was later replaced by the *panier*, which was high and wide enough for the arms to rest on. The wide *panier* was, however, only used for formal dresses. For dresses worn in the home, smaller and more practical *paniers* were preferred. At first a single framework with three hoops, one above the other, sewn to the material of the skirt, and held in place at the waist by a hoop exactly the same size as the waist, the *panier* later became a double structure, separated into two convex shapes attached to the belt. This fashion then slowly disappeared, partly because the wide skirt was uncomfortable and impractical for wearing in theatre boxes, coaches, or gondolas, but also because of the whim of an actress who decided to appear on the stage without the discomfort of the cage of *paniers*. Women began to remove the whalebones from their *paniers*, and use them for their corsets, which became the next instrument of torture in the wheel of fashion.

Dressing from head to toe was a very long business. Madame de Staël in one of her plays has a marquise

182

'Louis XVI'. A. F. Callet. Versailles Museum

cardboard painted black and white. The black silk *tabarro* and accompanying *bautta* (the half mask) were joined by the *rochetto* (worn by women)—a little cape in silk or lace which fell from the head and swathed half the body under its three-cornered hat. Because the *bautta*, which concealed half the face, allowed one to talk confidentially, it lent itself to all sorts of misuses (of which Casanova was the master);

The Gardens at Versailles. Engraving. Eighteenth century

of the time say, 'It is enough to observe the details with which we are preoccupied each day. Every morning, all those discussions with artisans and tradesmen to choose our apparel! What care in choosing the latest dress, in the effort to keep abreast of fashions! And then we have the arduous task of performing our toilette with all the attention to detail needed for good grooming.'

In Italy fashion was dictated not only by France but also by Venice, where women covered their head with the *zendado* and *linzioletto*. The former consisted of a scarf, usually black, which covered the head, reached down to the waist and was tied in front, covering the arms. The *linzioletto* was more often worn; made of white cotton, and tied round the waist like a skirt, open in front and thrown back over the head, it covered the shoulders and arms. In Genoa the favourite head-covering was the *mezzero*, an embroidered shawl, or the *pezzotto*, a large white handkerchief, the ancestor of the modern *foulard*. For men, Venice created the *tabarro*, which was initially a fancy-dress mask, made of material or

however, it could only be worn during a few months of the year, and to certain festivities: it was permissible to wear it from the first Sunday in October until Lent, for the feast of the Ascension, or the election of the Doge or his procurators.

After the high clogs women had been wearing were abolished, little shoes became fashionable, which were without heels, but had an upturned toe, and a diamond or paste buckle. Paste was the invention of a jeweller who had succeeded in preparing a particularly limpid and transparent glass, which he used in the manufacture of artificial diamonds or strass. The little Venetian shoes which made it so much easier for ladies to walk were considered by the Doge Contarini 'too comfortable, unfortunately', as they allowed high-born women, hidden by the *bautta*, to mingle with the crowd in the Piazza San Marco, and to attend the gaming rooms without being recognised.

In France the King was the only man allowed to wear a great cloak in brocade, lifted on one shoulder to reveal his costume: the rich, puffed, embroidered

183

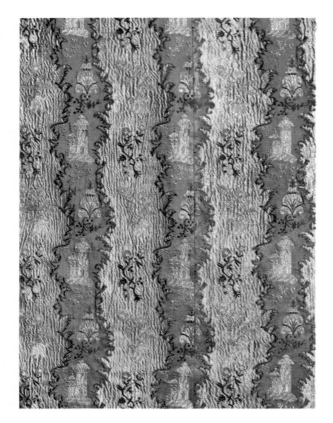

Striped Venetian brocade. Chigi Collection, Venice

breeches, the silk stockings and the little shoes. Other men modified their dress, which consisted of a *gilet* or waistcoat and breeches. The waistcoat became a rich garment, made of damask, satin or velvet, embroidered in *petit-point* with landscapes, flowers, animals and symbolic patterns; it was adorned with a great number of gold buttons, closely set, which could also be silver or enamelled; only the first few buttons were in fact used, so that the waistcoat stayed partly open, reaching halfway down the thigh, that is about thirteen inches shorter than the coat; it had lateral pockets and long sleeves. The collar of the shirt was tied like a scarf and embellished with lace. The breeches were close fitting, and ended above the knee, where white silk stockings were fastened with laces.

The coat was fitted closely to the body (the waist was made slimmer by a corset), and widened on the hips to the fullness of a half circle; it had a slit at the back from the waist down, and was without a collar. Trimmed with braid, it was always worn open.

A white tie hemmed with lace which was part of

'L'Enseigne de Gersaint'. Detail. Antoine Watteau. Dahlem Museum, Berlin. This painter had a great influence on fashion at the beginning of the eighteenth century, and gave his name to the pleats on the backs of dresses

Marie Adelaide of Savoy, Duchess of Burgundy. Pierre Gobert. Private collection

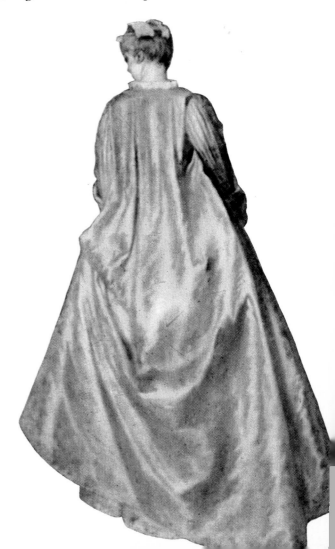

184

A long coat with embroidered front and large cuffs. 'Portrait of a Gentleman'. Ghislandi. Brera Museum, Milan

the shirt was replaced by a true tie, often made in black silk. The long coat was lined with silk of the same colour as the material of which the waistcoat was made. The tails were flared and held stiff with whalebones. The white waistcoat, embroidered with multicoloured flowers, such as the one Casanova wore when visiting the Princesse d'Urfé, was trimmed with a decorative silver braid, which cleverly hid all the seams.

In England came other changes in masculine dress. Lace and ribbons were abolished, and the lace *jabot* was replaced with a black silk tie, which in turn was abandoned in favour of a white muslin scarf tied round the neck. The sleeveless waistcoat of coloured silk was shortened to waist length, where it ended in two rounded points. The coat on the other hand reached mid-calf length, and was called a *frac*; its sleeves were long and narrow, with the lace on the shirt peeping out below a little velvet cuff. The velvet

Left: Coats were tight fitting above the waist, flaring out over the hips. 'Family Concert'. Detail. Pietro Longhi. *Below*: 'The Governess'. Detail. Chardin. 1739

186

Hair styles of the eighteenth century. Engraving. Circa 1740

collar was straight and doubled. The *frac* was generally pale green or pale yellow in colour, but later was made also in black. In Italy the *frac* was called a *goldoniana*. Towards the end of the century, breeches were held up by braces and became longer to cover the knee, extending over the stockings. Though braces were considered a novelty in the eighteenth century, they were not really new to the field of masculine fashion, for they had been worn in Scandinavia as early as 1500 B.C., when men were dressed in a seamless piece of material which covered their shoulders, and ended in two points to which leather straps were attached, straps which had the same function as braces.

There were many eccentrics who adopted ostentatious and bizarre costumes. One courtier presented himself to Marie Antoinette dressed in a long coat of scarlet cloth trimmed in blue, and with mother-of-pearl buttons; underneath it the satin waistcoat was seen, in pink and green stripes; his trousers, of a soft pale blue material, were very close fitting, fastened by garters embroidered in white silk, as were the buttonholes, and reaching below the knee; his stockings were of silk with vertical stripes in blue and poppy-red, he had silver buckles on his shoes, dogskin gloves, and a three-cornered hat embellished with a silk rosette. The ensemble was completed by an enormous muff in grey and black fur, trimmed

Portrait of Vergniaud. Durameau. Lambinet Museum, Versailles

Long waistcoats were worn under calf-length coats. 'A Gentleman'. Drawing by Watteau

187

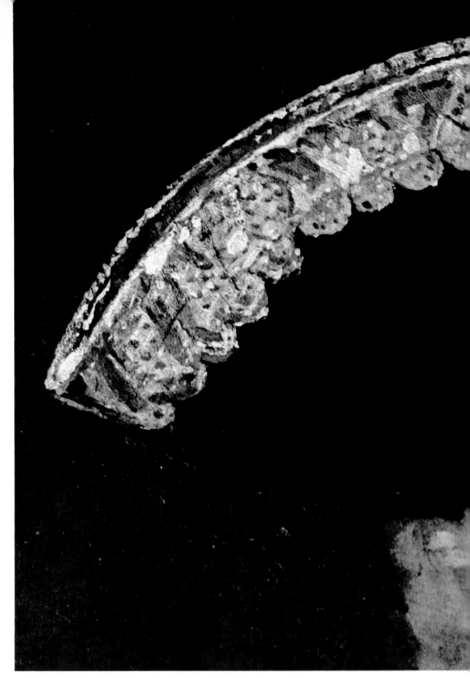

Below: 'Portrait of a Gentleman'. Detail. Ghislandi. Poldi Pezzoli Museum, Milan. *Right*: Detail of the portrait. Before the Revolution men's hats were bicorne or tricorne, embellished with gold braid, lace or cockades

188

in the middle with a large poppy-red bow; at his neck a wide tie in white embroidered muslin; and he sported an overcoat in lemon-yellow cloth with green stripes, and spangled buttons. His wig was very elaborate, with large curls symmetrically placed one on top of the other at the sides of the head, 'high and saddle-shaped in front, and shaped like a horse-shoe behind'. The hair was tied very low on the nape of the neck, and fell down his back.

Before the French Revolution hats were almost always three-cornered, often trimmed with lace rosettes and edged with gold braid. The Three Musketeers wore elaborate hats trimmed with white plumes. Soldiers preferred felt hats with little brims, trimmed with gold braid or rosettes.

Left: Illustration from *A History of Fashion*. M. A. Racinet

Watteau pleats remained fashionable on women's dresses for a long time, especially at the back of the dress, where they started from the shoulders, widened on the hips and came down to the hem of the dress, thus giving an appearance of greater fullness. Cloaks too were 'à la Watteau', with great pleats and a hood. Spanish women preferred to wear the *mantilla*, a silk shawl which was often embroidered.

Feminine dress always included the corset, trimmed with lace and ribbons. The bow pinned in the middle of the neckline, which was wide and deep, was called a '*parfait contentement*'. The overskirt was attached to the corset, and pulled up on each side to increase the volume of the *paniers*. The underskirt, of a different colour, was often embellished with ribbons, frills and gathered lace.

189

When the hooped skirt was born it was received with jeers, but soon triumphed everywhere. It was introduced by the actresses of the Comédie Italienne, which the Duke of Orleans had imported from Italy. The skirt was supported by five round hoops one over the other and joined together by stiff waxed cloth. The hoops, first round in shape, later became oval, but the skirt was always so huge that ladies were obliged to turn sideways in order to go through doors, and found it impossible to reach the hands of the gallants who escorted them everywhere.

Materials

Brocades and velvets were among the most popular, but lighter fabrics also became fashionable and were given very curious names: the *camelot*, a silk cloth with a wool warp; the *ferrandina* or bombasine, a silk and cotton mixture; *cartek*, a lining material; the *grisette*, silk mixed with grey cotton (as this was the favourite material of working-class girls, the term was later applied to working-class girls of loose morals).

There was a certain breaking down of class distinctions. Louis XV, on the occasion of the wedding of the Dauphin and the Infanta of Spain, organised a great ball in Versailles, where he decided, perhaps to gain the sympathy and support of the middle classes, to invite the most beautiful Parisian women, even if they did not have titles. The ball was to be in fancy-dress, and it was soon rumoured that the King would appear as a fir-tree. When the doors of the Royal apartment opened, seven men dressed as fir-trees emerged to join the crowd of Columbines, Harlequins, Chinese and Turks who were dancing. They surrounded the newcomers, and the ladies did their best to recognise the King, perhaps hoping to conquer his heart, as his favourite Madame de Châteauroux had died recently. The woman who succeeded in gaining the affections of Louis XV was Madame d'Etoiles, née Poisson, the daughter of a provincial weaver.

Gentlemen took great pains with their appearance and employed servants to help them dress. '*La Grande Toilette*'. Engraving. Moreau the Younger. Bertarelli Collection, Milan

Left: 'Portrait of Madame Pompadour'. François Boucher. Rothschild Collection

The Marquise de Pompadour

Blonde with blue eyes, Jeanne Antoinette Poisson had a fresh and delicate face, with rather pale lips. Intelligent and gifted, cunning and fond of intrigue, she soon learned to dominate the King, and she even made herself acceptable to the Queen, Maria Leczinska. She had been schooled for her role of court favourite since her childhood, so much so that her mother had always called her La Reinette. She had enormous power over the King which enabled her to meddle in State affairs: she obtained the nomination of ambassadors, founded the manufacture of Sèvres

Metal hoops were placed under the full skirt to make it wider. Engraving by Fragonard

Portrait of Maria Louisa of Parma. A. R. Mengs. Circa 1770. Prado, Madrid

'Portrait of a Lady'. Verri. Miniature. Circa 1760. Private collection, Milan

Right: 'The Hairdresser'. Detail. Pietro Longhi. Ca' Rezzonico, Venice

porcelain (delicately coloured in blue, yellow and gold), and organised theatrical performances. She was a friend of Voltaire and loved dancing, music (she played the clavichord extremely well), painting and sculpture. She kept her beauty for a long time; twice a week, in order to keep her clear complexion, she would apply an astringent lotion made with cypress cones, pomegranate and strawberry roots, walnut leaves and alum, boiled in three litres of rain water, and strained through a linen cloth. On her hair she used a pomade made of beef marrow, veal fat, hazelnut oil, Peruvian balsam and vanilla; all this was warmed up in a double boiler, filtered and scented with rose or musk.

She was very elegant, and remained faithful to the *robe à la française*; this had a bodice cut with a downward point in front, a wide neckline either V-shaped or square (with rounded corners), trimmed with a pleated lace border artfully called *tatez-y* (touch here). In the middle of the neckline there would be a

parfait contentement made out of the same ribbon that trimmed the sleeves, which were close fitting to the elbow, and adorned with frills of pleated lace called *petits bonhommes*. The huge overskirt opened in front in the middle to reveal the skirt beneath, which was attached to the bodice and embellished by a deep embroidered border decorated with braids, frills and

Jewel case belonging to Madame Pompadour

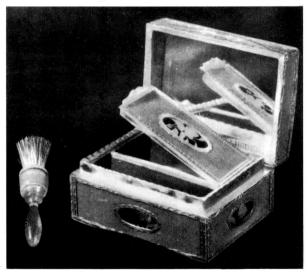

flowers. These decorations, *les garnements*, which often ornamented the upper part of the skirt, were extremely rich and expensive, and often cost more than the material and the making of the dress. *Les robes à la française* were publicised in the *Mercure Galant* and in the *Galerie des Modes*.

The fashion *à la polonaise*, created at the time of the war with Poland, had an overskirt with two cords which allowed one to lift the skirt as high as the wearer wished, so as to form deep folds. Then a new dress became fashionable: the dress *à la circassienne*, launched by Mademoiselle Aisse, a beautiful young Circassian girl whom the French Ambassador in Constantinople, Monsieur de Ferriol, had bought in the slave market. The dress named after her had three cords which lifted up the ankle-length overskirt; the sleeves of the under-bodice reached down to the wrist, and were longer than the sleeves of the dress.

As well as dresses for formal occasions, *négligés* for wear at home or on a journey became fashionable: bodice and skirt were all in one piece, to form a complete and practical dress. The actress Dancourt was the first to launch this fashion, when she wore a *négligé* in the play *Adrienne*; because of this the *négligé* was often called Adrienne. *Caraco*, on the other hand, was the name given to a different type of *négligé* brought from Nantes by the Duke of Anguillon, which had a double flounce falling down the back of the skirt.

Then came the fashion for the *robe à l'anglaise*, a simpler garment than the *à la française*. This consisted of a redingote similar to the masculine one, a short jacket with wide lapels at the collar and long sleeves. There were no *paniers*, but an underskirt of stiff horsehair, and the *cul de Paris*, a little cushion which was placed on the buttocks and tied at the waist to

Elisabeth of Württemberg. Lampi. Pitti Palace, Florence

Some elaborate hair styles of the eighteenth century. Engravings. Bertarelli Collection

à la Comode

a l'inconstante

a la Parisienne

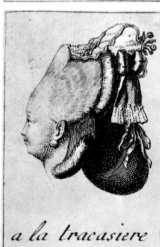

a la tracasiere

Espèce de Pouf couvert d'un voile de gaze transparent.

Cyr, two hundred and fifty young ladies of noble birth but limited means. The boarding-school of St Cyr had been founded by Madame Brinon, a nun and a friend of Madame de Maintenon, mistress of Louis XIV. The young ladies attending it were taught science, arts, music, dancing, and domestic subjects so that they might become good housewives. Their uniform was black, and on their heads they wore *fontanges*, which were a headgear made of starched and fluted linen, pleated like the pipes of an organ. For manual work they had little black aprons, trimmed just like the bodice, with blue, red, yellow or green ribbons, according to their rank.

Hair Styles

At the beginning of the eighteenth century hair styles became very simple again for a time: the hair was puffed up on top, and two curls fell back behind the ears. Later Leonard, the fashionable hairdresser,

increase the width behind. The dress consisted of a very close-fitting bodice, pulled in tight with whalebones, which was joined to a rich skirt, cut slightly longer in the back than in front, to form a little train. At the neckline of the bodice was a linen scarf trimmed with lace, like the masculine *jabot*. The fashion for lace became so excessive that in almost every country there were laws passed to limit its use. An Englishman named Hammond invented a machine to make tulle, which to some extent replaced the more expensive lace. Little aprons made of tulle or silk often completed the dress.

These aprons were worn by the schoolgirls of St

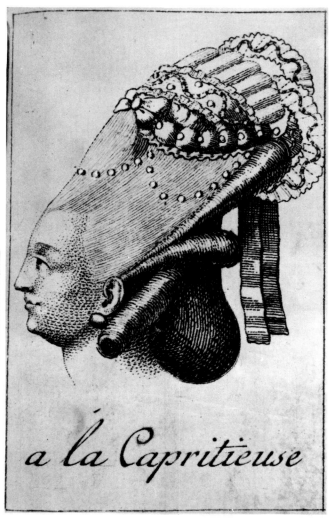

à la Caprieuse

à la bonne Feme

à la Magisienne

'Portrait of Marie Antoinette'. Janinet. 1777

'*La Petite Toilette*'. Engraving. Moreau the Younger. Bertarelli Collection

introduced far more elaborate hair styles; the head was now loaded with real or artificial hair, bedecked with a battery of veils, flowers, ribbons, plumes, stiffened by pomades and then powdered. Hair styles grew to be the most important feature of eighteenth-century fashion. They changed continuously, according to the dictates of fashionable hairdressers. Every hair style had a name; when they had the added complication of *poufs* they might be called *à la belle Poule*; some hair styles had decorations as elaborate as sailing ships placed on top of the edifice; even the *poufs* had names which distinguished them. Every occasion prompted Leonard to invent new hair styles, like the one called 'Inoculation', when Lady Montagu, the wife of the English ambassador in Constantinople, came back with the news that in Turkey and other countries inoculation against smallpox was widely known and practised.

There was also a 'Mesmer' hair-do, inspired by the founder of mesmerism, a new cure for illness through the power of hypnotism. This Doctor Mesmer, of German origin, claimed that through his power of healing convulsions and migraine, rheumatic pains and fever would disappear. The hair style inspired by him was very high, strewn with magnets and little figures of men and women, the patients he had cured, and flowers.

Hair was always carefully powdered. To keep the hair style in place when they were at home ladies wore little caps made of lace and also very large silk hats. When hair styles again became simpler, the hair was not powdered any longer and the emphasis changed from hair to hats, which were very varied indeed, and changed shape continuously. There were close-fitting caps and hats as large as sunshades; there were even some 'satirical' hats, like the one made of black veils and called the 'Discount Bank'; this hat was commenting on the very poor state of the royal finances, and on the banks which had stopped making payments. During journeys, large velvet berets, linen caps, handkerchiefs, little shawls or hats with a large brim upturned at the side were fashionable.

Men were somewhat more modest than women in their hair styles. They wore their hair in a halo of curls over half of the head, and the rest of the hair gathered into a little black silk bag tied with a ribbon of the same colour; or else they wore their hair 'knotted', that is, with three curls on the nape of the neck; or with curls tied by a ribbon; or they wore a

Right: Portrait of Maria Theresa of Savoy, wearing her hair built up on top and curls behind the ears. Van Blarenberghe. Versailles Museum

Venetian lady. Teodoro Viero. Print. Bertarelli Collection

A fashion plate. 1779. Bertarelli Collection

A Swedish lady. Teodoro Viero. 1783. Bertarelli Collection

wig with a tail; or large wigs with *cadenettes*, hanging locks tied and plaited with ribbon. Wigs were at first completely white, but later they were merely powdered, an operation so complicated that it could take several hours. While men wore simple hair styles, in all else they competed with women. Villeroi *le charmant*, the favourite of the King, later Maréchal de France, was a professional dandy. Though he never proved himself a great Maréchal, he was an innovator in the world of fashion: it was he who invented most

Fashion plate. 1781. Bertarelli Collection

of the sentimental romanticisms of eighteenth-century society. He was the first to offer a single rose to his lady, to cry in public for love, to write love verses and admire the sentimental novels which had begun to appear, as classicism lost its appeal and its place was usurped by the literature of sentiment, typified by Rousseau. Villeroi's tastes changed, however, when the *Contrat Social* appeared on the scene. Although it could not be said that its author, Jean Jacques Rousseau, was particularly elegant, his preference for the simplicity of nature had an influence on the disappearance of over-tight corsets and the excessively ornate dresses of the time, decorated at neck and wrists with numerous ruffles of lace.

Marie Antoinette

The most elegant lady in the eighteenth century was Marie Antoinette. She had very definite tastes in fashion; she hated the corset, but liked wearing 'considerations', which were two half circles used to widen the skirt, in a much more simple and practical manner than the usual *paniers* or hoops. Her mother, the Empress Maria Theresa did not object to the 'considerations', but she forbade her daughter to abandon the corset lest she ruin her figure. This Queen of France, with innate good taste, succeeded in blending the rococo style, with its curved lines and florid ornamentation, recognisable in dress as well as in furniture, with the new trends introduced from

Venetian costume. Engraving. Teodoro Viero. 1783. Bertarelli Collection

Fashion plate. 1779. Engraving. Bertarelli Collection

Genoese lady. 1783. Engraving. Teodoro Viero. Bertarelli Collection

England. The new way of dressing had the romantic grace of the English gardens, where imagination had free play. This new freedom gradually supplanted the cold if elegant symmetry of French design. The new dresses appeared to be inspired by nature, that nature loved so well by Marie Antoinette; in her model farm, the Petit Trianon, she would receive her faithful, platonic lover Axel Fersen, dressed in light muslin, with a big straw hat to protect her hair.

Lady-in-waiting wearing a *panier*. Engraving. Moreau the Younger. Bertarelli Collection

Hoops were now abandoned, and the skirts fell in soft pleats, held at the waist by a wide belt tied at the back. The absurd hair styles with *poufs*, which were done once a week, were abandoned in favour of soft curls falling back on the shoulders—curls that were still powdered grey. The fashion for grey hair passed quickly, however, because Marie Antoinette had very beautiful blonde hair (blonde, not red, as Madame Du Barry had obliquely hinted on many occasions, for the mistress of Louis XV was quite jealous of the radiant beauty, simplicity and elegance of the Dauphine).

A handkerchief, knotted like a fichu, covered the neckline, leaving the narrow, close-fitting sleeves quite free. Large Florentine straw hats, tied with pastel coloured ribbons, were worn. Long blue redingotes on white dresses were also very popular. In order to balance the *cul de Paris*, the little saddle fixed to the underskirt under the waist, the curve of the breast was made more prominent by a special corset, which had a piece of triangular iron or wire, curved and padded, which formed the 'pigeon's breast'. The handkerchief crossed over the neckline, and was held up stiffly so that it reached the chin, giving the appearance of false breasts.

Mademoiselle Bertin was Marie Antoinette's Minister of Fashion. The daughter of a provincial *gendarme*, she came to Paris from Picardy. With her natural good taste, her lively spirits and her skill, Marie Jeanne won the esteem of the Princess of Conti, who aided and protected her. In her shop in the Rue

199

'Marie Antoinette'. Detail. Perin–Salbreux. Beaux Arts Museum, Rheims

Engraving. 1780. Chodowiecki. Bertarelli Collection

The *panier* was often elaborately embroidered. Fashion plate 1779

Portrait of Marie Josephine
of Savoy. Jacques Gauthier
d'Agoty. Versailles Museum

The exaggerated *panier* became
cumbersome and impractical.
An elegant couple. Chodo-
wiecki. Engraving. Bertarelli
Collection

Fashion plate. 1779. Bertarelli
Collection

To keep the hair in place while at home women wore huge bonnets or silk hats. Fresco. Gian Domenico Tiepolo. Correr Museum, Venice

'Le Billet Doux'. Detail. Fragonard. Metropolitan Museum, New York

St Honoré, Mademoiselle Bertin slowly acquired the best Parisian clientèle, from Madame de Polignac to Madame de Guiche, but Marie Antoinette was always her most faithful customer, and the fashionable milliner created little masterpieces for her. Mademoiselle Bertin was also an able business woman, and she founded an association of tradesmen, of which she became the self-elected chairman. Twice a week Mademoiselle went to Court to give her advice, and she was loyal to the Queen to the very end.

Accessories

The eighteenth century was the century of elegant accessories. There were little umbrellas and sunshades of pink, yellow, or apple-green taffeta; or they were natural coloured and made of leather, oiled cloth or painted paper. At that time the fashionable Dr Tronchin advised long walks in the open air to encourage a fresh complexion and good health. For these walks special shoes were needed, stronger than the silk or velvet shoes of the time, so fragile they did not last even a few steps. (When Madame Du Barry complained to her shoemaker because her little shoes

had lasted such a short time, the artisan scolded her: 'But Madame, you must have walked in them!')

Other accessories were fans which were attached to a little gold chain worn round the waist. The fans were made of hand-painted parchment, of Alençon or Arles lace, of precious feathers or of embroidered silk. There were also little boxes and containers for beauty spots, cosmetics, scented lozenges, tobacco, perfumes. These boxes were shaped according to their function: little *nécessaires* in enamelled metal containing two perfume bottles; sheaths and boxes in which to keep a little watch key, a pair of tiny scissors, a penknife, an ear-cleaner, a nail-cleaner (ladies wore their nails very long and polished) a pencil and little ivory plates on which to make notes. Amongst the perfumes the Cologne water of the Farina brothers was a novelty. These two brothers, Italian by origin, had settled in Cologne where they invented a new formula, which consisted of bergamot, flowers and the peel of oranges and lemons, lavender, rosemary and neroli mixed with water and alcohol in proportions which they kept a close secret.

The use of Cologne water spread all over the world, not only as a perfume but also as a remedy against headaches, vapours, indigestion. A few drops were

'Portrait of Lady Haverfield'. Detail. Gainsborough.
Wallace Collection, London

Above and below left: Fashion plates showing skirt before
and after hoops were abandoned. Teodoro Viero. 1783.
Engraving. Bertarelli Collection

supposed to ensure the easy digestion of heavy food
like chocolate, which at that time had become extremely fashionable, so much so that Marie Antoinette, after the theatre or a ball, used to go to the dairy
des Lilas to sip a steaming cup of chocolate and cream.

Jewellery

Jewels at that time were wrought into little masterly
designs which showed off the jeweller's skill. In this
time of widespread frivolity and ostentation,
trinkets had more importance than in any other
period. The most popular technique was the *sbalzo*,
the art of engraving on the outside of raised metal
work. This offered great scope, and was very popular, especially with semi-precious stones in rings,
bracelets and earrings. Earrings were not much worn,
mainly because the very elaborate hair styles tended
to hide the ears. Even so, matching earrings and
necklaces that formed a *parure* were owned by rich
women. Diamonds, either by themselves or set with
other precious stones, were highly valued. Bracelets
were also very fashionable, usually made of laminated
gold or silver ribbons worked *a sbalzo*, and often

203

Portrait of Maria Theresa of Savoy, Countess of Artois. Jacques Gauthier d'Agoty. Versailles Museum. *Right*: Detail. A silk purse. *Far right*: Detail. The skirt.

enriched with gems or diamonds. Women also wore bracelets formed by four or five wide thin plates of gold or silver, almost always rectangular or square in shape and embellished with diamonds or other gems. The thin plates were joined to each other by small flexible hinges. Other bracelets were mounted around a miniature painted on ivory and encircled by coloured precious stones.

Necklaces were usually made of strands of pearls of varying sizes. A lady often wore a little velvet ribbon round her neck from which hung a drop-shaped pearl. On formal occasions ladies adorned their hair with gold filigree diadems, strands of pearls, hair slides and combs encrusted with diamonds, or covered with enamel or delicate miniatures. Watches were also worn by women; often they were tiny, covered with diamonds, enamelled and attached to a little filigree chain.

Men also used jewels lavishly, particularly rings with large precious stones set in gold. Fashionable too were signet rings of solid gold with the initials of the family engraved on them. Noblemen displayed heraldic symbols or emblems of knighthood, while military men made a great display of their decorations. The gold or silver watch became an accessory of great importance. It was usually kept in the small pocket of the waistcoat, attached to a small gold chain. A second watch, with no functional purpose and only an imitation, was kept in the breeches pocket, attached to a heavy precious chain to which it was secured. Other beautiful jewelled objects were snuff boxes and the hilts of smallswords. The handles of walking sticks and umbrellas were often of ivory. And men had clasps or buckles of gold either on the little strap which fastened the breeches below the knee or on their shoes.

Women's shoes, often like slippers, and sometimes without any heels, were made either of silk or velvet. They were almost always embroidered in gold and encrusted with gems; leather shoes were adorned in the same way, with precious buckles and gems. Shoes also were made with high heels and long points, slightly turned up. Stockings were white, knitted in a lace-pattern. Working-class women wore slippers of cloth or velvet.

Portrait of Domenico Annibali. A. R. Mengs. Brera Gallery, Milan. *Right*: Detail. Men wore waistcoats embroidered like women's dresses

Women of the Time

Not all eighteenth-century women were frivolous
and interested only in fashion and intrigue. In Italy
Gaetana Agnesi was a child prodigy; at the age of five
she spoke perfect French; at the age of nine she translated into Latin a discourse written in Italian on the
question of whether the education of women should
include the study of the humanities. The answer was
in the affirmative, as she asserted that women's intellectual capacity is in no way inferior to that of men.

Left: Tailor's workshop in Arles.
Raspail

The English style of *frac*. Fashion
plate. Bertarelli Collection

Frach.

Styles in the United States were considerably simpler
than in Europe. 'Portrait of American Lady'. Anonymous.
Gunston Hall, Virginia

This statement was supported by the intellectual
achievement of Isabella Rosales degli Ordegni, who
over a century before had debated her theological
thesis before the Holy College presided over by
Pope Paul III.

Another woman of great intellectual ability was
Madame Dacier who had translated and illustrated
the poems of Homer. She knew seven languages
fluently, could play the viola, sing charmingly, ride a
horse and manage her home capably. She wrote
several books, including one entitled *Analytical In-
stitutions for the use of the Italian Youth*, which she
dedicated to the Empress Maria Theresa. Because of
her contribution in this book, the University of
Bologna appointed her lecturer in mathematics. In
her later years she dedicated herself wholly to religion
and the care of the sick.

Rosalba Carriera, also from Italy, was a great
painter. She came from a humble family and as a child
she made designs for her mother who in turn made
them into lace. In those times a painted snuff box was
more valuable than a gold one, and Carriera became
an expert miniaturist of snuff boxes. She then began

Right: 'Mr and Mrs Andrews'. Detail. Gainsborough.
National Gallery, London

207

to study the technique of pastels, and she learnt English and French, music and singing. She became famous in Venice for her portraits, and later went to live in Paris, where she enjoyed the friendship of Watteau and François Rebel, the director of the Opéra. She became a well-known Parisian personality and her salon was filled with famous men.

Another great woman painter was Madame Vigée-Lebrun, a French woman who painted a portrait of Marie Antoinette during her first pregnancy. The Queen sat for her portrait in a special dress designed for the occasion, a comfortable, voluminous robe. When this portrait was hung in the Salon, it provoked such a scandal that the painter was obliged to withdraw it and replace it with another one portraying the Queen in formal attire, with a pointed bodice and an ample, rich skirt covered with a mass of *garnements*.

Women of this period were involved in science, the arts, philosophy. theology and even in heresy. Maria Francesca de Porto-Carrera de Montijo, a highly educated Spanish woman, appeared before the Inquisition and was denounced because she was too friendly with the Jansenists. The Princess of Lamballe, the most loyal friend of Marie Antoinette, and superintendent of the Royal Household, was elected Great Mistress of the Scottish Mother Lodge of Adoption. After joining this Masonic Order, she called herself the 'Serene Sister of Lamballe', while the Duchess of Chartres, also a Mason, chose the name 'Candour'. During the ceremonies, a Masonic Sister wore a formal white dress, a white leather apron and white gloves; a blue cordon, from which hung a blazing heart, crossed the breast from left to right.

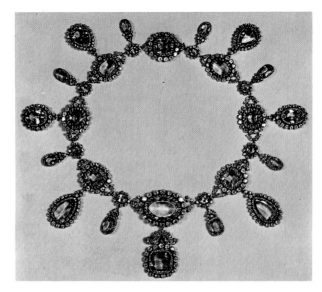

Jewellery which belonged to Catherine of Russia. Necklace, and brooch and two earrings with topaz and diamonds. Jewellery was often matched, especially earrings and necklaces, to form a *parure*

During the last years of Marie Antoinette's reign, simplicity became fashionable again. *Chemises à la reine* and *négligés* were no longer made of silk but of muslin or *indienne*, which was a fine cotton, in white or in pastel colours. White was the rage, a forerunner of neoclassicism, in simple, comfortable, inexpensive fabrics. Men continued to wear embroidered waistcoats in the English style of *frac*.

Left: 'Portrait of the Infanta Maria Ludovica'. Detail showing heavy bracelet and rings. A. R. Mengs

Marie Antoinette's tiara and necklace

In this century there were continuous changes in styles of architecture and furnishing. After the Baroque period, which was characterised by elaborate scrolls, curves and carved ornaments, came a period in French architectural style called Regency, which roughly corresponded to the term of 1715–1723, when Philip of Orleans was regent. This period was called the 'Queen Anne' in England. More fragile and delicate than the Baroque, it is epitomised in the work of Jean Bérain, who rediscovered the grotesques of the Italian Renaissance and combined them with graceful arabesques and fanciful linear decorations interspersed with monkeys, jesters or strange mythological creatures. Also fashionable during this period was *chinoiserie*: furniture in black and red lacquer and walls decorated with landscapes and figures in delicate pastel colours—all in a decorative design characteristic of the Chinese.

When Louis XV came to the throne, the Rococo style made its appearance, combining in profusion rocklike forms, scrolls and crimped shells used lavishly as decoration. The taste for *chinoiserie* still continued. The Rococo was a profoundly original and voluptuous style which captivated Europe, with its subtle play of curves, swirling, asymmetrical forms and free-flowing lines, especially in furniture design. Mirrors contributed to give a new character to rooms, covering walls and ceilings and creating a series of surfaces that seemed to melt into each other. Madame de Pompadour had mirrors to reflect her beauty from every possible angle, in an attempt to be fascinating every moment of the day.

There was at this time a passion for masks, carnivals, parties, plays by Goldoni and operas by Metastasio and Mozart. Eighteenth-century taste pursued a rich riot of fantasy in ornaments, colours, fashions, rococo trifles, until the French Revolution put an abrupt end to it all.

The French Revolution

Fashion, which in the reign of Louis XV had started to be more informal, now decreed that *paniers*, silks and brocades should be abolished altogether. Dresses were now made of muslin, with fichus of white cotton, called *à la citoyenne* or *à la Charlotte Corday*; these were crossed on the breast and fastened with a brooch, or crossed at the back and knotted in front. The long gloves of silk or very fine leather were

Dress accessories included fans of hand-painted parchment or lace, and gloves. 'Portrait of Maria Carolina of Naples'. A. R. Mengs. Prado, Madrid

replaced by the less elegant half-gloves of cotton, net, or lace.

Both feminine and masculine fashions changed little, but were given new names such as 'Constitution' or 'Camille'. New features were the tricoloured motifs used to trim the *indienne* dresses, rosettes or fringes on belts and plumes on hats of red, white and blue. The *négligé à la patriote* for ladies consisted of a royal blue redingote worn with a white dress and a red collar striped in white. The Royalists, however, dressed exclusively in black, as a sign of mourning for the loss of their privileges. The great men of the Revolution, from Robespierre to Saint-Just, dressed just as the elegant men of the old regime had done. The working classes and the *tricoteuses* wore wide trousers or *sansculottes*, identical with sailors' trousers, ankle length and with an extra panel buttoned on at the front, usually made in a red and white striped material; and the *carmagnole*, a short woollen jacket with two pockets and a wide collar with red lapels. This outfit was completed by a red beret.

The Revolutionary ideology which urged a return to Spartan simplicity again took up the Grecian style which had appeared a few years before. The most influential painter of the period, David, attempted to introduce a male fashion of togas, but worn with boots and a plumed toque on the head. These innovations had no real following, except with the pupils of the School of Mars or, under the Directoire, from the members of the Council of the Ancients and of the Five Hundred, in whom the power of government was invested after the Constitution of 1795. The costume for the French citizen devised by David was not popular, and was worn only by those who took part in the public festivities he organised. At this time all dress was extremely simple, an expression of the ideal of equality; wigs were abolished, and hair styles became equally simple, with a parting in the middle and locks falling over the ears. Once again costume reflected the ideas of the age.

The Revolution had from the start declared war against all the fetters and chains imposed by the tyranny of fashion: corsets, *paniers*, wigs, high heels, powder, beauty spots and ribbons. These became the symbols of the tyranny of the aristocracy, which had at all costs to be destroyed. A uniform dress was created that would be the same for all, drawing no distinctions between the classes: for men the bourgeois fashion, and for women extreme simplicity, influenced by English fashion.

Since the time of Colbert in the seventeenth century, France had had unchallenged supremacy in

Marie Antoinette's fan. Versailles Museum

Jewel box. Italian school. Eighteenth century

The parasol came into vogue in the late eighteenth century. Fashion plate. 1780. Bertarelli Collection

'Promenade à Trois'. Detail. G. D. Tiepolo. Ca' Rezzonico, Venice

the world of fashion, just as Italy had in the sixteenth century. In the last decade of the eighteenth century France, preoccupied with political problems, left the field to England. In 1791 a German traveller, passing through Paris, noted that interest in fashion in this city appeared to be dormant. The *élégantes* had become emigrants, followed abroad by their dressmakers. Even Mademoiselle Bertin had left the capital, and taken refuge first in Vienna and then in London, where she found some of her former clients had become milliners, maids or darning women.

French women were obliged to give up wearing silks, brocades and velvets and to replace them with printed materials which they named 'Equality',

Fashion plate. 1791

'Liberty' or 'Republican'. Even the names chosen for new-born babies expressed revolutionary ideas—names like République, Civilisation or Marat and, with the help of the new calendar invented by Fabre d'Eglantine, such names as Thermidor (this was the name of Madame Tallien's daughter) or Amaryllis.

Another sign of the change in customs were the advertisements for marriage, appearing for the first time in a newspaper called the *Indicateur*. On Tuesdays and Fridays lonely men or women could choose a companion from the list of candidates for matrimony. After choosing one of the loyal republicans available it was enough to post an announcement of marriage in the town hall: the religious ceremony

'Madame d'Aumont'. Detail. Elisabeth Vigée-Lebrun. Private collection, Paris

212

was abandoned, and the marriage was contracted with a few words pronounced by an official with a tricoloured scarf across his chest; two individuals thus were united for the better, but not for the worse, because a law made in 1792 allowed divorce to be easily obtained on the grounds of incompatibility of temperament or other slender grounds.

In the field of fashion there were other minor revolutions. In Paris the first shops selling ready-made dresses were opened. These shops were swiftly imitated in Hamburg and in other parts of Europe. Fashion during this period was strongly influenced by trends in England. When the Duchess of York realised that she was expecting an heir, she launched a fashion with a new line, the 'false stomach', obtained by moving the *cul de Paris* from the back to the front. This made the waistline of the frock rise up under the breasts, foreshadowing the Empire line. The 'false stomach' introduced into Paris was quickly all the rage, and was worn by young girls as well as by married women expecting babies.

The waistcoat, which had gone out of fashion, was brought back by Robespierre, who wore one made of white material, with large lapels and buttons engraved with tiny guillotines. The guillotine was also reproduced on the lids of snuff boxes, often made with the lead taken off the roof of the Bastille. Then the *Muscadins* appeared on the scene, elegant young dandies who rebelled against the simplicity of dress and lack of ostentation; they adopted the *frac* with the opening cut at an angle and buttoned in various ways. Their breeches were usually striped and their boots had turned-down cuffs and were lined in different colours and trimmed on one side with ribbons.

Following pages: 'Promenade at the Palais Royal'. Philibert Louis Debucourt

Drawing of an elegant man with a cockade in his hat

Their hats either had stiff horizontal brims and were shaped like truncated cones, or else were very low three-cornered hats with tricolour rosettes. Knobbly walking sticks *à la jacobin* replaced the slim ones carried by elegant pre-revolutionary men, which in turn had replaced the little sword. Monocles and lorgnettes returned to the favour they had enjoyed at the beginning of the century.

The Chemise

At the time of the Directoire, French women abandoned the false exaggeration of their figures and adopted a line inspired by the garb of women in Greek and Roman times, which showed the natural shape of their bodies. They gave up corsets and underskirts, and dressed themselves in light, flowing transparent chemises. Long tunics of linen, of very light cotton or muslin, were pulled in under the breast and trimmed with Grecian designs; these were called

à la Vestale and *à la Diane*. Some women wore this provocative dress open on the right side up to the waist so that their legs and tights could be seen. This alluring outfit was completed by bracelets around the ankles, rings on the toes, sandals and buskins. The fichu was replaced by a shawl, and by the English *spencer*, a short waist-length jacket with a shawl collar and close-fitting sleeves. Hair was worn shorter and arranged in little curls which gave the feminine head a vaguely masculine appearance. Hats also underwent changes; shapes varied from turbans or cylinders to bonnets with or without brims, but were always heavily bedecked with ribbons and plumes.

The *Incroyables*, the successors to the *Muscadins*, excited ridicule with their exaggerated style of dress. The *frac* they wore was very close fitting, with sleeves with no cuffs and a very high waist. The waistcoat, of a different colour, had two huge lapels. The breeches, indecently tight and knee-length, were fastened at the bottom with bright, coloured ribbons; usually they were made in a striped material with the stripes in contrasting colours from the *frac*. Round the neck these men wore an enormous necktie wrapped around six times, which covered the chin and formed a type of pedestal on which the head rested. Gold earrings adorned the *Incroyables'* ears, and very low shoes barely covered the heels and toes of their feet.

These eccentric fashions were only typical of a privileged class, who could afford them. Ordinary people could not hope to emulate these fashions. For a few years a large number of tailors, dressmakers, embroiderers and lace makers were unemployed. This was the end of the epoch in which the death of a fashionable tailor, André Scheling, caused a public sensation. Previously in Lyons the manufacturers of braids and materials had waited with baited breath for Scheling's decisions. The industry was brought to a standstill until the *très habile, très élégant, très merveilleux* André Scheling let his decisions be known.

As dressmakers and tailors closed their shops with the disappearance of their former rich clientèle, even Marat became perturbed, commenting about the crisis in fashion that within a few years it might be difficult to find anywhere in Paris a working woman capable of making a hat or a cobbler capable of making a pair of shoes. This was why, just as Richelieu had decided to encourage the art of lace-making in France by prohibiting the import of lace from abroad, so Napoleon Bonaparte, though busy with his wars and political manœuvres, decided to restore luxury and splendour to the world of fashion in Paris, in order to stimulate the economy.

NEW OMNIBUS REGULATION.

"'Werry sorry 'm, but yer'l 'av to leave yer Krinerline outside."

A cartoon from *Punch*

The Nineteenth Century

'The Consecration of the Emperor
Napoleon I and the Coronation of
the Empress Josephine'. Detail.
J.-L. David. Louvre

The nineteenth century, considered as an historical epoch, really begins with the French Revolution. With the reorganisation of society and the rise of the bourgeoisie, clothes changed and became more alike for all classes of society, allowing for the inevitable differences in material and workmanship between the clothes of the rich and the poor. To express the republican ideals which had originated in classical times, fashion became imbued with a passion for imitating all things Greek.

Women welcomed the opportunity of dressing differently. They abolished corsets, shifts (which they replaced with flesh-coloured, knitted vests), skirts and stockings and dressed in fewer and simpler garments: an extremely light and transparent *chemise*, which later lengthened into a train as long as six yards for a town dress, and as long as fourteen for a gala dress, as if compensating for the nakedness of bosom and shoulders. 'An elegant woman'—wrote one fashion chronicle of the time—'should not wear more than eight pounds of clothing, including jewels and shoes.' Shoes were either flat slippers or shaped like Roman sandals. As protection against cold weather, a second tunic of heavier material, usually in a colour, became fashionable; this allowed most of the classic white tunic below to show. Apparently simple, many of these tunics were very richly embroidered and expensive; a dress of embroidered percale with a train might cost a small fortune. Lace was greatly admired.

The arbiter of fashion during the Directoire period was Madame Tallien, nicknamed *Notre Dame de Thermidor*, the first woman to adopt the reticule, a

Styles of dress showing the evolution of the crinoline in the nineteenth century

1810   1830

handbag made of various materials including papier-mâché and painted tin, shaped like an urn or Etruscan vase, and coloured yellow, green or grey. Her most successful outfit was a *chemise* which was open at the lower edge of the skirt to show her legs. She wore bracelets on her ankles and rings on her sandal-shod toes, as well as on her arms and fingers. On her head, dressed in a Grecian hair style, she wore a head-dress of coloured feathers.

Women were constantly changing the colour of their hair, and when not wearing plumes dressed their hair in silk turbans, lace bonnets, or tulle bonnets with oval brims, trimmed with lace, *ruches*, or flowers. All these varieties of headgear were usually tied under the chin with a silk ribbon.

In the spring of 1810 the French Empire was at the zenith of its power. Napoleon had reached his forties and, absorbed in conjugal life, was putting on weight. Though he had more serious problems, he found time to take an interest in fashion, not so much because he had any taste for frivolity, but because he wanted to increase the production of fabrics and, thereby, the economic prosperity of the nation, thus challenging England in this field. England had an advantage in the fact that, at the end of the eighteenth century, Watt and Arkwright had invented machines for the manufacture of textiles, while in France spinning and weaving were still done by hand.

Spurred on by Napoleon, machines similar to those in England were installed in Sedan and Louviers. In St Quentin the production of linen and muslin was increased, and in Valenciennes the production of

1855   1874

tulle, batiste and lace was started. Thus France recovered her primacy in the field of fabrics, and the Emperor wrote to General Caulaincourt, 'I have created French industry', and claimed in his memoirs written on St Helena that the ban on importing English textiles was a *coup d'état*. Only one item of imported fashion enjoyed Napoleon's favour, the shawls woven from the fleece of the wild goats in Kashmir. He discovered these during his Egyptian campaign, and immediately sent several in different colours to Josephine, who found them very ugly and expensive, but light and warm. The fashion for shawls blazed up overnight, to cover bare shoulders, to make dresses, to serve as bed covers, and even as cushions for pet dogs. These shawls were eventually manufactured in France.

To further his ambition to found a dynasty as well as to advance French industry, Napoleon imposed on

'Les Incroyables'. Charles Vernet. Cartoon. 1795

his court a pomp similar to that of the *Roi Soleil*. He ordered that ladies should not present themselves at

The *chemise* dress became fashionable during the Napoleonic period. '*Point de Convention*'. L. L. Boilly. Rothschild Collection

the Tuileries wearing the same dress twice. He summoned to Court a famous tailor, Leroy, and entrusted him with the task of developing French fashion, asking him to put the emphasis on brocades, velvets, precious embroideries and lace. No detail was overlooked by him—he even ordered that the fireplaces in the Tuileries should be bricked up, so that the ladies had to give up wearing flimsy materials.

Leroy guided the Emperor along the byways of fashion, just as he had done before with the Revolutionaries and before that with the aristocrats. He was of humble origin (the son of an employee at the Opéra) and in his early youth became a hairdresser, who was so fashionable that eventually he dressed the hair of Marie Antoinette. At the very beginning of the Revolution, loyal to his aristocratic connections, he continued to dress in pink satin, powder his hair and wear pointed shoes. He was then invited to appear before the Convention. Although at first he feared for his life, thinking he was about to be denounced

because of his Monarchist sentiments, he was reassured later by their invitation to design a costume worthy of the Republic. He had immediate success with a tricolour dress, trimmed with a border on which were embroidered the words 'Liberty, Equality, Fraternity', while on the belt appeared the words 'Liberty or Death'. Having succeeded in becoming the favourite tailor of Josephine, he also reached the position of secret adviser to Napoleon.

After months of patient study among the archives, he found inspiration in the fashions of the past. An able business man, but a misogynist, he was scornful of the poor and a flatterer of men in power. In the course of a few years, Leroy accumulated an immense fortune and gave back to France its leadership in the world of fashion. Under his reign, women wore crêpe, cashmere, satin, taffeta and velvet produced by

'Cornelia Adrienne, Gräfin Bose'. Detail. J. F. Tishbein. National German Museum, Nuremberg

Jean-Baptiste Isabey was the Court painter and designed clothes for the Empress Josephine. Portrait of Isabey and his daughter. F. Gérard. Louvre

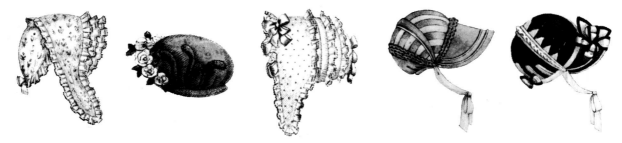

Bonnets from *Courier des Dames*. 1809. Bertarelli Collection, Milan

the factories at Marseilles and Lyons. The waist was raised to just below the bust, which was deeply décolleté; the neckline, round or square and V-shaped at the back, was trimmed with lace. A very short sleeve barely covered the shoulder or came down to the elbow, and was shaped either with a fold fastened with a button or a slit fastened with three buttons, in the English style. If the sleeve was long enough to cover part of the hand, it was called *à la Mamelouk*; it was sometimes puffed up like a balloon in the upper part, then narrow and close fitting.

The seam which joined the skirt to the very short bodice was hidden with fringed braid or with an embroidered belt, often fastened in the front with a precious brooch. The skirt, generally draped at the back, had a slight hint of a train, but later became shorter, usually an inch from the ground and conical in shape. To keep the skirt stiff a little padded roll was sewn in the hem, which was often trimmed with frills and ribbons. A genuine train was abolished, surviving only in dresses worn at Court, where it was a separate garment, very long, and in a different colour and material from the dress, fastened to it just under the breasts; made in heavy satin or velvet, this train was always embroidered, like the train of blue velvet embroidered in silver worn by Marie Louise when she became Duchess of Parma.

The Empire Style

The Empire style was inaugurated with the coronation of Napoleon and Josephine in the Cathedral of Notre-Dame in 1804. The dresses of the Empress

Six fashion plates. 1803–1804. Bertarelli Collection, Milan

An Italian advertisement for chocolate. Castello Sforzesco, Milan

were designed by Isabey, the Court painter, but made by Leroy. Court dress, which became fashionable by Imperial command, consisted of two models. One costume for informal occasions was in blue satin, with a very small design of scattered flowers, long sleeves and a velvet cloak lined with satin and fastened on the left shoulder and the right hip. The costume for great occasions was in silver brocade with short sleeves, and a velvet cloak embroidered in gold and silver and lined with ermine, fastened at the waistline and worn with a train. For everyday wear over the tunic there was the spencer, of English origin, in black or green velvet, a garment already fashionable by the end of the eighteenth century, hemmed with fringes or fur, with a high collar, and heavy with embroidery. Sleeves became longer, until they covered the hands, but two buttons were always left open. The redingote of Marie Antoinette's time returned to fashion in the shape of a long overcoat with a high collar and long sleeves. Hats had new shapes; conical with wide or narrow brims turned up at the sides, with trimmings of lace plumes or ribbons; bonnets with the oval brim very high in front or lowered to shade the face; *pamelas* worn very far back and fastened with ribbons under the chin; or shaped like turbans.

Over fashion, Leroy reigned supreme. His models, published in the *Journal des Modes*, were seen all over Europe. The entire Imperial family were dressed by him, and the most elegant women in the land competed to obtain his models.

However, there was one woman who stood aside

'Portrait of the Empress Josephine'. Pierre Paul Prud'hon. Louvre

'Empress Marie Louise'. Detail. Lefèvre. Louvre

Detail of the head

from the general adulation: Madame Récamier, the intelligent and beautiful enemy of Napoleon. Madame Récamier was elegant, cultured and refined. She loved to surround herself with beautiful objects which were the talk of all Paris. Her bed of mahogany, inlaid with gold and supported by two bronze swans, had curtains and a canopy of bronze silk, heavily fringed with gold and pearls. On her night table stood a golden lamp, and on the tables strewn round the room there were other lamps which diffused the soft light of candles. Even the bathroom of Madame Récamier was elegantly designed, with the bathtub in a niche entirely walled with mirrors and

Portrait of Madame Récamier, one of the most elegant women of her time. J.-L. David. Louvre

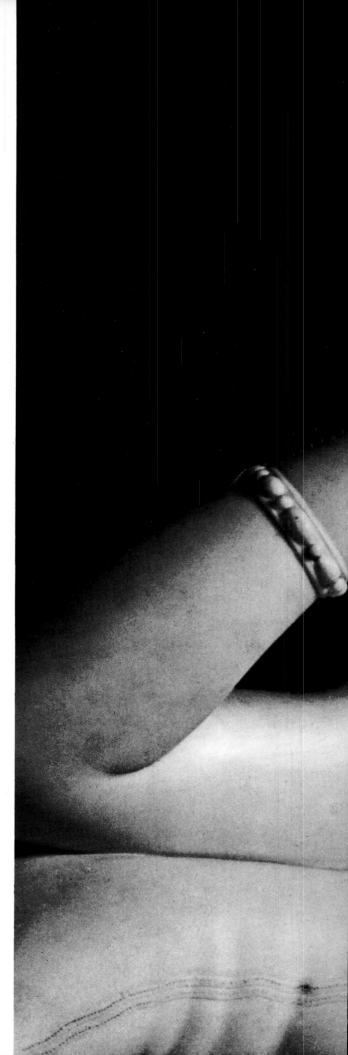

'Portrait of Pauline Borghese'. Detail. Antonio Canova.
Borghese Gallery, Rome

hidden behind a sofa upholstered in red morocco.

The best clients of Leroy were still Josephine and
her daughter, Queen Hortense of Holland. The
former had a weakness for sequins, veils, frills and
hats, but the famous tailor was able to guide her and
transform her into the first lady of the Empire, and
she was always grateful to him, remaining his client
even when no longer Empress. In her retirement at
Malmaison she was never able to give up her old
passion for dress, and continued spending with gay
extravagance and abandon.

Marie Louise, on the other hand, was never very
interested in fashion, even during the three years that
she lived in France. However, during the Hundred
Days, when she fell in love with Count Neipperg,
she too turned to Leroy to acquire elegance, following the example of her sisters-in-law and of the two
step-daughters of the Emperor, Hortense and
Stephanie. Caroline, Queen of Naples, also used
Leroy for her gala and hunting dresses, her fans and
even for her jars of pomade. Leroy in fact procured
for his clients every accessory in their wardrobes,
from stockings to eau de Cologne. Nor was Leroy's
fame confined to France. His clients included the
famous singer Grassini, the Countess Toschini and
Maria Walewska, who was anxious to retain the

Caroline Bonaparte, wife of Joachim Murat, had all her
dresses designed and made by the famous Leroy

with, furs were the rage, together with cloaks and hats inspired by military uniforms. Shawls, no longer as large as in Josephine's time, and triangular in shape, stoles and loose jackets all tended to make women look like bundles. The climax of this period was reached between 1804 and 1817, but after the Congress of Vienna in 1815 fashion began to return again

Left: Italian fashion of 1822. *Courier des Dames*
Below left: 'Portrait of Josephine la Croix'. Detail of drawing. J. D. Ingres. Bertarelli Collection, Milan
Below right: Fashion plate. Vernet. 1814

affections of the Emperor, who was then her lover.

When Napoleon fell, the great tailor yielded to the flattery of the new clients who were arriving in Paris. The names of the victors joined the names of the defeated: the Duke of Berry, who ordered gloves, hats and ribbons for a secret mistress; the Princess of Metternich; the Duchess of Wellington. Clients from all over Europe, Austrian and English, Polish and Italian—Leroy satisfied them all. To him the fall of an Empire was no more important than a change in hair fashion. The formidable fight between Napoleon and Metternich meant simply a change of client. Marie Louise could not do without him, and he was indispensable to the Duchess of Wellington as well as to the Princess of Metternich. So the frivolous wheel of fashion was linked to the cycle of history in Leroy's ledgers, as if the veils of the Empire style had the importance of a Napoleonic campaign.

With the end of the Empire, fashion changed once more, and the feminine body was again imprisoned in a corset and smothered with garments. To begin

Fashion plate from *Le Bon Genre*. Vernet. 1810

Lady's toilette. Vernet. 1814. Bertarelli Collection, Milan

to a slim line, with narrow, straight, ankle-length skirts, and tall, cylindrical hats that elongated the feminine figure.

The Restoration

The return of the Royal family to Paris brought the first signs of romanticism in the high collars and Henry IV hats, laden with plumes and tassels. Then the first Mary Stuart belts appeared, which tended to lower the waist. When the waistline returned to normal, corsets also returned. Skirts became twice as full as they had been, and were embellished with pleats, frills and ribbons. Whatever the fabric they were made of, dresses of the time entailed considerable work in the trimmings. There were no more raised trimmings of the same material as the dress, called 'wolf's teeth'. Now frills, gathered and flounced in two or three horizontal rows to give width at the hem of the skirts reaching to the floor, were favoured.

Sleeves, which up to the time of the Congress of Vienna had been narrow and long, became shorter and swelled up into strange shapes, like 'hams' and 'legs of mutton'. Shoulders became wider and drooping, broadened by immense triangular collars. The waist grew smaller and smaller, but skirts remained full, so that the female body at this time acquired the shape of an hour-glass.

An American woman, Amelia Jenks Bloomer, attempted to banish the corset, by now an instrument of torture. She tried to introduce her reforms to London, in a costume consisting of a jacket and a short skirt to be worn over baggy breeches, Turkish fashion. Her victory was limited to seeing her Turkish breeches adopted as an integral part of European costume for physical exercise; but this was not to be until the end of the nineteenth century.

In the nineteenth century many former styles were echoed and reintroduced. Just as the Directoire period saw a revival of Greek fashion, and the Empire period reintroduced the spencer and redingote, so the Second Empire revived the fashion for the hoop.

An obscure Hungarian doctor, Ignatius Philip Semmelweiss, observed that women in childbirth did not contract fever if those who helped them during labour first washed and disinfected their hands. Three Americans, Wells, Jackson and Morton, discovered that a few drops of chloroform or ether were enough to ease the pain of tooth extractions, and thus invented anaesthesia. Their method was later used to ease labour pains, and Queen Victoria was the first to try this, initiating the trend for labour *à la Reine,* or painless childbirth.

Fashion, however, did not keep pace with the scientific and practical discoveries of the industrial revolution. Instead it went rather wild, with wide stiff jackets *à la Malakoff,* Polish style bootees, mittens of open-work cotton, miniature umbrellas with long handles and complicated mechanisms, posies of fresh flowers worn on the head, tucked in the belt or sewn on the dress.

A style of cloak inspired by Italian opera. *Courier des Dames.* Bertarelli Collection, Milan

The Rise of the Bourgeoisie

After the Restoration, the bourgeoisie rose to new positions of power. They became financiers, industrialists, merchants and members of the Stock Exchange. They began to collect paintings and precious books. To express their sense of self-importance they embarked on a life of conspicuous consumption, to the gratification of their womenfolk who nostalgically imitated the past, particularly the fashion for fancy-dress balls with historical themes. Architecture and furniture as well as fashion were affected by a nostalgia for the past. A new sensibility was born, melancholy and languid. The romantic ballets of Taglioni and Fanny Essler, the poems of de Musset and the music of Chopin were the moving passions of the day. Literature began to show an interest in fashion, and fashion in literature. Balzac wrote '. . . her gown was adorned by three frills, which fell down in adorable pleats and betrayed the hand of a fashionable tailor'. This tailor was called Victorine, and was admired even by Stendhal for her skill.

The Crinoline

Fashion under Napoleon III decreed the crinoline. Over long lace pantaloons a woman wore a flannel petticoat covered by the crinoline. A special underskirt kept the skirt stiff and wide; over this were worn three more percale underskirts, and finally the dress. The middle-class woman contentedly wore a little silk apron over her crinoline, and protected her hair style with a lace cap while attending to her domestic chores or doing her embroidery. When she went shopping she threw a mantilla over her dress and hid her face under a bonnet. Her evening dress had a wide neckline, modestly veiled by the ever-present shawl, or by the *bayadère,* a scarf with multicoloured stripes. In summer the dress was often made of organdie embroidered with sprigs of flowers.

Fashion, however, as it continued to evolve, gave birth to the *lionne* style, designed for eccentric mannish women, who were able to handle the pistol and whip, to ride well, to speak the slang of the turf, to smoke and to drink alcohol. By day they would wear an outfit influenced by English fashion, with loops on their jackets, blouses with *jabots* and yellow leather gloves. In the evening they would swathe themselves in Eastern materials, usually with Turkish sleeves, with Grecian bonnets on their heads and their hair falling in curls on the nape of the neck. George Sand, who dared to dress like a *lionne,* with

Romantic fashions, with wide but modest necklines gave women a fragile look.
'Portrait of Margherita Verdi'. Mussini. Museum of La Scala Opera House, Milan

The Empress Marie Louise, Napoleon's widow. Miniature. Private collection

her masculine garments and cigars, was nevertheless an intelligent, active woman.

At first the crinoline was an underskirt starched and lined with horsehair, but later this went through various changes. Hoops of compressed horsehair and padded frames were added. Finally an ingenious man replaced the horsehair padding with steel springs, an invention that had such success that in four weeks he earned a huge fortune. The steel hoops allowed women to reduce the incredible number of underskirts they had formerly been obliged to wear, to do away with all padding, and to effect a considerable saving, as his springs were not very expensive. A crinoline with twenty-four hoops cost only a few shillings, but women who could afford it bought the Thompson crinoline, which weighed only ten ounces, and was considerably more comfortable. Then Delirac invented a seemingly magic crinoline, which could be expanded or contracted as desired.

Crinolines were the secret of elegance, and choosing the right one became a matter of great importance. One fashionable lady asked no less a man than Bismarck himself to get her an oval crinoline from Berlin, which would make it easier for her to go through doors. Crinoline shapes were oval or round, or flat in front and extended at the back, or a crinoline might have a cord to raise or lower the draping. The craze for crinolines spread throughout the world; they were worn in the theatre, in the 'salons',

Men's dress coats were double-breasted and trousers were long enough to cover the top of the shoe. Fashion plate. 1830

In the mid-nineteenth century shoulders were accentuated by wide necklines. 'Portrait of a Lady'. Berry.

'Portrait of the Archduchess Sophia'. Josef Kriehuber. 1836. Bertarelli Collection, Milan

Portrait of Countess Emilia Sommariva. Detail. C. B. Boulanger

Fashion plate. 1830. Bertarelli Collection, Milan

235

The crinoline became very popular during the reign of Napoleon III. Twelve variations are shown above. Little fringed shawls and trimmed bonnets were also fashionable at this time. Bertarelli Collection, Milan

MARIA   OLYMPE   CÉLESTE

ERNESTINE   ALPHONSINE   ADELINE

and in the street. As its width steadily increased, bows, puffs, fringes, frills and laces were added to it, until it became so exaggerated that it was a target for the wit of all the satirists of the age.

The leader of fashion during the Second Empire was the Empress, Eugénie de Montijo, a Spanish woman who launched the fashion for blonde hair a generation after Josephine had made black hair fashionable. However, she never adopted bizarre or eccentric fashions, even if she was nicknamed '*Falbala première*' because of her love for ribbons, frills and lace. Only a few intimates knew of her goodness, her interest in many charitable works, her piety (she attended Mass regularly but was not a bigot), her pain at the unfaithfulness of the Emperor, her remorse

for having encouraged Maximilian and Charlotte in their tragic Mexican venture, and her sorrow at the death of the Prince Imperial.

All these qualities were hidden behind her elegance, seeming frivolity and sophistication. The nobility and even middle-class women imitated her, and she was admired by everyone for her good taste, not only in her dress but also in her graceful gestures and attitudes. Eugénie in turn was a great admirer of Marie Antoinette, who was her romantic ideal, and with whom she felt a great secret affinity.

The Empress loved variety in her life, and frequently made drastic changes in her apartments and her wardrobe. She loved silk shoes, and never wore the same pair twice, even though they lasted much

Illustrations from 'The Art of Knotting a Tie in Sixteen Lessons'. Conte della Salda. Milan, 1827. Bertarelli Collection

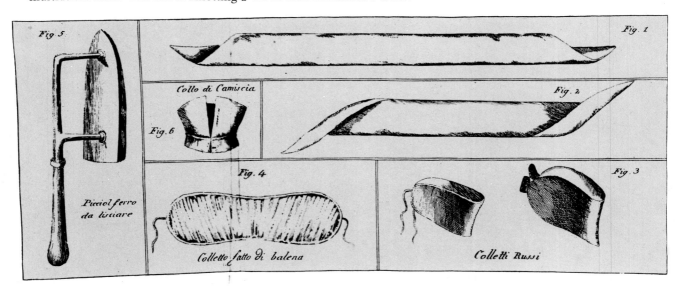

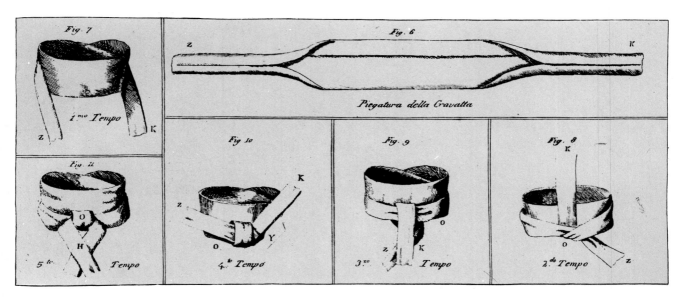

Fashion plate. 1845

longer than the light ones fashionable in the eighteenth century, so fragile they could not withstand
even the shortest walk. As the Empress had tiny feet,
all her old shoes were sent to a school in which she
took an interest, as a gift for little girls about to take
their First Communion.

Fashions for Men

Men's fashions in the nineteenth century were much
more practical and less fantastical than they had been.

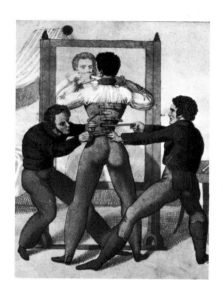

Caricature of a dandy. 1838

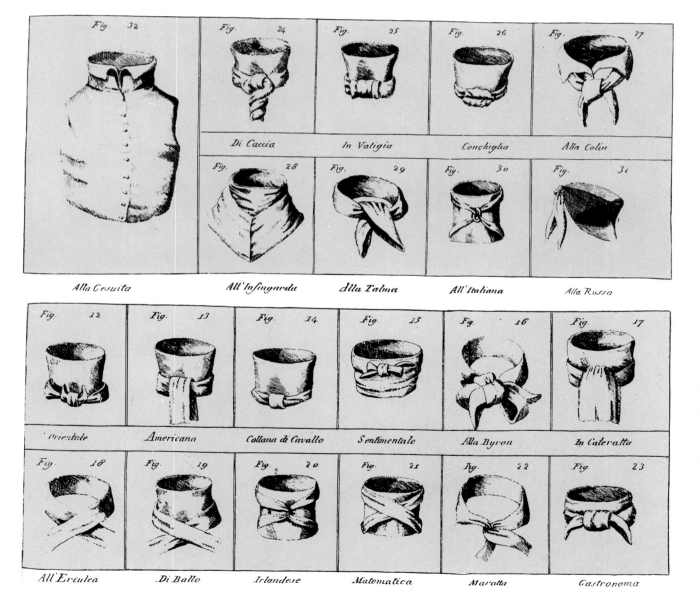

Alla Cesuita — All'Infingarda — Alla Talma — All'Italiana — Alla Russa

Orientale — Americana — Collana di Cavallo — Sentimentale — Alla Byron — In Cateratta

All'Erculea — Di Ballo — Irlandese — Matematica — Maratta — Gastronoma

Fashion plate. 1840. Bertarelli Collection, Milan

Fashion plate. 1845. Gavarni. Bertarelli Collection, Milan

The only ornament was in the detail of the waistcoat, which was made of velvet, satin or embroidered silk. This waistcoat was the basic item in the masculine wardrobe, so much so that Balzac is known to have ordered thirty at a time, all exactly alike, and de Musset had thirty-one made for him, each one

Furnishing fabric. Circa 1850

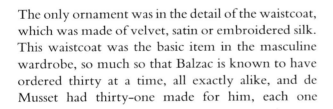

different. The collar of the waistcoat was either shaped like a stole, or it had large lapels; and it was usually worn buttoned to the top. The coat reached mid-thigh and was open in front. The *frac* was double-breasted, closed at the collar and fastened in front with a belt. The redingote had one or more buttons; initially ankle-length, it was later shortened to mid-thigh. Trousers were so long they covered the heel of the shoe, and had a leather strap under the foot to keep them taut. The white shirt, pleated in front, had a high pointed collar and was worn with a black or white cravat.

During the winter men wore a cloth overcoat decorated with braid and a velvet collar, and sometimes lined with otter or beaver. Very fashionable were circular cloaks with deep collars and little over-capes, which later became the uniform for postilions. A major development was the dramatic sleeveless cape, which had vertical slits for the arms, a double, pointed collar and double-breasted buttoning. This came from Italy, and was inspired by the Carbonari. Popular colours for men's clothes were dark green, blue, black, and purple, but brighter colours were also worn very often.

Two young men presenting jewellery to young ladies in romantic setting. 1840. Bertarelli Collection, Milan

As time passed, men's coats underwent certain changes: shawl lapels became smaller, rounded in front, and deepened at the back by extra fullness; a small pocket high on the left side was added to the two side pockets. The overcoats changed too, becoming as long as the coats, and cut straight in the front. The 'raglan', a circular cloak, was later supplanted by the 'plaid' in one of the Scottish tartans, and by the 'talma' cloak (launched long before by the famous actor Talma), which was semi-circular. There was also the dust-coat of grey alpaca for protection during journeys. The *burnous,* a full knee-length coat, had a hood purely for decoration. (A *burnous* worn by women looked like a sleeveless shawl, ending in two long tassels at the front, fastened with a couple of loops and provided with a hood.)

Trousers, still long and narrow with a strap under the foot, were made in a different material from the coat, either striped, checked or plain. During the Restoration the Monarchists, in order to demonstrate their loyalty to the King, had always worn knee-length silk breeches at Court, but by the middle of the century the use of trousers was universal. Around 1850 they were buttoned down the front rather than the side. The silk band which even nowadays runs down the side of trousers worn for evening or ceremonial dress is simply part of the old tradition of side-buttoning. Trousers underwent further changes: the underfoot strap disappeared, and they were cut

'Portrait of the Duchess of Orleans'. Detail. Winterhalter. Versailles Museum

Bonnets and hair styles. Circa 1840. Bertarelli Collection, Milan

to the modern length. However, creases in trousers did not appear until the very end of the nineteenth century, and permanent turn-ups until early in the twentieth century.

The Age of Dandies

English fashions influenced all of Europe. Beau Brummel was a leader in this field. He had three hairdressers, two glove-makers, and bought his clothes only from the most exclusive and expensive tailors: his coats from one, his trousers from another, his waistcoats from a third. According to the time of the day he changed from a frockcoat to a spencer to a cutaway tailcoat. He asserted nevertheless that a person is all the more elegant, the less he is noticeable. One problem which exercised these very elegant men and all their imitators was how to tie the neckcloth,

which could be knotted in a number of ways. In Paris an enterprising Italian founded a school where he taught the art of knotting ties. Each lesson lasted for six hours and cost nine francs an hour. The dandies were much ridiculed in the satirical prints and journals of the time but they took no notice, and continued their search for bizarre subtleties.

Men's hair was at first cut very short. In Palermo a certain Giacomo Perollo, who insisted on wearing his hair long, was condemned to have it cut in public, in the stocks. Styles varied, and many different fashions were worn, from the shaven face of Napoleon to the 'imperial' of his nephew Napoleon III, the rounded beard and whiskers of Cavour, the thick but well-groomed beard of Verdi and the flowing beard of Tolstoy.

Masculine hats varied from the top hat, and its evening form, the collapsible *gibus*, to the 'wide-

Fashion plate. Circa 1840. Bertarelli Collection, Milan

'Madame Moitessier'. Detail. J. D. Ingres. National Gallery, Washington

'The Empress Eugénie and her Ladies-in-Waiting'.
Winterhalter. Musée de la Malmaison

English print. Circa 1840

French fashion plates. Styles of 1848, 1850 and 1860. *Courier des Dames*. Bertarelli Collection, Milan

awake' and the bowler, with its rounded crown, invented by William Coke of Norfolk and first made on the instructions of Lock's, the famous hatters of St James's Street. Artists preferred a romantic velvet toque, the Renaissance beret, or a felt hat with a very large brim. In Italy there was a new fashion for the

Comic magazines made fun of the extreme examples of the crinoline craze. Cartoon. *Punch*. 18th September, 1858

STUDY OF PERSPECTIVE.—AFTER NATURE.

hat of Calabria, with a high conical crown and large brim; this was derived from the costume of the brigands who infested the South.

Hair Styles for Women

Women abandoned the fashion for classical hair styles and increased the volume of their hair on the sides and at the back. For these styles hair-pins were invented and were used to secure plaits, which sometimes had as many as seven strands stiffened with wire. The accompanying locks and tufts of hair were arranged on the top of the head, leaving the nape of the neck bare. Usually, however, the hair was

The name of Worth became established as a leader of
fashion. The Empress Eugénie and the Empress Elizabeth
of Austria were among his clients. Drawing by Worth.
Private collection

gathered from the sides and drawn up into a high
topknot of curls, secured by combs of gold, enamel
or tortoise-shell, and embellished with feathers,
flowers and ribbons.

By way of a hat women wore the toque, covered
with veils and feathers, or else a town turban. At
home they usually wore a lace cap rather than leave
their hair uncovered. Later hair styles became simpler, with curls on the forehead and a parting in the
middle. Then even curls were abolished, styles became smooth and flat, with the bulk of the hair

Maximilian, Archduke of Austria and Charlotte of Belgium. Miniature

arranged in plaits or rolls between the ears and the nape of the neck. For many years hair was worn puffed out at the sides and adorned with ribbons and lace. Sometimes it was gathered into a thin net on the back of the neck, with a great lock of hair in front, and a little velvet ribbon was worn around the neck. A special type of hair-pin was used to hide the joining of real hair from false. Then hair-clips came into use. With the crinoline it was fashionable to wear a great chignon on which rested a tiny hat with a flat crown and narrow brim. Sailor hats also became fashionable, made in oil cloth (the technique of water-proofing had recently been invented) with a ribbon at the back falling down on to the shoulders. There were hats called *capotes à la cabriolet*; these had very deep brims under which the face almost disappeared and were worn far back on the nape of the neck, with the usual arrangements of feathers and flowers.

Madame de Castiglione, favourite of Napoleon III, dressed as Queen of Hearts. Miniature.

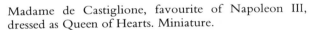

'The Empress Eugénie'. Dubufe. Versailles Museum

'Portrait of Elizabeth of Austria'. Winterhalter. Miniature

Worth

The middle of the century saw the rise of a great dressmaker who was to set the pattern for the *haute couture*. He was an Englishman, born in Bourne in Lincolnshire, the son of a woman of modest birth. His name was Charles Frederick Worth. He started work at the age of thirteen as an apprentice to a printer, but left to become an accounting clerk at Lewis and Allenby, a London shop specialising in 'fashion novelties'. Fabrics and lace, however, attracted him far more than figures, and he decided to leave England for Paris, where he immediately found work with Gagelin, the owner of one of the most famous boutiques in the city. Before long he entered into partnership with his employer, and later started in business on his own in the Rue de la Paix.

Jewels of the Empress Eugénie

The next milestone in his career was his marriage to the most successful *vendeuse* at Gagelin's. After this he started to make dresses and hats for his wife. With fine political instinct, he began a carefully planned campaign to acquire rich and prominent Parisians for his clientèle.

He sent Madame Worth to call on Princess Metternich, who was as thin as a rake but extremely elegant, and therefore nicknamed 'Madame Chiffon'. She was a highly cultured woman, and very much feared at Court, both because of her noble birth and her disconcertingly outspoken manner. Worth's aim was to get the Princess as his first client. Sooner or

Queen Victoria as a young woman. Winterhalter. Miniature

later, he was sure both her friends and enemies would follow her example. Pauline de Metternich chose two of the sketches shown to her by Madame Worth, one for the evening and one for the afternoon, but she demanded a considerable discount on the price. However, she promised that at the next ball at the Tuileries she would wear a ball dress of tulle and silver lamé, adorned with red daisies, created for her by Worth. Its success was immediate, and the Empress Eugénie demanded to know the name of the magician who had conjured up such beauty. She sum-

The Duchess of York and the young Duke

250

moned him to Court, forgetting her own dress-makers, Palmyre and Vignon, and after this became Worth's best client. For the Empress, Worth created a town dress in grey taffeta, trimmed with black velvet ribbons, worn with a blouse and jacket in a matching colour. This was the ancestor of the modern tailor-made suit, but it was too advanced for the Empress. The Countess of Portalès was the first to appear in this type of outfit, which she wore at the races, and only six months later did the Empress feel safe enough to wear it herself.

In the Worth *atelier* new ideas followed each other with amazing speed. When crinoline hoops became oval, reaching knee-length so that attention was drawn to the hips, Worth gathered the folds at the back and lengthened them into a train. His talent lay in predicting what would become successful. This happened with the *polonaise*, a puffed tunic reminiscent of the *paniers* of the old regime. He also created the *tournure*, accurately described by Mallarmé, who was then a journalist on the *La Dernière Mode*, writing under the *nom de plume* of Miss Satin, with these words: 'Without knowing it we all dreamed of a model like this, but only Monsieur Worth has been able to create a *toilette* as fragile as our dreams . . . a long gown with a silk repp train of a translucent blue, that shimmering opal blue that sometimes shows behind silvery clouds. The front of the skirt is of pleated voile; the side panels are trimmed from top to bottom with pompons lined with pale yellow silk. Over a *pouf* (a small saddle) trails an enveloping scarf of periwinkle blue. The bodice is medieval in style, with

Elizabeth of Austria

slashed sleeves lined with pale yellow. The sleeves are trimmed with more pompons. The richly pleated fichu has the colours of spring.'

The Bustle

The *pouf* or small saddle, which shaped the bustle, consisted of a horsehair cushion or one or two starched frills, but later developed into an actual support composed of several hoops in the shape of a horseshoe, held in place horizontally by laces or bands. This was suspended like a cage between the skirt and the underskirt at the back. Over this cage the material of the dress would be draped, with the same fullness that appeared in the drapery of curtains. In fact fashion often had an influence on furnishing; when the crinoline was in vogue, furniture makers invented a decorative 'pouf', a round or rectangular stool on which women could sit down comfortably.

When the bustle went out of fashion, skirts became so narrow that they hampered the movements of the wearer, and women were obliged to walk in a series of little hops as if they were sparrows. These narrow skirts were in turn supplanted by the *crinolette*, a sort of miniature crinoline, which once again was supplanted by the bustle, although now it was more voluminous, with even more bows, ribbons and

Right 'Girl with a Veil'. Renoir. Jeu de Paume, Paris

drapery. This was the last expression of an idle womanhood, for new fashions that allowed freedom and were suitable for sports followed. Women had recently learnt to ride the bicycle, to swim and to fence; now there appeared the first breeches, puffed and tight round the knees, the first peaked caps, the first sports shoes. High fashion was to become mainly the province of actresses, from Sarah Bernhardt to Réjane, and women in high society.

Degas drawing showing a bustle. Fogg Art Museum, Harvard University

Fashion plates from *Il Giornale delle Signore Italiane*, 1877-1878. Bertarelli Collection, Milan

Men adopted the top hat and frock coat. Drawing. Detail. R. Sernesi. Brera Gallery, Milan

252

Jacques Doucet

Doucet was typically Gallic. At the beginning of the century, his mother had opened a boutique for hand-made lace of great delicacy. Monsieur Doucet père had opened, also in the Rue de la Paix, a shop for men's underwear, to which was attached a special-ised laundry, which did very good business. At that time, French and Italian dandies used to have their shirts washed in England, where they had mastered the art of washing and starching the elaborate pleats, *ruches* and lace of men's shirts, the costumes of a by-gone age. The clients of Doucet père included Beau Brummel and D'Orsay, the inventor of the jacket that bears his name. Extremely elegant in his outfit of white spats and matching waistcoat, with his beard carefully combed, Jacques Doucet adored frou-frou, lace and the eighteenth-century manner. He collected paintings by Watteau and Chardin. He perfected the *tailleur* created by Worth, making it more practical and suitable for the grand tours which were becoming fashionable in that period. Doucet was the first to treat fur as if it were a fabric, and from his *atelier* came the first otter coats, designed in imita-tion of the fur coats of Prussian officers.

Doucet's favourite client and also his friend was the French actress Réjane. She co-operated with him in creating the models that she could wear on the stage, and often gave her own name to a line or a dress. There was a coat in velvet and pleated satin 'à la Réjane', just as there were 'Réjane hats', made by Caroline Reboux, the milliner to Eugénie de Montijo. For Eugénie this skilful milliner created a delight-ful little hat with the crown covered with pink and white flowers. Caroline Reboux was the first person in the history of fashion to think of adding a little veil to the hat, swathing the feminine face in a mist.

Postiches became fashionable again after the fall of Napoleon III. Women arranged their hair in plaits and curls falling on the shoulders, while the bulk of hair was drawn to the top of the head in heavy plaits or cascades of curls, sometimes real and sometimes false. It was also fashionable to plait fresh flowers in the hair, in a colour which matched the dress. A few years previously the *ferronnière* had been reintro-duced; this was a ribbon round the forehead with a jewel attached to the ribbon. In this century the jewels women wore were imitations of ancient de-signs; the only true innovations were in the use of coral and cameos. Necklaces, brooches and long ear-rings were made in smooth or carved coral, repre-senting flowers, animals, tiny human figures and

Fashion plate. 1840. Bertarelli Collection, Milan

Fashion plate. 1840. Bertarelli Collection. *Below*: Fashion accessories from the shop of Herbaut and Van Acker, Paris. Bertarelli Collection

'Portrait of Eleonora Duse'. Kaulbach. Private collection

arabesques. Cameos were used for brooches and bracelets, which were worn over long gloves, and for rings and necklaces. Enamel was still very popular, especially in the making of bracelets. Marie Louise, ex-Empress of France and Duchess of Parma, had one in gold and blue enamel, in the centre of which there was a delicate miniature of her lover Neipperg. 'Sentimental' bracelets were fashionable such as the one, also belonging to Marie Louise, made of very fine blonde hair interwoven with gold threads. This was made of the hair of her son, the King of Rome, later Duke of Reichstadt. Also fashionable were gold chains, with little trinkets, medals, medallions, crosses and charms hanging from them.

Men wore jewels in their tie-pins, made of gold with a diamond inset; or in their watch chains, with trinkets worn prominently displayed across the stomach; or large gold rings set with diamonds or precious stones. White shirts with long sleeves and starched cuffs were fashionable, which brought about the vogue for cuff-links, usually simple little buttons in gold, silver or ivory, or else gold set with diamonds.

Children's wear continued to reflect the styles of adults. Although their clothes were less complicated, they were still rather clumsy and unpractical. Little boys wore skirts up to the age of four or five, and then

'Woman Fishing'. Georges Seurat. Museum of Modern Art, New York

The Marchioness Landolfo Carcano. L. G. Ricard. 1878. Petit Palais, Paris

255

graduated to long trousers and little bowler hats, or long trousers and little straw hats, after these were introduced towards the end of the century. Even for children it was still Paris that dictated the fashions, though the influence of the more comfortable English fashions also made themselves felt. Adult and children's clothes could be bought ready-made towards the end of the century in the large department stores, which sprang up in even greater numbers than the stores born in the years immediately after the French Revolution.

The ready-made dress originated in the nineteenth century, after the invention of the sewing machine by Barthélemy Thimonnier, an event which caused much unrest in factories from workmen who rebelled against the use of the 'infernal machine' because of the fear of unemployment. An American, Mr Singer, then perfected his famous sewing machine and launched it on the world with immediate success.

Wanamaker's was opened in Philadelphia, and in Paris the *Louvre, Le Bon Marché, La Samaritaine* and *Printemps* opened their doors. In these stores one could buy everything from stockings (manufactured on the new circular machine) to shoes, hats and dresses. One could also find toys, lace, knick-knacks and tableware. Merchandise was exhibited on stalls with the price clearly marked. Shoppers could thus choose, compare and even return purchases; women could browse without buying anything, weigh themselves, or admire themselves in the mirrors. For the first time, the poorer classes could enjoy the sight of beautiful and often useless objects.

At the beginning of the century clothes echoed the past, as did the architecture and furniture of the period. The 'Directoire' style, which developed from the classical influence introduced in the reign of Louis XVI, lasted only a decade. Houses were filled with furniture that reflected this 'Directoire' taste. Classical architectural styles were repeated in many buildings, especially in the Arc de Triomphe, which was a copy of a Roman arch, and in the church of La Madeleine, built in Paris in imitation of a Greek temple. Egyptian motifs were also used, for example sphinxes and lions' paws in gilded metal on furniture

Left: Birreria Cornelio. Detail. Riccardo Nobili. Modern Art Gallery, Florence

Portrait of Bernardo Celentano. Domenico Morelli. National Gallery of Modern Art, Rome

At the end of the nineteenth century women's clothes showed little sign of emancipation. They still clung to the self-inflicted tyranny of the artifices illustrated here. Illustrations of *La Vie Parisienne*. 1881. Bertarelli Collection, Milan

in mahogany, an exotic wood which had recently become fashionable.

After 1820 there was a reaction against the Empire style and the Graeco-Roman imitations. Furniture was no longer designed on vertical lines, as during the Empire, but was rounded, carved in dark mahogany, hollowed, quilted, or covered with heavy woollen materials in dark colours, sometimes em-

Illustration from *La Vie Parisienne*. 1881. Bertarelli Collection, Milan

broidered with large bunches of flowers. There was a profusion of fringes, bows, tassels and acorn-shaped buttons. Interior decoration was characterised by heavy ornamentation.

Towards the end of the century, a *mélange* of styles flourished: Renaissance for the bedroom and dining room, Chinese for the smoking room, neo-rococo for the boudoir. Curtains and door curtains were draped in deep folds, through which light and air seldom penetrated; padding grew more and more cumbersome and heavy; little baubles of silk or wool

appeared everywhere, especially in the *atelier* style launched by Makart, who also created the fashion for bunches of wax flowers, varnished reeds and peacock feathers, which were often kept under a glass dome. Table cloths usually came down to the ground, hiding the legs of the table. Each room was crammed to the full with mass-produced knick-knacks of all kinds.

During the last decade of the nineteenth century and the first decade of the twentieth, a new style was born which had roots in the Pre-Raphaelite Brother-

258

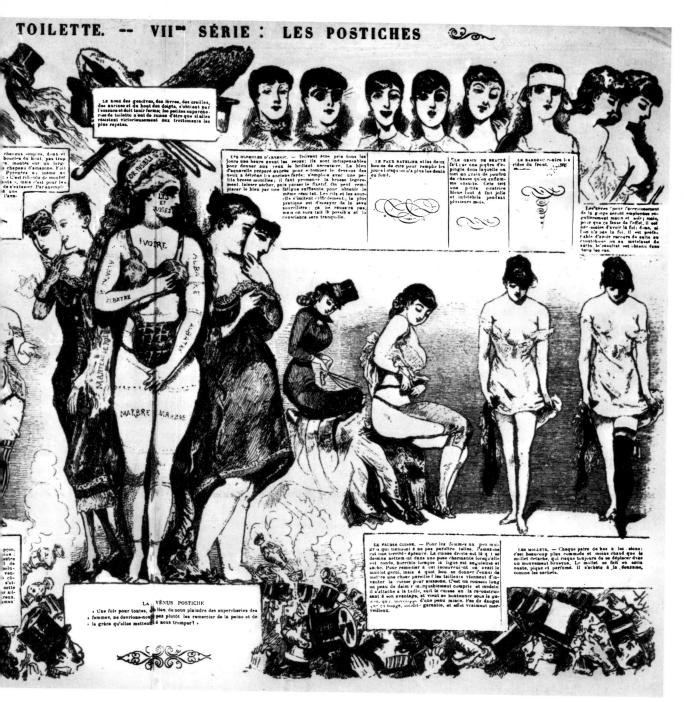

hood, founded in 1848 in England by the poet Dante Gabriel Rossetti. The Rossetti movement sought to escape from the present, finding its inspiration in pre-Renaissance Italy. To this end William Morris started the Morris Company, with the aim of reforming the decorative arts which had been debased by the invention of the machine. His theories gave a new impetus to craftsmanship in England. He founded professional art schools and set up exhibitions of arts and crafts.

However, the influence of the machine-age was not curbed by the ideas of William Morris; on the contrary it was accelerated. In London, the Crystal Palace raised its dome of glass and steel; in Paris the Eiffel Tower soared in metal scaffolding over the International Exhibition. Henry van de Velde, a Belgian who was influenced by a functionalism which he saw even in the curve of flowers on their stems and in the water weeds on ponds, created a modern style which in Germany was called *Jugendstil*. At the Paris Exhibition his sketches and completed works were christened 'Art Nouveau', the style which, with its strong Japanese influence, is characterised by a long, curved sensitive line, as in the curves of plants.

After the Battle of Waterloo there was peace in Europe for a generation, but the year 1848 saw revolutions in many continental countries. A year or two later all the monarchs were restored to their thrones. In France the short-lived Second Republic was replaced by the Second Empire. The nationalist movement in Italy succeeded in driving out the Austrians and the country was at last united under the House of Savoy. Austria suffered from troubles at home and abroad; her defeat in the war of 1866 meant that the leadership of the German states was henceforth assured by Prussia. Russia, needing an outlet on the Mediterranean and anxious to play a more dominant role among the Slavic countries, tried to destroy the Turkish Empire. In 1878 the Congress of Berlin restored the balance of power in Europe. Serbia and Rumania gained their independence; Bulgaria became a Princedom; Bessarabia was granted to Russia; Bosnia and Hertzegovina to Austria. Three great powers were the leaders of Europe: England, Russia and Germany. The balance of power was maintained by a system of alliances, England, France and Russia forming the Triple Entente and Germany, Austria and Italy the Triple Alliance.

Between the invention of the steam-engine and the start of the movement for political equality with men the social status of women changed radically, and during the century many women distinguished themselves. When the King of Rome was born, the first woman aeronaut, Madame Blanchard, spread the news from a balloon. The Princess Cristina di Belgiojoso, a beautiful and aristocratic woman, helped the Carbonari, befriended Mazzini and Garibaldi, and travelled far and wide, even across the continent of Africa. The Countess Clara Maffei was the first woman in Italy to start a literary *salon*, which was attended by Giuseppe Verdi, Alessandro Manzoni, Carlo Tenca and Ugo Foscolo. Less aggressive than the Princess of Belgiojoso, but more sensitive, she dedicated all her energy and power to the support of the patriots of her time.

Mary Claire Dawes was the first Englishwoman to become a Master of Arts, and collected many other degrees in ancient and modern history, mathematics and political economy. Her example was followed by a Russian woman, Madame Kovalewsky, who obtained a degree in mathematics and taught at the University of Stockholm. In Turin, Lidia Poet took a degree in Law but was not allowed to practise her profession as she wished.

One of the greatest women of the time was Maria Sklodowska, the wife of Pierre Curie. In collaboration with her husband she discovered radium in 1898. She was the first woman to obtain the Nobel prize, which was awarded to her twice. She was a reformer in many fields, including sea bathing. However, being modest and simple, she never adopted the extraordinary bathing costumes which were the fashion of the time, with shorts half way down the leg, trimmed with frills, ribbons and lace, and very low-necked blouses.

Another woman endowed with great character and high moral principles was Florence Nightingale. She was born in Florence of an aristocratic English family, and she dedicated herself to the task of taking care of the sick and the wounded. Against the wishes of her family, she studied nursing and organised first aid and nursing services on the battlefields of the Crimea. The lamp which Florence Nightingale carried around the wards in her hospital when she was on night duty caused her to be called 'the Lady of the Lamp.' On her return to England she renounced marriage in order to devote herself to public service. From her fight against disease was born the International Red Cross.

Progressive women at this time fought a hard battle for feminine emancipation, a battle which was to be won in the twentieth century. But they did not manage to banish such feminine artifices as make-up and the many different kinds of adornments of this period: wigs to hide baldness; postiches to puff up hair; false hair attached to the hat to simulate long hair; artificial eyelashes and beauty spots; anti-wrinkle bandages and pills; and padded brassières to suggest a larger bosom.

At the end of the nineteenth century women's clothes showed little sign of emancipation. Waists were still excessively tight, and skirts were long and hampering. Nevertheless the 'New Woman' movement of the 1880s had not been without its effect. In the 1890s the craze for bicycling opened new vistas of freedom. The seeds of emancipation had been planted.

When women began to take part in energetic sports their clothes became less hampering. Bloomers were worn by cyclists. '*Les Gens Chics*'. Gyp. 1895. Bertarelli Collection

The Twentieth Century

262

The First Three Decades

From 1871 to 1914 the world enjoyed a period of peace between the Great Powers, during which material wealth increased prodigiously. The twentieth century was born in the midst of flowers strewn everywhere, on dresses, on furnishings and in architecture. The Liberty style was launched by Arthur Lasenby Liberty, an English dealer in Oriental *objets d'art,* whose *chinoiseries* created a new fashion, especially in oriental and oriental-inspired fabrics, with their light colours and flat, stylised patterns.

Women at the beginning of the century changed the style of their corsets. Instead of exerting pressure on the abdomen, the ones they wore were straightboned in front, thus enhancing the opulence of the bosom and of the hips. The woman of the period swathed herself in a feather boa and wore hats loaded with ornaments, such as stuffed birds and false fruit. Her boleros were trimmed with cascades of lace, muslin frills and *ruches*. Her bodice was strewn with shining sequins and bead embroideries. Beads were the rage. Bead fringes adorned lamp-shades and screens, as well as women's clothes.

The early years of the twentieth century were very much influenced by literary fashions set by Gabriele d'Annunzio, Paul Bourget, Maurice Maeterlinck and Oscar Wilde. The duchesses described by Matilde Sergo, the Italian novelist, wore dresses entirely embroidered with daisies (a flower brought into fashion by Marguerite, the Queen of Italy), topped by hats trimmed with the same flowers, and in their gloved hands clasped great bunches of still more daisies.

Scandals were created by women who smoked or displayed painted lips in public. In Berlin, Czarina Alix, Queen Victoria's granddaughter, shocked the Smart Set by appearing on an official visit to the Austrian Court wearing a black outfit (at a time when fashion decreed water-green, lilac or pastel blue) cut like a man's suit, with a little white collar and a black tie. In the evening at the gala dinner she again appeared in black, wearing a dress of crêpe, with long sleeves, high up at the neck, with only one Russian Order, thus breaking every rule of etiquette.

More conventional was Alexandra of England, who arrived in Berlin draped in an ermine cloak. During her drive in the Kantnerstrasse in Berlin, the horses pulling her gilded coach went out of control, so that she had to make her way on foot, passing

Left: 'Girl at the Mirror'. Federigo Zandomeneghi. Private collection, Milan

between crowds of Berliners who stopped in the street to admire her elegance. When Alexandra appeared in her box at the Opera dressed in lilac-grey silk, with a sapphire tiara on her blonde hair, the applause of the audience was deafening.

Paul Poiret

The fashionable tailor from 1910 to 1914 was Paul Poiret, an extreme non-conformist. Jacques Doucet had employed him at the beginning of his career as an apprentice in his firm. At the end of the first month Doucet paid Poiret five hundred francs which the youth immediately spent on a splendid pair of cufflinks from Cartier's. Poiret's whole career was extravagant and sensational in this manner.

With 50,000 francs borrowed from his mother, the youth inaugurated his *Maison* in the Rue Auber in Paris, and soon began to exercise his influence. Corsets became much less constricting under his guidance. Women who were dressed by him no longer had attacks of the vapours, brought on by the difficulty of breathing in their tight-laced dresses. They learned to walk freely. The waistline was higher than it had been; sleeves, which had been wide at the shoulder and narrow at the wrist, now were tight from shoulder to wrist; the conical skirt lengthened

An early sewing machine. Advertisement

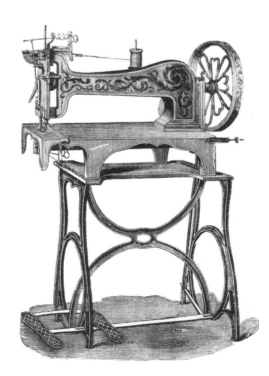

Following pages: 'Lady with a Red Hat'. Maillol

at the back and completely hid the underskirt. Hats with low crowns were made with much wider brims and were even more heavily loaded with feathered trimmings. Umbrellas and sunshades, often made of lace, became indispensable accessories.

Poiret perfected and launched the masculine-inspired walking skirt, which he called the *trotteur*. He shortened skirts to ankle length, against the wishes of conservative women. He introduced huge muffs and fur stoles. He also designed underwear, replacing the muslin or flannel underskirt with petticoats of light cotton material or silk.

The high waistline, however, did not last long after three-quarter length coats became fashionable; these were full from the waist downwards and reached beyond mid-calf. Hats once again were made with high crowns and small brims, which came down low on the forehead and hid the eyebrows. Some of Poiret's dresses were positively pyrotechnic: evening cloaks in brilliant colours and *culottes* which provoked a scandal when they first appeared.

Taking his inspiration from the Far East, Poiret

Woman with parasol. Bonnard. Lithograph

Fashion plates. 1893. Bertarelli Collection, Milan

266

introduced the fashion for kimonos in exotic fabrics and bright colours: red, green, lemon, orange, violet, the whole range of the palette of the Fauves. Painters such as Raoul Dufy collaborated with him. In the *atelier* run by Martine, one of Poiret's daughters, young women studied folk and oriental art, as well as African and Polynesian sculpture, in order to gain inspiration for designs for Poiret's fabrics. This prolific tailor also created and launched a perfume, Rosina, named after his second daughter. For the first time a fashion designer had produced a perfume which reflected his own image, an example that was later followed by Lanvin and Chanel and all the great couturiers in Paris.

Poiret introduced many other innovations: the long, slender sheath; the *entrave*, a ribbon tied half-way down the skirt, which at any sudden movement would break and which made any strenuous activity difficult; amazon dresses; narrow skirts, broken

Fashion plates. 1893. Bertarelli Collection, Milan

267

'*The Diseuse*'. Picasso. Museum of Modern Art, Barcelona

by short minaret-shaped tunics, ending in trains; and belts as wide as the Japanese *obi*. Extravagant and original, he looked for new ideas in the ballets of Diaghilev, in Stravinsky's *Fire Bird,* in Rimski-Korsakov's *Scheherazade*.

The first tailor to travel round the world in order to spread French fashions, Poiret was indefatigable. Accompanied by nine mannequins, he visited the capital cities of Europe and America. He also had a flair for publicity, and would appear on concert platforms where, with a roll of material, a box of pins and a pair of scissors, he would create a dress in a few minutes of skilful improvisation.

Lavish too in his private life, he gave splendid parties attended by the élite of Paris. One such party was given at Versailles, a *fête* with a classical theme: gods and nymphs, dryads and satyrs fluttered around Jove (who was Poiret himself) made taller by his *cothurni* and swathed in a long toga, his hair and beard gilded. On that occasion the three hundred guests drank nine hundred bottles of champagne.

Fashions for Men

In the first decade of the twentieth century, masculine dress was a uniform black in colour, but it distinguished itself by the variety in overcoats: the Ulster, double-breasted and with detachable cape; the inexpensive *loden,* named after the material of which it was made, with a cape and hood attached; the *paletot,* often made of wool, lined with fur, with a shawl collar and double-breasted; the silk or woollen cloak to wear over tailcoats; the *Don Carlos,* a waisted overcoat, double-breasted with a deep pleat in the back; the *Prefect,* a single-breasted coat with side pleats; the frock-coat and the long overcoat were all variations of the redingote.

Trousers were striped, checked, and often of white linen in summer, made without turn-ups. These were an English fashion, which became very popular at this time.

Hats were also varied: bowler hats, soft hats (generally worn on informal occasions) and black felt hats with wide brims, adopted by intellectuals and

Women sometimes imitated male dress. 'The Bar at the *Folies Bergère*'. Georges Bottini. 1907. Ghez Collection, Geneva. *Right*: Portrait of Count Robert de Montesquieu. Giovanni Boldini. Museum of Modern Art, Paris

also artists who favoured the black, fluttering ties *à la Lavallière*. Later the fashion turned to boaters, at first worn only on holiday, but soon adopted for wear in town as well, although the most typical headgear for summer remained the panama hat.

For years the dress of fashionable men consisted of the following items: a vest, a shirt with high starched collar; long pants reaching down to the ankles; knee-length socks held up by suspenders; braces; a tie and tie-pin; morning coat and trousers. In winter a fur coat was worn with a top-hat. Gloves were *de rigueur* —Boldini, the painter, always wore yellow gloves —and walking sticks were carried by everyone. Thus clad, professional men, business men and civil servants went about their work, the poorer among them protecting their sleeves with half-sleeves of alpaca.

Men had special clothes designed for sports such as striped knee-length bathing suits and cycling suits with knickerbockers. The last of the dandies distinguished themselves by the outlandishness of their accessories and their taste for idleness, an attitude epitomised by Oscar Wilde's witty comment: 'Work is the curse of the drinking classes'. Edward VII, the most fashionable of elegant men, launched a new fashion every season, and was imitated by crowds of stylish idlers. This was the epoch of romantic adventures, of suggestive perfumes, of the rustling under-

skirts of the French can-can, the whirling dance of the *Moulin Rouge* and the *Folies Bergère*, and of all those ladies of pleasure who were at the same time admired and despised. These were women on whom scandal centred, especially concerning their wild extravagance. At a time when a newspaper cost a penny and a tram ride twopence; when a few shillings would pay for a dinner and a theatre, Cléo de Mérode, Carolina Otéro, Lina Cavalieri and Diane de Pougy were

English fashion plate. 1907. Bertarelli Collection, Milan

Illustration from '*Journal des Demoiselles*'. 1907. Bertarelli Collection. *Below right*: The muslin or flannel underskirt was replaced by petticoats of light cotton or silk. Photograph. 1905

beauties who squandered fortunes, and whose lovers belonged to the highest ranks of society.

Emmeline Pankhurst

Women were not, however, content to be engaged only in the world of fashion; many of them fought against the masculine prejudice which excluded them from political activities and the right to vote. In England the leader of the Suffragettes was Emmeline Pankhurst, who had started her fight towards the end of the nineteenth century. She organised processions, broke shop windows, threw a bomb at Lloyd George's house and, together with her companions, actually stopped the traffic by lying down in the street. She organised conferences throughout Europe and North America to enlist support for her movement. She was helped by her daughters Christabel and Sylvia. Her own indefatigable fighting spirit was remarkable, and she lived to see her ideas realised; she died in the year 1928, a decade after English women were given the right to vote—although the first time they went to the polls they did not elect one single representative of their own sex.

Other women founded clubs (women's clubs had been started as early as the French Revolution) and won the right to enter a café without an escort. They played tennis (with their faces covered in cold cream to protect them from the sun). They learned to skate, row and also to cycle. But for a long time the bicycle caused controversies because it obliged women cyclists to wear breeches. These notorious breeches excited much criticism, such as: 'difficult to wear, unaesthetic, anti-feminine, anti-family'.

The invention of the telephone, the electric light, the first aeroplane and the cinema changed the quality of life in the twentieth century. After the brothers Lumière invented the first movie camera, a few years passed before the experimental showing

Illustration from 'L'Art et la Mode'. 1909. Bertarelli Collection, Milan

Luxuriant beards were in vogue. The sculptor Vibert. Ferdinand Hodler

271

Fashionable lady. Bas-relief. 1907. Bertarelli Collection, Milan

Right: Portrait of Duchess of Montellano. Giovanni Boldini. Duke of Montellano Collection, Madrid

given in the basement of a Parisian café on the Boulevard des Capucines. The programme showed workmen coming out of the Lumière factory, children quarrelling, goldfish in a bowl and the arrival of a train. The performance was a great success but the appearance of a locomotive on the screen so upset a woman in the audience that she fainted. Gaumont made his first film, called *La fée aux Choux*. Arturo Ambrosio made the first newsreel of the Susa–Mount Cenis Motor Race. Audiences usually talked loudly without paying attention to the piano that accompanied the events on the silent screen. Soon the first film stars were born: Douglas Fairbanks, Mary Pickford and Lillian and Dorothy Gish, among others. All the actresses had heavily made-up eyes and wore thick layers of powder covering their faces. People began to be alarmed at the spread of motoring—Marinetti, in the columns of *Figaro*, announced: 'A new beauty has been born. A car is more beautiful than the Victory of Samothrace.' For some years the car was still spoken of in the masculine gender. Then after the war d'Annunzio changed its sex with this description: 'This car has the grace, the slim lines, the vivacity of a seductress; she also possesses a virtue lacked by many women—perfect obedience.'

Women too began to familiarise themselves with cars: with cranking handle, carburettor and gears.

Photographic portrait. 1885. Bertarelli Collection, Milan. *Below*: Material with design of water lilies. Annesley Voysey

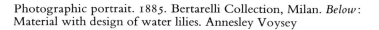

While some women cultivated elegance and femininity, the suffragettes had no time for such trivialities. Photograph. Circa 1903

In many hitherto male provinces, women sought to compete with men on equal terms. Photograph. Circa 1903

Above: A suffragette being forcibly removed from an outdoor meeting at Enfield in 1914

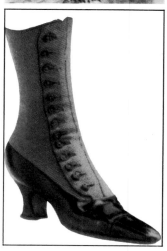

New fashions were introduced as the sport of motoring became popular: caps, dustcoats, button boots and goggles became *de rigueur* for the motorist. Photographs. 1905

Left: Suffragettes selling their magazine at Henley regatta

Clothes began to allow freedom of movement for sport. 1905

The bravest of them took the wheel themselves. The Duchess of Uzès was the first European woman to learn how to drive. Fashion, in order to protect women from the dust and wind, introduced the perfect car-suit: a long-skirted tailored suit, a blouse with *jabot,* a grey dustcoat and, on the head, a toque with a short veil to protect the face and neck. Men also bundled themselves in dustcoats and pulled peaked caps down over their faces, while protecting their eyes with special goggles, enormous objects shaped like dragonfly's wings.

All over Europe fashion designers accepted the decrees of the Parisian couturiers, often expressing themselves through the inspiration they found in the paintings and sculptures of the old masters. Models were created that recalled the patterns of the San Vitale mosaics in Ravenna; some designs had collars composed of multicoloured embroideries imitating the graded strands of the necklace of Nefertiti; other models had very wide sleeves bordered with ermine, copied from fourteenth-century miniatures; still other models had short tunics over evening dresses with a train, taken from a Florentine costume of the twelfth century. There were cloaks copied from the

Illustration from '*Album des Blouses Nouvelles*'. Circa 1910. Bertarelli Collection, Milan

Tanagra figurines. Fra Angelico and Giotto inspired designs for children's frocks with short skirts slit at the sides and embroidered with geometrical patterns. Finally there was a dress inspired by the Egyptian costumes of the Old Kingdom: a redingote buttoned below the waist, trimmed with silk and worn over a straight embroidered dress. The same redingote had an ingenious system of buttons which could be undone to reveal the lower leg. The costume was completed by an odd hat made of feathers with a shape vaguely reminiscent of Mercury's winged helmet.

A new dance, the tango, had arrived from South America and Mistinguette immediately launched it, after it had been introduced into Europe by Argentinian women escorted by sun-tanned men with thick side-whiskers, wearing striped trousers, long double-breasted black coats, highly polished shoes and butter-coloured gloves. In London, Paris, Berlin and Milan, young people and old people, middle-class and upper-class, all went crazy about the tango. With their hair combed down over their foreheads, wearing turbans trimmed usually with osprey, with their skirts clinging, ankle length and slit on one side to give them freedom of movement, with their eyes blackened with kohl, and their hands on their hips, the pelvis thrust slightly forward according to Poiret's instructions, women danced until the disaster of war overwhelmed Europe.

During the four years of the First World War, fashion design came to a virtual standstill, although at the beginning of the conflict the shoulderline became sloping, the waistline went up, the neckline was round and deep and colours were bright. *Broderie anglaise* trimmed blouses and dresses and

Illustration from *'La Chic Parisienne'*. Bertarelli Collection, Milan

Right: Portrait of Lina Cavalieri. Cesare Tallone. Private collection

277

hats assumed a military shape. Then women became absorbed in the events around them and dressed themselves for their work as nurses, postwomen, tramway conductresses, often preferring to wear the overalls worn by factory workers. They replaced men in every field of activity: they drove trains and ambulances, they became factory managers, electricians, mechanics and plumbers. Society life in Europe came quickly to an end, and lasted only a little longer in America.

At a party Wallis Warfield, who later became the Duchess of Windsor, appeared in a cloud of chiffon, a knee-length tunic, with the hem trimmed with pearls. The dress was cut on Empire lines, decorated with two single American Beauty roses. In the same season, the future Duchess created a sensation in another model with a gold brocade bodice, trimmed with large flowers, and a very full flame-coloured georgette skirt.

Women writers of the time, like Katherine Mansfield, wore somewhat more sober clothes, such as romantic sweeping dark cloaks and white em-

Right: Fashion plates by Ventura. 1912. Bertarelli Collection, Milan

broidered jackets patterned with loops and gold epaulettes, rather short skirts, boots, and hats trimmed with feathers. Eleonora Duse always wore grey when she was visiting wounded soldiers on the battlefield. Queen Elizabeth of Belgium wore cloches like soldier's helmets when she was not wearing a nurse's uniform. Queen Helen of Italy favoured dark, coarse fabrics for her severe dresses; she organised hospitals and canteens, and knitted balaclava helmets and woollen socks.

The Boyish Look

Towards the end of the war, as though it were an augury of peace, the waistline dropped to the hips and was overlaid with frills, often made in a different material from the dress. Overcoats became longer and spindle-shaped, with wider sleeves. A ribbon or a band was worn round the forehead; a slave bangle was worn on the arm above the elbow, and a thin gold chain round the ankle. The tailored suit was still popular. Mata Hari, who in her private life preferred almost masculine dresses, wore a dark redingote with feather boa and little hat to face the firing squad. Cécile Sorel, when visiting the front line, wore knee-high boots and a fur coat of military cut, which showed up the ribbon of the Légion d'Honneur.

Then the bombshell exploded: hair was cut short, the first feminine rebellion against the state of subjection in which women had been kept for centuries. During the war, women had become aware that they

Illustration from '*Journal des Dames et des Modes*'. 1913. Bertarelli Collection, Milan

Left: Fashion model. 1912

Paris model from '*Journal des Dames et des Modes*'. 1912. Bertarelli Collection, Milan

Below and right: In the years preceding the war, a craze for the tango swept Europe, with the fashion for osprey plumes and tight skirts. Illustrations from '*Journal des Dames et des Modes*'. 1912 and 1914. Bertarelli Collection, Milan

were the equal of men and, as a first reaction, they cut their hair short. This new hair style was unpopular with men, even though some women, out of shyness, were content merely to shave the nape of the neck, and to allow their plaits to remain. The *garçonne* haircut was a sign of change not only in women's fashion but also in their whole way of life.

After the long gestation period of the first eighteen years, the true personality of the twentieth century emerged, and the prejudices of previous decades were abandoned. A kind of madness followed, the madness of the roaring years of the charleston and jazz, of *nouveaux riches* eagerly thirsting for amusement, of negro singers like Betty Smith, of prohibitionism and of a frantic interest in sport. This was the age of sports cars and plastic surgery, of Marcel waving and the cinema. In 1927, silent pictures gave way to the 'Talkies'. Women too made their mark on this age,

through their rebellion against tradition, and their struggle to free themselves from the fetters that had held them for centuries.

After the innovation of short hair, women started another revolution in the field of fashion: corsets were discarded and replaced by suspender belts; and the underbodice which supported the breasts was replaced by a *brassière* which flattened the breasts. Women began to display their legs as skirts became shorter. Belts were worn low on the hips, giving clothes a boyish look. There was also the 'Tutankhamen' line, inspired by the Egyptian excavations. Scarves were draped round the neck of every kind of dress; zip-fasteners replaced buttons and the little veil became more voluminous. Evening dresses grew shorter while necklaces grew longer. The fashion for necklaces reached the point where women wore them everywhere: with bathing costumes on the

Immediately before the war ankles began to make their appearance. Illustrations from '*Journal des Dames et des Modes*'. 1913 and 1914. Bertarelli Collection, Milan

Illustrations from '*Journal des Dames et des Modes*'. 1914.
Bertarelli Collection, Milan

beach, in cafés, or at home with the lounging pyjamas which had now become fashionable.

The amount of underwear was reduced, becoming less bulky and lighter in weight. Combinations such as thin camiknickers were introduced, easily washed, requiring no ironing, and with shoulder straps made of little gold chains that needed no laundering. Women achieved boyish figures by dieting strenuously. Most underwear was cut straight to emphasise the straight lines that were fashionable.

Before the war, fashion magazines had always shown special models for ladies over forty, but after the war a woman was considered young at forty, and was offered the same designs as her younger sisters. Modern medicine, plastic surgery and diets helped people to keep fit and retain their youth.

The 'little boy' theme was developed with a number of variations by the Dolly Sisters, with their small round heads and flat hair styles, and by Greta Garbo with her page bob and her soft, large-brimmed hats. Skirts continued to get shorter, and belts were worn almost at the knees. The great couturiers who had tried to reintroduce drapery and ornament at last submitted to defeat, preached simplicity and launched a geometrical, flat, angular line; the influence of Picasso's cubism was felt in fashion. In order to accentuate the new trends, dress collections were presented by American mannequins, who were extremely tall and thin. Evening gowns were worn above the knee, as short as afternoon or morning dresses, and hair continued to be short.

By this time women had learnt that careers could be part of their lives; they learnt to be independent, to drink cocktails, to smoke and to engage in active sports. At last, free to love or to have a career, they were no longer obliged to marry as the only way of life open to them. Divorce, too, became easier to obtain in many countries and divorce laws favoured the woman.

After a few years of being extremely short, skirts became longer again, but were irregular; above the knee in front and longer behind; evening dresses now sometimes reached to the ground. The waistline returned to its natural place. In 1929, shortly before the Wall Street crash, long evening dresses made a

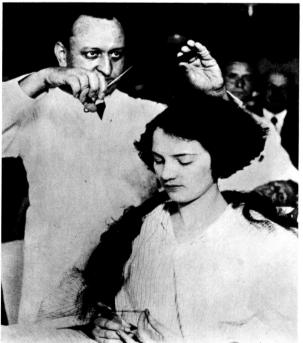

The war swept away all the traditional concepts of elegance. Hair was cut short in bobs and shingles, as the boyish look became popular

definite comeback. The 'roaring twenties' were at an end, and the conflict between boyishness and femininity ceased.

Fashion Designers

The world of fashion had always been dominated by men until, in the reign of Louis XIV, the prudish Madame de Maintenon persuaded the King to allow fashion design to be controlled by women, because 'it was not decent that men's hands should touch the body of women, or that men's eyes should see their most intimate secrets'. After the long period in which Rose Bertin acted as adviser to Marie Antoinette, men regained their power and did not lose this until the twentieth century allowed the weaker sex, if not superiority, at least equality in this field. In the 1900 Paris Exhibition, Madame Paquin displayed a wax mannequin of herself, dressed in the latest fashion, sitting in front of her *coiffeuse*, putting the finishing touches to her toilette. Among her clients were the Queens of Belgium, Portugal and Spain, and the queens of the *demi-monde*. An able organiser, she was elected chairman of the *haute couture* of the Paris dress trade.

Her contemporaries, the Callot sisters, the daughters of an antique dealer, introduced the fashion for lace blouses and gold and silver lamé evening dresses. Madame Vionnet, who served her apprenticeship in the Callot sisters' *atelier*, went to Doucet's for a short time, and then started her own shop. She was very able and created 'individual' models, finding for each woman the right fabrics and the line that would suit her best. She tried to express the different personalities of clients, and also studied their proportions on wooden mannequins of their exact dimensions. She based her success on the weave of fabrics, and on the precision, cut and balance of her patterns.

Coco Chanel

Chanel, inspired by the example of Lily Langtry, launched the simple jersey dress. She made her suits in jersey, and used jersey woven with gold or silver thread for more formal dresses. The revolutionary quality of Chanel dresses lay in their expensive simplicity and classic line.

Gabrielle (Coco to her friends) Chanel was born in poor circumstances. During her childhood she was supposed to have cut up the curtains of the aunts who brought her up to make dresses for her doll. She was still very young when an Englishman, aware of her talent, opened a millinery shop for her in the Rue Cambon. During the war, Coco became a nurse in a

During the war fashion came to a standstill. Women wore overalls and did men's work. Red Cross parade in New York

Following pages: The cinema was a new form of entertainment which had a great influence on fashion. Illustration from '*Journal des Dames et des Modes*'. 1919

The boyish figure came into vogue; corsets were used to flatten the bust and hide feminine curves. Fashion plates. 1925. Bertarelli Collection, Milan

hospital in Deauville. At this time another friend offered to set her up in a boutique. Chanel, with her infallible instinct, created for all the women who were replacing men in offices and factories blue sailor skirts and mannish pull-overs. She was her own mannequin, making her own costumes and wearing them, sometimes adding a touch of femininity in the form of a brooch. With these outfits she immediately became a huge success.

On her return to Paris after the war, she met the Duke of Westminster, who was also the owner of a splendid yacht on which Coco took a long holiday. When she landed in Cannes her suntan immediately became fashionable, a fashion which still continues. Unable to stay inactive, Chanel left the yacht to re-

turn to the world of fashion. Every collection she created was a personal triumph, even if her subsequent models were only variations of her first line. She dressed the most elegant women in the world in simple grey, black or beige pull-overs, trimmed with white piqué collars and cuffs; or in tricot jersey suits and coats.

She launched the fashion for costume jewellery made of crystal or coloured glass, often the only ornaments her models wore. When her pearl necklace broke one day, it is said that she had neither the time nor the patience to grade the pearls according to size when rethreading them; she thus launched the fashion for necklaces of pearls or semi-precious stones of different sizes. She created a perfume and called it Chanel Number Five because five was her lucky number: she was born on the 5th of August and invariably presented her collections on the 5th of August (for the winter) and the 5th of February (for the summer).

Jeanne Lanvin became *haute couturière* after her success with the dresses she made for her daughter, who later became the Countess of Polignac. She found her inspiration in the greens of the landscape, in the colours of Renoir's palette, in the ethereal figures of Botticelli, in the stained glass windows of churches (which inspired the famous Lanvin blue), in the woods lit by autumn sunshine. She imported gold and silver fabrics and precious brocades from the East. Among her clients were the Princess de Lucinge and the four wives of Sacha Guitry. When Yvonne Printemps returned to the United States after her separation from her husband, she took with her in her trunks eighty Lanvin models.

Maggy Rouff, after taking a degree in medicine, fell in love with the world of fashion. She was the daughter of the tailor who had created the white riding habit for the Empress Elizabeth, and who had made for the Princess Czartyoryski, one of the first woman pilots, 'a pale, soft dress, almost golden, fastened at the ankles with drapery, so that it seemed

Dresses became shorter and necklaces longer. Fashion plates. 1925. Bertarelli Collection, Milan

'The Tango' from 'La Gazette du Bon Ton'. 1922. Bertarelli Collection, Milan

like turkish trousers'; a gold belt, a beret with a flattering veil and a leopard jacket completed the ensemble. Maggy Rouff studied every aspect of the art of dressmaking. She opposed the popular black and beige colour scheme introduced by Chanel. She created a style for formal occasions which suggested the fashions of the past.

Of all these couturières, only Coco Chanel continues today as a force in this field. Her work continues to be of importance in the years after the Second World War.

Cosmetics

After many years of not being used, make-up again became fashionable for respectable women. (Courtesans and actresses had of course never abandoned the use of cosmetics.) Cléo de Mérode used kohl to make her attractive eyes even more mysterious. She claimed to be the daughter of the Baronne de Mérode, Princess of Trelon, and said that she had been educated in a convent of Ursulines. She used rice powder on her face and a touch of red on her cheek-bones, lips and on the lobes of her ears. Actresses often wore bizarre make-up. Lily Elsie, a star of musical comedy, shaded her eyelids in purple and grey for the stage, and darkened her nostrils with red and purple and her cheeks in different shades of red, from coral to wood-rose. She applied ochre-coloured powder to her chin with a rabbit's paw, and coloured the tip of her nose and the lobes of her ears with salmon-coloured paste. Her face thus acquired the immobility of a Chinese doll.

'The Lady Wants No Children'. Kees van Dongen. 1925. Private collection. *Right*: It was smart to wear jewellery even with bathing suits. 'The Bather'. Kees van Dongen. 1924. Private collection

After the First World War, it was a woman who launched cosmetics as big business. Elizabeth Arden had long been aware of the need to care for feminine beauty by scientific methods. Formerly, women had covered their faces with rice powder and used kohl or burnt matches to blacken their eyebrows. Apart from a few really elegant women who knew how to apply coloured paste on the lips, the great majority of women reddened their lips as Madame de Pompadour had done—by biting them. Elizabeth Arden introduced new creams into the field of cosmetics, prepared according to a prescription obtained from Elizabeth Hubbard, who had found this among Madame Récamier's notes on beauty. With the help of chemists and other experts at the start of the twenties, Elizabeth Arden began to experiment with lanoline, benzoin, almond oil, hamamelis and other extracts, with which she made cleansing milk and nourishing creams, tonics and lotions. These were used to combat wrinkles, to cleanse the skin and to nourish and rejuvenate it. The company she founded now also makes facepowders, lipsticks, nail varnish and massage creams, and has spread a network of beauty clinics throughout the world.

Helena Rubinstein, a contemporary of Elizabeth Arden, was born into a well-to-do family in Cracow, but left her parents and her country to emigrate to

Advertisements in 'La Gazette du Bon Ton'. 1924. Bertarelli Collection, Milan

A tiara and necklace by Cartier. Illustration from 'La Gazette du Bon Ton'. 1924. Bertarelli Collection, Milan

A fur coat by Weil, and an advertisement for the jewellery shop, 'Tecla', in Paris. Illustrations from 'La Gazette du Bon Ton'. Bertarelli Collection, Milan

Right: Designs by Doucet. Illustration from '*La Gazette du Bon Ton*'. 1922. Bertarelli Collection, Milan

Left: Designs by Jeanne Lanvin. Illustrations from '*La Gazette du Bon Ton*'. Bertarelli Collection, Milan

'The Jungle'. Fabric design. Raoul Dufy. Illustration from '*La Gazette du Bon Ton*'. 1922. Bertarelli Collection

Australia. She also built up a vast empire manufacturing cosmetics. She started by producing a cream her mother had given her to protect her skin from the Australian sun. This cream was such a success that Madame Rubinstein started to manufacture it on a large scale; from this beginning a chain of factories and beauty clinics has grown. She married Prince Gourielli, and at her death in 1965 she left a personal fortune of one hundred million dollars. Like

Model by Madelaine Vionnet. Illustration from '*La Gazette du Bon Ton*'. Bertarelli Collection, Milan

Elizabeth Arden, she owed her wide success to her initiative and her hard work. These were two typically modern women, though they were born in the last century, who developed a new profession for women, that of the 'beautician'.

Another profession born in the twenties was that of the interior decorator. This field was developed by Elsie de Wolfe, an American actress who left the stage to become Lady Mendl. It was she who aimed at giving more appeal to contemporary furniture, which at the time was functional and lacking in warmth. Her decorative designs were complementary to the short skirts and straight lines of women's clothes reflecting the mood of this period.

Illustration from '*La Gazette du Bon Ton*'. 1922. Bertarelli Collection, Milan

In general the decade from 1920 to 1930 is almost invariably thought of as extravagant: prohibition, jazz, a new sexual morality. These were also years of enormous achievement in the field of literature: Virginia Woolf, F. Scott Fitzgerald, Thornton Wilder and William Faulkner are but a few of the names that shaped the age. This decade also produced unrivalled

In the twenties skirts were worn knee-length and even shorter. Fashion drawing. 1927. Bertarelli Collection, Milan

actors from Greta Garbo to Charlie Chaplin, from Gloria Swanson to Rudolph Valentino. Dadaism, Picasso's cubist period, Klee and German expressionism had all had their influence. This was the age of mass culture. Magazines of huge circulation began to reach millions of readers. The radio from 1920 onwards devoted more and more time to literary, artistic and musical activities. Negro rhythms created new dances like the charleston and the black bottom. Al Jolson won enormous popularity with young people; his song 'Sonny Boy' was a huge success. Josephine Baker took Paris by storm. Women stood out, tall and slim, in their narrow sheaths, with their short hair hidden under cloches drawn down over the eyes. They plucked their eyebrows, wore long earrings and held immensely long cigarette-holders.

Chinoiserie was still fashionable. Rare pieces of Ming or Tang dynasties were highly prized; lacquered screens, ivory statuettes, vases decorated with lotus flowers and bowls filled with gilded poppy seeds were used for decoration. Mah-jong, of Chinese origin, was a favourite game.

This was an age of emancipation and also of flux between the different classes. Chanel's dresses were elegant without appearing expensive in an obvious way. Whereas before the war ten yards of material went into the making of a skirt, now only one was

Fashion plate from *La Rinascente* autumn and winter catalogue. 1926-7. Bertarelli Collection, Milan

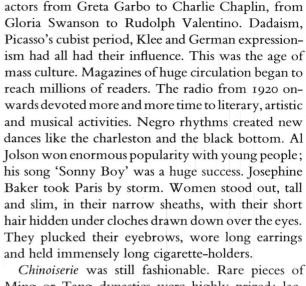

Close-fitting cloche hats made of felt helped to give women the boyish look. Fashion drawing. 1927. Bertarelli Collection, Milan

required. The comfort and freedom of movement to which women had become accustomed would never have been possible in the costly, cumbersome clothes of the early years of the century.

The psychological explanation for the clothes of this period can be found in the struggle for feminine emancipation. Most women had gained the right to vote, and had improved their legal position and economic status, and their clothes became more masculine, as an expression of this change.

The Honourable Mrs Reginald Fellowes was one of the exceptional women of this period, and also one of the most elegant. Her elegance was achieved with the utmost simplicity. One typical outfit of hers had a jacket covered in sequins, cut like a man's dinner jacket. She wore this with a green carnation in the button-hole. She often arrived at an elegant cocktail party in a simple silk dress. She had dozens of these silk dresses in different colours, which she adorned with jewels, large gold cuff links and Indian neck-

Fashion drawings from 'Femina'. 1928 and 1929. Bertarelli Collection, Milan

Fashion drawings. *Above*: From 1929. *Above right*: From 1927. Bertarelli Collection, Milan

laces. She wore jewels even when dressed for the beach. She loved to shock people through her unconventional dress, for example by appearing bareheaded at Ascot when everybody else was wearing a hat. Once at a dinner-dance, she became aware that another woman was wearing the same dress as she; this was of black tulle, trimmed with a large spray of ostrich feathers. She asked the waiter to bring her a pair of scissors, and quite calmly, without interrupting the conversation, cut off the ostrich feathers, and used them as a fan.

Another eccentric personality of this period was the Marchesa Casati. Deathly pale, with orange coloured hair, her eyes enlarged by *belladonna* and with a heavy black line, she liked to walk round the streets of Rome leading a leopard on a leash, or followed by

a black servant extravagantly dressed. She sometimes dressed in white flannels, gold sandals and an enormous cow-boy hat. Despite all her eccentricities, the Marchesa had an influence on the decorative art of her time, with her taste for alabaster vases filled with roses, or pieces of rock crystal or amber as ornaments in her unusual home.

Anita Loos, an American woman writer, was enormously successful with her book *Gentlemen Prefer Blondes*. She too was typical of the twenties. Being a tiny woman, the stoles, wide skirts and huge hats of the pre-war period did not suit her. In the twenties she found her true self: she cut her hair very short, bought her hats and dresses in the children's departments of the big stores, and suddenly a new, fascinating personality emerged.

296

Fashion drawing. 1929. Bertarelli Collection, Milan

Side by side with this international group of eccentric women, gifted with taste, elegance and intelligence, who influenced the fashions in London, New York, Paris, Berlin and Milan, the youth of the period danced the charleston and displayed the uncouth manners that were typical of the time. Their language was vulgar, their attitude aggressive. They drove cars too fast, and smoked too many cigarettes, but their obtrusive bad manners helped to break down the excessive formality that was a residue from the nineteenth century.

At the end of this decade the world was stricken by an economic crisis which had momentous results. The slump began in the autumn of 1929, with the crash of the New York Stock Exchange, which shook the financial structure of the whole world to its foundations. No continent escaped the catastrophe, and the consequences were tragic. The 'roaring twenties' closed with a slump that swept the world like a hurricane, and left everywhere a wreckage of despair. Towards the close of this period dress designers made every effort to bring in longer skirts. They tried a whole series of devices: side-draperies, skirts longer at the back than at the front and transparent overskirts, but it was not until 1930 that they succeeded. Skirts suddenly lengthened to mid-calf or lower, and the waist slipped back into its normal position instead of being round the hips, where it had stood for nearly a decade.

Unless we believe, in defiance of all the evidence from the past, that fashion is purely arbitrary, and at women are 'dictated to' by a handful of Paris designers, we can hardly fail to see in this a real change in the social climate. There had been an air of gaiety about the twenties, but people all over the world were beginning to realise that the party could not go on for ever, that, in fact, the Great American Slump had sounded its death-knell.

If we are interested in historical analogies we can compare this period with 1820, when waists, having been abnormally high ever since the French Revolution, suddenly slipped back to their right place. Waist-lines in the right place indicate a desire for normality, even an acceptance of paternalism, and a reaction against female emancipation. It is no accident that the fashions of the early 1930s coincided with the rise of Hitler.

Yet it is necessary to make a distinction between these two periods. In 1820 and on all previous occasions, the return of the waist to its natural position presaged a return to tight-lacing, and, in an attempt to make waists look even smaller, either wide sleeves or voluminous skirts, or both. In the early nineteen-thirties this did not happen. There was a passing vogue for wide sleeves *à la Toulouse-Lautrec*, but hips remained obstinately slim. Indeed, the wide sleeves themselves might be said to have had the effect of making the hips rather than the waist look small. There was obviously a conflict between the tendency towards tight waists and the tendency towards small hips. In psychological terms tight waists mean that women are content to accept some degree of paternalism, narrow hips that they are reluctant to bear children. It has been suggested that it was fear of war that kept hips slim throughout the decade which saw the outbreak of the Second World War.

In the years to come, women tried to recover the femininity they had set aside during the twenties. They began to grow their hair again after the eccentricity of the 'Eton crop', and longer hair made it impossible to wear the cloche hat. This type of headgear therefore disappeared. All kinds of new experiments were tried. Schiaparelli created a sensation by sticking what looked like a sock on her head and calling it a hat. Most of the new hats were extremely small and perched forward over one eye.

Drawing by Steinberg. From 'The Art of Living'

Fashion Today

From the Thirties to the Sixties

Schiaparelli was one of the most influential dress designers of these years. (The story of Chanel's success has already been told; a woman in the highest ranks of *la haute couture*, she has inaugurated something of a revolution by her introduction of 'working-class modes'. She was accused of having introduced the apache sweater into the Ritz, but her genius lay precisely in making ordinary clothes into high fashion by some significant touch.) Schiaparelli entered the field almost by accident with variations on the sweater mode already launched by Chanel. She flew in the face of what had been considered good taste, but the results were oddly attractive and she soon had a fashionable clientèle, including Greta Garbo whom she dressed for years. Even Schiaparelli's highly individual taste in colour was accepted and her 'shocking pink' became famous.

In one sense the innovations of both Chanel and Schiaparelli reflected a general tendency towards the disappearance of class distinction in women's daytime clothes. Women of all classes were now engaged in some sort of work, and there had evolved for this purpose a kind of working uniform, consisting of that essentially English costume, the tailor-made. Trousers, in the form of rather full slacks, were sometimes worn for sports, but not yet for shopping.

Right: Culottes were fashionable for beach wear. 1930. Bertarelli Collection, Milan

Underwear had become lighter and the one-piece foundation garment gave women the new sleek line. Fashion drawing. 1930

Marlene Dietrich in 'Blonde Venus'. 1932

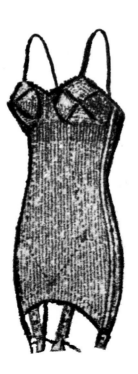

Left: Greta Garbo. 1932

Fashions in 1937. Bertarelli Collection, Milan

There was a marked distinction between day clothes and evening clothes. Even girls in the lower income groups, although they might wear factory dungarees during the day, assumed some kind of 'glamour' dress, based usually on a simplified version of that worn by a favourite film star, for going to a dance hall at night.

This approach of the clothes of lower classes to that of the wealthier classes was made possible by two factors: one was the increasing efficiency and speed of mass production; the other was the development of technology. The American depression had hit hard at the profits of designers in Paris. In the twenties fashion had become big business, the export market in 1925 being worth nearly 2,500,000,000 francs. The principal fashion houses, such as Lanvin, Lelong, Molyneux, Patou, Piguet, Vionnet, had added new workrooms, some of them employing as many as five hundred people to cope with the demand, and until 1930 it was the habit of American buyers to

purchase several dozen copies of each selected model in Paris and retail them to a wealthy clientèle. After the slump prohibitive customs duties began to make this luxury trade almost impossible, for a duty of up to 90 per cent might be imposed on the cost of the model. Models imported, on a temporary basis, for the purpose of copying, were however allowed into America duty free. The main American market therefore began to consist of those mass producers who purchased *toiles* (that is, patterns cut out in linen). These were sold for about 100,000 francs each, with full directions for making them up. Simplified versions could be sold to a wide public through the chain stores for as little as fifty dollars, and firms like Macy's of New York disposed of thousands of them.

In the last thirty years, however, the French designers have not had entirely their own way in the United States. Many American names have come to the fashion fore. Charles James was already recognised in the thirties as a vital influence in *haute couture*,

302

Fashion in 1937. Bertarelli Collection, Milan

Evening dress by France Vramant. Fashion drawing. 1937. Bertarelli Collection, Milan

together with Mainbocher, Valentina and the well-known Hollywood designers Gilbert Adrian and Howard Greer. Among the most successful designers of ready-to-wear clothes (both in the expensive and the medium price brackets) have been Hattie Carnegie, Arnold Scaasi, Pauline Trigère, Galanos, Claire Potter, Norman Norell, B. H. Wragge, Anne Fogarty, Rudi Geinreich, Bill Blass, Geoffrey Beene, Ben Zuckerman, Adele Simpson and Bonnie Cashin. The numerous fashion groups and fashion awards given in America are evidence of the American interest in fashion, and perhaps there is no country in the world where the innumerable fashion magazines command a larger sale.

The other factor which helped to bring fashion

Top right: Mrs Wallis Simpson, later the Duchess of Windsor. 1937. Bertarelli Collection, Milan. *Centre right*: A hat of 1938. Bertarelli Collection, Milan. *Below right*: Wide trousers were the fashion for men throughout the twenties and thirties. Jean Harlow and Robert Taylor. 1930

Bette Davis

Maggy Rouff design. 1938

within reach of a wide public was the growing use of synthetic fabrics. Even in the twenties, it would have been impossible for the mass of women to wear the new short skirts to good effect without the invention of artificial silk stockings. At the present time, the use of man-made fibres has reached an unprecedented level, even in the production of *la haute couture*: in fact they are no longer regarded as cheap substitutes but are accepted in their own right.

Men's clothes, never so quickly modified as women's, continued the steady progress towards informality which had been noticeable since the end of the First World War. The frock-coat disappeared altogether, and the morning coat and silk hat were seen only on ceremonial occasions. The ordinary daywear was now the lounge suit, and from 1924 until the end of the thirties it was worn with the very wide trousers known as 'Oxford bags'. Soft collars replaced the stiff white linen variety, and for golf and other sports, men wore baggy knickerbockers called 'plus fours', often with a gaily coloured 'Fair Isle' sweater, a fashion popularised by the Prince of Wales, who loved striking patterns.

Women's sports clothes became far scantier than they had ever been, even in the twenties. In 1930 we find the first backless bathing costumes which were, however, no more backless than the evening dresses of the period. And in 1931 Mrs Fearnley-Whitting-

Claudette Colbert. 1937

stall, playing tennis at Forest Hills in America, appeared on court with bare legs. But it was not until 1933 that Miss Alice Marble of San Francisco ventured to appear in shorts above the knee. Women began at this period to play golf in trousers and to ride horseback in breeches instead of the traditional side-saddle costume.

As the cataclysm of the Second World War approached, the minds (perhaps one should say the unconscious minds) of the leading designers seemed to be divided between the unacknowledged fear of war and the hope of peace. The first was shown by a sudden shortening of the skirt, until it was almost as

Coco Chanel. 1937

A beauty parlour

Styles of 1940

and femininity.' Other slogans of the time were: 'Grandmother was right, because she concentrated on slimming her waist.' In Paris all the designers seemed to be of the same mind, and in London, Lachasse, having displayed his slim-waisted collection, sent his mannequins out again, without the dresses, to show that they had been wearing boned corsets underneath. It is tempting to think that really tight waists and expanded skirts might have swept the world of fashion—if there had been no war.

At first the war seemed to make little difference, and in March 1940, when all the great Paris houses launched their collections, they found plenty of buyers, both American and French. Social life went on, and one reporter recorded that in the Ritz 'they are all dining gracefully again, in skirts that touch their toes'. The Battle of France put an end to that, but the victorious Germans made every effort to win over artists of all kinds during the Occupation, and the dress designers produced some extravagant fashions. *The export trade, however, was dead.*

Great Britain was as completely cut off from French *haute couture* as it had been during the Napoleonic wars. Indeed, once clothes rationing was introduced in June of 1941, fashion in England almost ceased to exist. Women were compelled to wear

short as it had been in the late twenties; the second by a determined effort to bring in tight-lacing, and even a revival of the crinoline. Fashion commentators, returning from Paris in 1938, announced that 'Paris has decreed a new woman . . . She will be veiled and gloved and corseted—and even button-booted. [Schiaparelli had invented eight-button boots for evening in coloured kid.] There must be frou-frou

A woman pilot in the Second World War

Fashions during the war were influenced by military uniforms. Auxiliaries training at the Duke of York's Barracks

An embroidered dress worn in 1943

what clothes they had, and housewives as well as factory workers took to wearing slacks, thereby making stockings unnecessary. Even with skirts, many women began to go about with bare legs; some of them even painted their legs and drew lines down the back to imitate the seam of the stocking. Hats were replaced by head-scarves and in wet weather by plastic hoods.

Reactions in Italy were somewhat different. It was at the most difficult period of the war that Biki, the granddaughter of Puccini, launched herself in Milan as a dress designer. Another talented woman, Germana Marucelli, fought to establish a distinctive Italian style. Both during the war and after, the 'King of Fashion' was Farcioni. When the hostilities were over, a number of society women founded *maisons de couture*. Aristocratic ladies like Simonetta Colonna (who with her husband Fabiani, himself a talented de-signer, migrated to Paris) and Giovanna dei Principi Caracciolo-Giretti entered the fashion field. Three little dressmakers from Parma, the Fontana sisters, created a couture house of international reputation, with branches in New York and London. Other names were Federico Emilio Schubert, Austrian by origin but Neapolitan by birth; Gattinoni, Maria

General Montgomery's duffle coat influenced designs for women's coats

Antonelli, Jole Veneziani in Milan; Emilio Pucci in Florence; and Enzo, the couturier of the *nouvelle vague*.

All these challenged French supremacy in design. But after the war Paris once more reasserted herself, leading names being Balenciaga, Balmain, Carven, Dior, Grès, Givenchy, Griffe, Jacques Fath, Jean Dessès, Jean Patou, Lanvin, Castello, Mad Carpentier, Manguin, Paquin and Nina Ricci.

In England, too, fashion revived. The Fashion Group of Great Britain, which had been founded in 1935, was encouraged by the Board of Trade in 1941 to form an Incorporated Society. This was done in the following year, the original group of Norman Hartnell, Peter Russell, Worth, Madame Mosca, Digby Morton, Victor Stiebel and Hardy Amies, being joined by Molyneux and Charles Creed. Later additions to the membership were Mattli, Michael Sherard, Lachasse, John Cavanagh and Ronald Patterson. Clothes rationing, however, continued in England for some years after the end of the war. Even when, early in 1949, a large range of garments became 'coupon free', there was still a shortage of materials and prices were high.

This shortage of materials made all the more astonishing the success of Dior's 'New Look', launched in the spring of 1947, which was a deliberate attempt to break away from women's short-skirted, tubular

Christian Dior, 1947

In 1947 Dior launched the revolutionary New Look which swept the Western world

appearance and from square, padded shoulders. The new silhouette had narrow shoulders, the waist in the right place, a new emphasis on the bust, and a longish skirt with a wide hem. In England the Board of Trade appealed to women not to waste material by adopting the new fashion. This was all in vain, for the 'New Look' swept the world. It was part of the nostalgia of women for what seemed the more settled world of the past.

The 'New Look' was, however, essentially a throw-back, and it was not long before a typical 'post-crisis' dress made its appearance. Balenciaga was first in the field with his chemise or sack dress, and some nine years after his 'New Look', Dior produced first his H-Line and then his A-Line. Since then the general silhouette of women's clothes has more and more resembled the modes of the mid-

twenties, that is so long as they do not abandon skirts altogether and adopt trousers. In some cases the clothes of young men and women today are almost indistinguishable, and equally informal.

In the period immediately after the Second World War, however, men's clothes showed a curious reaction (comparable with the feminine throw-back of the 'New Look') to Edwardian modes. For the upper classes, this meant an attempt to reproduce the styles of fifty years before: narrow trousers and close-fitting jackets buttoned rather high. With these was worn a small bowler hat perched forward on the head. These modes were exaggerated and modified by the East End 'Teddy Boys'. Their trousers were even narrower than those of fashionable young men. Their jackets were longer, having a much more pronounced shoulder line. They did not adopt the bowler hat: indeed they abandoned hats altogether and wore their hair rather long.

However, by the beginning of the sixties both the neo-Edwardians, who had their clothes made for them in Savile Row, and the 'Teddy Boys', who bought theirs in Whitechapel, were already outmoded. The bulk of young men belonging to the newly prosperous lower middle-classes never took to these styles. There was nothing nostalgic about *them*: they had no desire to return to 'the bad old

After the war nylon stockings became an essential part of every woman's wardrobe. Nylon factory

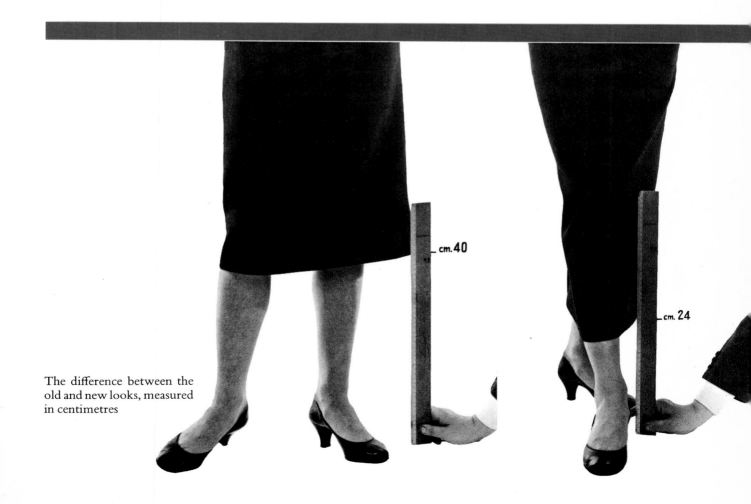

The difference between the old and new looks, measured in centimetres

cm. 40

cm. 24

days', and their clothes were no longer an attempt to imitate those of the gentry. They had their own ideas, on which they insisted.

Fifty years ago social differences were shown more by the condition of a man's garments than by their shape. Clothes quite literally filtered down, passing from hand to hand until they ended with the rag merchant. Class distinction was often merely a matter of personal cleanliness. All this has vanished today in England; nobody wears rags and everybody is clean. The new difference that shows itself is not a difference in degree but a difference in kind. For clothes have shaken off (or are beginning to shake off) the superstition of gentility.

We seem indeed to be on the eve of a revolution in masculine attire just as drastic as that which occurred around the year 1800. The essence of that revolution was to substitute, for the embroidered coats, knee-breeches and ruffles of the eighteenth century, a tightened and smartened version of country clothes—that is, the clothes of the fox-hunting country gentleman. The innovation of Beau Brummell and other Regency dandies was to wear this outfit *in town*.

Today it seems as if men's clothes can only be modified in this manner: by promoting sports clothes into the category of 'ordinary wear'. But ordinary wear tends (or has tended in the past) to formalise itself. By the second half of the eighteenth century, the cut-away tailcoat of the sporting squire had become the tailcoat of full evening dress. Ordinary wear became a new smartened version of country clothes, that is the lounge suit. After the First World War, this lounge suit had itself become formal, and

The age of the great couturiers. *Above left*: Jacques Fath. 1957. *Left*: Coco Chanel poses on the left. 1955. *Right*: Emilio Schubert. 1955

something else was required for energetic pursuits. Once again a sports outfit was brought in, this time from golf: the 'plus fours' of the twenties. Sometimes the 'sports coat' was worn with flannel trousers. Just before the Second World War, young men were wearing this combination even in town. After the war the process was carried a stage further and was much aided by the shops selling 'Government Surplus Stores'. The duffle-coat was the Navy's contribution; the battle-dress blouse or Eisenhower jacket, the Army's. The motor cyclist found in Surplus Stores a whole collection of useful garments, of which the sleeveless leather coat is an obvious example. He also seized upon flying kit, finding the airman's kapok-lined jacket just the thing for high speed on the roads.

Twenty years after the end of the war, we can see the kind of picture that is emerging. In some ways the situation is simply an echo of what has happened before: the increasing use of sports clothes as ordinary dress. But now a far wider range is available and greater variety is possible. There are belted sports coats, leather jackets, 'pilot coats', 'campers'' cardigans, ski 'anoraks' or parkas with hoods.

The significant thing about all this is that the long reign of gentility is over. What kept men's clothes formal for more than a century was the idea that there was something 'caddish' in any departure (at least in town) from a very rigid norm. This restriction seems at last to have been overcome. Today a man no longer feels it necessary to show by his clothes that he belongs to a certain social caste, though most men,

A Fath model. 1957

A Givenchy design. 1957

Stiletto heels were an Italian contribution to fashion

in the upper income bracket at least, still cling to the dinner jacket for formal occasions. The way is open to every kind of innovation. We shall certainly see some startling changes in the years that lie ahead.

Perhaps we are on the eve of a drastic reassessment of our whole attitude to clothes. Looking back over the long history of fashion we see many beautiful and extravagant garments both for men and women. Are we ever likely to see them again? Anthropologists and social historians are agreed that clothes in the past have been worn for three main reasons: for warmth and protection, to mark the social status of the wearer, and to attract the opposite sex. It is pertinent to ask which of these three reasons is still valid.

The early civilisations enjoyed hot climates, and it was not until men migrated to colder regions that what are called 'arctic clothes' became necessary. The people of the countries of Northern Europe still require protection against the cold, but we can already see, in the United States, where central heating is now almost universal, that indoors such protection is no longer necessary. The cities of the future may be roofed over and the streets themselves artificially warmed, so it is probable that our descendants will wear clothes lighter than we do.

The second motive, that of indicating social status, is plainly obsolescent. In the past it was taken for granted that the clothes of the noblemen should be more splendid than those of ordinary folk. Even the sourest seventeenth-century Puritans conceded this,

A new development in fashion, in the fifties and sixties, was the appearance of 'boutiques' which specialised in slightly off-beat clothes. Fashions from the Ken Scott Boutique, Milan. 1965

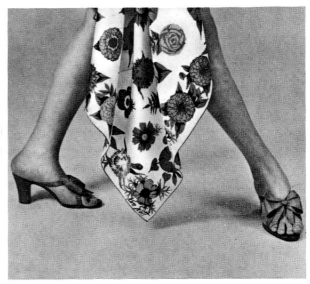

Following pages: Fashion shows have become great social gatherings evoking something of the glamour which surrounded court life in other times

and the notion persisted until the French Revolution. Even in the nineteenth century a gentleman enjoyed the distinction of a better material and better cut. But in recent years there has been such a tremendous improvement in ready-to-wear garments, and such a vast increase in the range of sizes available, that it is often difficult to tell the suit made by a bespoke tailor from one bought 'off the peg'. The clothes of all classes continue to resemble one another more and more. In Communist China this tendency has been pushed to an extreme. The men (and often women) in the streets are as alike as a colony of ants. Indeed, as 'class' is supposed to have been abolished, it would be suspect to show any class distinction in clothes.

There remains the third motive: the desire to attract the opposite sex. This, unless mankind is fated to die out, will probably be always with us. Naturally, it is most evident in women's clothes, but in many countries women are already adopting for work clothes similar to those of men. Even in the Western democracies this is so, and the question arises as to whether what we recognise as 'fashion' will survive.

It probably will, in a modified form. Women's clothes may divide into clothes for work and clothes for leisure; trousers and pullovers (or even dungarees) in the daytime, and in the evening something more feminine—clothes as glamorous and seductive as the designers can make them.

Above right: Culottes for entertaining at home, designed by Emilio Pucci.
Right: A brooch in white gold with sapphires, designed by Pomodoro

Fabric from the Ken Scott Boutique, Milan

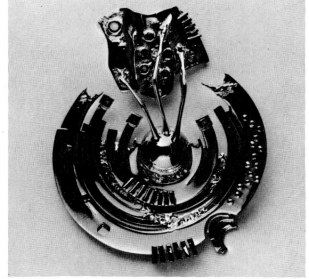

A Mary Quant dress, typical of the Chelsea fashions which have become popular in the United States and Europe. 1961

French leisure wear for teenagers from the magazine 'Vingt Ans'

An example of American leisure wear in suede, designed by Bonnie Cashin. 1964

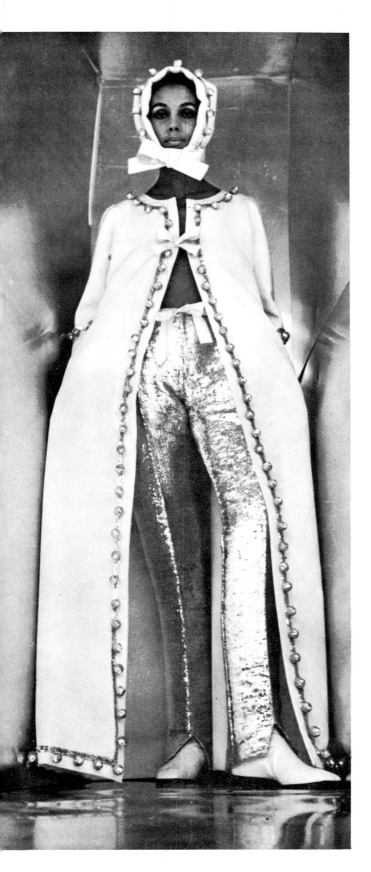

A cocktail dress, designed for teenagers from the magazine '*Vingt Ans*'

The clothes of the future: trouser suit by Courrèges, 1964

A sequined dress by Courrèges, 1965

INDEX
Numbers in italics refer to illustrations

PICTURE ACKNOWLEDGEMENTS

ALINARI: 5, 6, 9, 38 (upper left), 44,
45, 49, 56, (upper), 57 (upper), 69, 75
(left), 82–3, 86, 108–9, 112, 148 (lower
left), 167 (upper left), 183 (left), 210

ANDERSON: 64 (lower left), 128–9
(lower), 179

ARBORIO MELLA: 15 (lower), 20,
22–3 (upper), 29, 34 (upper right), 36
(centre), (right), 60 (left), 64 (right), 83
(lower right), 90 (left), 104 (lower
left), 124–5 (upper), 124, 125, 141,
144, 148 (upper left), 202 (upper right),
204 (lower left), 205 (right), 222 (lower).
233, 244 (lower left), 275

ARCHIVIO MONDADORI: 19 (left),
22 (upper and lower), 28, 32 (upper
left, lower right), 36 (upper), 37, 38
(centre right), 48 (lower left and right),
52, 53, 56 (left, centre left, right,
centre right), 61, 64, 65, 66 (upper and
lower left, lower), 68 (lower left), 70,
72 (lower), 73, 77, 78, 80, 95, 96, 97
(upper left and right, lower right), 100,
101, 104 (upper left, lower right), 105,
106, 107, 108–9, 118–19, 121, 125
(upper left), 136 (upper and lower left
and right), 149, 152, 153, 168 (right),
172 (upper left), 174 (lower left), 175
(lower), 178, 184 (lower left), 185, 186
(left and right), 187 (upper, centre,
lower), 188 (lower), 190 (left), 191
(upper left, centre left, lower left and
right), 194 (left), 196 (upper left), 203
(centre), 208 (upper right, centre,
lower left), 209, 212–13, 222 (upper),
225 (upper right), 249, 250–1, 251
(right), 251 (left), 255 (upper left), 263
(right), 264–5, 266 (upper right),
267 (upper right), 270 (lower right),
271 (lower left), 272 (upper left, lower
right), 273, 274 (upper and lower),
275, 277, 278 (left), 282 (lower left),
283, 288 (lower left), 289, 299, 300, 301
(upper right, lower right). 304, 305
(upper and lower right), 306 (lower
right and left), 308, 309, 310 (upper
left), 311, 314

ARSPHOTO: 168 (upper and lower left),
169 (right, upper right), 248 (lower
right)

ASSOCIATED PRESS: 303 (lower
right), 306 (upper left)

ATTUALFOTO: 239, 250 (left)

BEVILACQUA: 21 (upper and lower
right), 24 (lower), 27, 33, 85, 88, 92
(lower), 111, 130 (lower), 131 (upper
left and right), 161, 164 (centre)

BIASI: 19 (right)

BULLOZ: 14, 91, 158, 159, 170–1, 175,
241 (lower right)

CARPINACCI: 57 (lower)

ELECTA: 76 (right), 103 (lower right),
131 (upper), 154, 184 (upper left)

E.P.S.: 201 (right), 204 (upper left), 205
(upper left and right), 206 (upper and
lower left)

FILIPPI: 202 (upper left)

GIRAUDON: 203 (upper left), 214–15,
218–19, 223 (right), 226 (left), 245

GOMBRICH: 72 (left)

HORST: 305 (lower left)

INTERSTAMPA SCOOP: 310 (lower
right)

MARZARI: 54–5, 164 (upper), 193

MERCURIO: 13, 48 (upper left and
lower left), 59, 62, 63, 64 (upper right),
74, 77, 79, 81, 87 (right), 92 (upper
left), 134–5, 138 (lower right), 164
(lower), 177, 178, 184 (lower left), 268
(upper left), 268 (lower left)

MATCH: 310 (lower left)

MULAS: 313

THE OBSERVER: (photo John Cowan)
316 (upper left)

PAF INTERNATIONAL: 317 (below
right)

PUCCI: 313

QUEEN: (photo Helmut Newton): 317
(left)

SCALA: 10, 46–7, 51, 67, 71 (upper), 76
(left), 93, 98–9, 103 (upper right), 122
(upper left), 123, 127, 138 (upper
left), 146–7, 160, 161, 165, 168–9, 169
(left), 188 (left), 188–9, 200 (left), 223
(left), 252 (lower right), 253, 256 (left),
257, 269

SILLS & CO. INC.: 316 (right)

KEN SCOTT: 312

VAGHI: 75 (upper left), 234 (right)

VASARI: 229

VINGT ANS: 316 (below left), 317
(above right)